DATE DUE

SE 2 1 '09			

SURVIVORS

A dramatic poster harnesses public admiration and sympathy for merchant seamen to boost the National Savings Campaign. (*Imperial War Museum*)

Survivors

British Merchant Seamen in the Second World War

G. H. and R. Bennett

THE HAMBLEDON PRESS

LONDON AND RIO GRANDE

99

102 Gloucester Avenue, London NW1 8HX (UK)
PO Box 162, Rio Grande, Ohio 45674 (USA)

ISBN 1 85285 182 1

A description of this book is available from
the British Library and from the Library of Congress

Typeset by Carnegie Publishing, Chatsworth Rd, Lancaster

Printed on acid-free paper and bound in
Great Britain by Cambridge University Press

Contents

Illustrations

1. An unidentified standard fast cargo ship of late 1944.
(*Imperial War Museum*)

2. HMS *Vetch*, a 'Flower' Class corvette, at Liverpool, 9 August 1942.
(*Imperial War Museum*)

3. A bomb falls astern of the *Glenorchy* on 12 August 1942 during
the 'Operation Pedestal' convoy to Malta. (*Imperial War Museum*)

4. HMS *Spey*, a 'River' Class frigate on the 2nd Escort Group, with
convoy in early 1944. (*Imperial War Museum*)

5. *U–109*, a type IXB U-boat, at Lorient in May 1941. (*Bundesarchiv*)

6. The sinking of an unidentified merchantman, probably taken
from the conning tower of *U–107*. (*Bundesarchiv*)

7. A lookout on the conning tower of Korvettkapitän Erich Topp's
U–552 watches the British freighter *Beacon Grange* break in two after
being torpedoed on 27 April 1941 in the North Atlantic.
(*Bundesarchiv*)

8. Square-ended 'Chipchase' liferafts show their capabilities under
oars or sail. (*Imperial War Museum*)

9. British merchant seamen being rescued from a raft by a vessel of
the United States Coastguard. (*Imperial War Museum*)

10. Covered in oil, an exhausted survivor from a torpedoed British
tanker sits in the scuppers of the ship which rescued him.
(*Imperial War Museum*)

11. A boatload of survivors approaches *U–107*, commanded by Kapitänleutnant Gunther Hessler, the son-in-law of Admiral Doenitz. (*Bundesarchiv*)

12. Posed photograph from March 1942, showing the lifeboat radio transmitter, small receiver and other equipment.
(*Imperial War Museum*)

13. Specially posed photograph of March 1942, showing improvements in survival equipment. (*Imperial War Museum*)

14. A rescue ship manoeuvres to pick up a party of survivors from a raft. (*Imperial War Museum*)

15. A typical wooden lifeboat, with only two men at the oars, struggles to come alongside a rescuing warship.
(*Imperial War Museum*)

16. After thirteen hours adrift, survivors are hauled on board one of the former US four-funnel destroyers transferred to Britain in 1940.
(*Imperial War Museum*)

17. A rescued crew, relieved to be safe on shore after being picked up, 200 miles out to sea, by a Sunderland flying boat of RAF Coastal Command. (*Imperial War Museum*)

Text Illustrations

Abbreviations

ADM Admiralty files at the Public Record Office

BMVL *British Merchant Vessels Lost or Damaged by Enemy Action during the Second World War* (HMSO, 1947) reprinted in *British Vessels Lost at Sea, 1939–1945* (Cambridge, 1980)

DEMS Defensively Equipped Merchant Ships

FO Foreign Office Files at the Public Record Office

IMT Trial of the Major War Criminals before the International Military Tribunal, Nuremberg

IWM Imperial War Museum documents

MRC Medical Research Council

MT Ministry of [War] Transport files at the Public Record Office

MWT Ministry of War Transport

OA Ocean Archives deposited at Merseyside Maritime Museum

PD(C) *Parliamentary Debates* (Commons), Fifth Series

SR & O Statutory Rules and Orders

WO War Office files at the Public Record Office

Preface

For over fifty years historians have been writing books about the crucial importance for the United Kingdom of the struggle at sea during the Second World War. Most of them have concentrated on the the multiplicity of operational tasks which fell to the Royal Navy in the exercise of seapower. Among those tasks, the protection of merchant shipping has received considerable attention because major successes against enemy surface units such as the *Admiral Graf Spee*, *Bismarck*, *Scharnhorst* and *Tirpitz* were essentially actions fought for that purpose, as were some of the very gallant failures associated with such names as *Rawalpindi*, *Jervis Bay* and Convoy PQ17. Other studies have dealt exhaustively with the protracted campaign waged by enemy submarines and with the bitter battles fought around certain convoys, especially those in the North Atlantic and those destined for Malta and north Russia. Very properly those books have given prominence to the strategic importance of merchant shipping for an island power with a large empire. Tonnage available, tonnage lost, tonnage replaced and tonnage of cargo carried have featured as vital logistic elements of seapower; and the technological, strategic and tactical means employed in the defence of merchant shipping have been described and analysed in great detail.

Atle Thowsen, a Norwegian historian, has reminded us that, 'while the loss of Allied and neutral tonnage during the Atlantic campaign has been painstakingly computed, we still lack accurate data for the total loss of lives',[1] while Geoffrey Till, a British naval historian, has urged that other members of his profession 'should never forget that what they analyse is not some kind of giant board game, but cruel hard war in all its horrors'.[2]

We have set out to examine some perspectives on that 'cruel hard war' arising from the experiences of survivors from British merchant ships and the factors affecting their chances of survival. Although it has long been possible, thanks to certain personal narratives, a few films, published photographs and incidental references in books about particular ships or convoys, to form some appreciation of the merchant seamen's struggle to stay alive when their ships were sunk, the subject has received scant attention from historians as an aspect of warfare worthy of study in its own right.

Beyond the natural hazards of the sea and the dangers inherent in any marine casualty, the outcome of every wartime sinking involved a complex interplay between the location and nature of the enemy's attack, the vessel herself and the cargo she carried, the responses of her crew and the safety provisions made by both the owners and the British government. Wartime experience soon provided ample evidence of the very varied nature of survival problems. The daunting challenge for the seamen, the government and the shipping industry was how to devise ways of solving or diminishing those problems and how to ensure that promising innovations were actually implemented.

To set our theme in context we have found it necessary to give some consideration to the general development of the war at sea and how measures for the general defence of merchant ships inevitably contributed to the safety of their crews in an incidental way, but the emphasis is on the personal survival of seamen when the ships themselves could no longer be saved or when they had sustained very severe damage. Although this aspect of the war at sea is discussed almost exclusively from the point of view of British (including Commonwealth) ships and those who sailed in them, it must never be forgotten that the ships of Allied countries under enemy occupation made a distinguished contribution to the war effort, and their crews faced the same problems when their ships were sunk. To a large extent they tended to adopt, sometimes with their own national variations, the changes in survival equipment and procedures found on British vessels. It should also be remembered that many neutral seamen suffered when their ships were lost, and that from 1942 American experience and ingenuity made a significant input to the understanding of the problems of survival.

We could not have written this book without the evidence of merchant seamen who experienced at first hand the sinking of their ships and the struggle to survive which then followed. Their matter of fact and generally understated accounts, whether written immediately after the event, recounted in conversation or published more formally years later, can hardly fail to evoke both our pity at the suffering involved and our admiration of the dogged resolve shown by those who had to endure it. In many instances we have used the words of survivors themselves: it would have been presumptuous of us to do otherwise when they cry out to speak directly to the reader without an author's intervention. In that sense this book has many more joint authors than the ones whose names appear on the title page.

All quotations appear in their original form except for a few minor editorial adjustments to conform to current practice in regard to abbreviations, the use of upper case letters and giving certain numbers in words rather than figures. In all such cases, the actual words used, their order and their meaning remain completely unchanged.

In writing of the number of casualties or the number of survivors we have been acutely aware that, while figures may be helpful in giving some general indication of the scale of losses, they should not be regarded as a precise audit. Figures recorded in wartime may have been inaccurate because of such diverse influences as the fallible memory of survivors, slips in encoding or decoding signals, mishearing oral accounts in strange accents, simple arithmetical and typing errors, illegible copies made with poor quality carbon paper, lost documents or a failure to alter them when last minute changes had to be made to the crew of a ship just before she sailed. Even where casualty figures were recorded as accurately as they were known at the time, they may not have been amended to take account of later information about survivors who died after being rescued or who, although originally presumed lost, turned out to be safe as prisoners-of-war or after completing a long lifeboat voyage.

Another source of confusion is the variety of ways in which people on a ship or in a lifeboat might be classified into such categories as master, ship's officers, merchant seamen, lascars, navy gunners, army gunners, convoy commodore's staff, service passengers, civilian passengers, distressed British seamen, hospital ship medical staff, or rescued survivors from another ship. At other times they might merely be described by a more general term such as crew, passengers, service personnel or survivors. One then faces a problem in deciding whether, for example, the gunners provided by the Admiralty's Defensively Equipped Merchant Ships organisation (DEMS) have been counted as 'crew' in one place and 'service personnel' in another; or whether distressed British seamen and rescued survivors from another ship have been counted as 'passengers' or 'crew'. No doubt some of the uncertainties in the figures could be cleared up by more detailed research using a computer data base, but we have decided that, *pace* Atle Thowsen, we must leave that task to others as it would not really add significantly to the general theme of our book.

Like all historians, we are greatly indebted to the many archivists and librarians who have so readily placed at our disposal their valuable

collections, professional skills and cheerful assistance. For access to
archives we wish to express our gratitude to the staffs of Glasgow
University Business Records Centre, the Imperial War Museum, Mersey-
side Maritime Museum, the National Maritime Museum, NUMAST, the
Public Record Office and Warwick University Modern Records Centre.
We have received superb service from the British Library, Derbyshire
County Library (especially at the Ashbourne branch), the Guildhall
Library, Liverpool Reference Library, Manchester Central Library and
the libraries of the Universities of Derby, Exeter, Nottingham, and
Plymouth (Rolle Campus). For providing photographs we are grateful
to the staff of the photographic archive at the Imperial War Museum
and to Frau Martina Caspers of the Bundesarchiv, Koblenz. The author
and publisher are grateful to the Bundesarchiv for permission to repro-
duce plates 5–7; and to the Imperial War Museum for plates 1–4, 8–17
and the illustrations on pages ii, 76 and 176.

The names of some individuals who have helped directly by conversations or correspondence appear in the bibliography. Some, alas, are
no longer with us, and others may be surprised to find their names
there since some of the conversations took place many years ago before
this present book was even projected. In bringing it to completion
the detailed, patient and friendly advice of Martin Sheppard of The
Hambledon Press has been invaluable in improving the presentation
and eliminating many infelicities of style. Responsibility for any
inaccuracies which remain must, of course, be laid at our door rather
than his.

Quotations from Crown copyright documents in the Public Record
Office and from the publications of Her Majesty's Stationery Office are
reproduced with the permission of the Controller of HMSO. The
Imperial War Museum has permitted the use of a quotation from their
Sound Archive, and the Trustees of the National Museums and Galleries
on Merseyside have allowed us to quote from the Ocean Archive.

We are grateful for permission to quote from the copyright works
listed below: Charles H. Brown, *Nicholls's Seamanship and Nautical Knowl-
edge* (Brown, Son and Ferguson, Glasgow, 1938); Admiral Doenitz,
Memoirs: Ten Years and Twenty Days (English translation, Weidenfeld
and Nicolson, London, 1959; and reprint edition, Greenhill Books,
London, 1990); *Fuehrer Conferences on Naval Affairs* (Greenhill
Books, London, 1994); Stephen Howarth and Derek Law, *The Battle of
the Atlantic* (Greenhill Books, London, 1994); H. R. Trevor Roper (ed.),
Hitler's Table Talk (Weidenfeld, 1953); Robert Seamer, *The Floating
Inferno: The Story of the Loss of the Empress of Britain* (Patrick Stephens,

Wellingborough, 1990); Dan van der Vat, *The Atlantic Campaign: The Great Struggle at Sea, 1939–1945* (Hodder & Stoughton, London, 1988).

For permission to quote from periodicals, we are indebted to the following: the Editor of the *Journal of the Royal Naval Medical Service*; the Editor of *Lloyd's List*; Ewan MacNaughton Associates, on behalf of the *Daily Telegraph*; the *Guardian*, for quotations from the *Manchester Guardian* and *Observer*; IPC Magazines, for *Motor Boat and Yachting*; the Librarian of the Institute, for the *Journal of the Institute of Actuaries*; NUMAST, the National Union of Marine, Aviation and Shipping Transport Officers, for the *Merchant Navy Journal*, *Salt Spray Reporter* and *Signal*; and RMT, the National Union of Rail, Maritime and Transport Workers, for *The Seaman*.

While every effort has been made to trace owners of copyright, in a few cases that has not been possible, particularly where a periodical ceased publication some time ago or a publisher is no longer in business. We offer our apologies to the copyright owners. If they will get in touch with us, through our publisher, we shall remedy the omission in any future edition.

Finally, a special word of thanks is due to three groups of people: to our wives and families for tolerantly accepting our obsession with the subject matter and the disruption to household routine which authorship entails; to GHB's colleagues at the University of Plymouth for their interest and encouragement; and to RB's former shipmates, both European and Indian, on the merchant vessel *Olivebank* in gratitude for the learning experience provided by weekly lifeboat and fire drills which, happily, never needed to be carried out in earnest.

G. H. Bennett
University of Plymouth

R. Bennett
Ashbourne

1

The German Threat
to British Merchant Shipping

On 3 September 1939, within ten hours of the outbreak of war between Britain and Germany, the first British merchant vessel lay torpedoed and sinking in the Atlantic some 220 miles northwest of Ireland. This victim of a single torpedo hit from *U–30* was the 13,581-ton passenger liner *Athenia* of the Donaldson Atlantic Line. As her radio officers transmitted distress signals, her 1102 passengers and 315 crew found that the voyage begun in peacetime from Glasgow, Liverpool and Belfast would not end in Montreal, as expected, but in a struggle for survival in 56°44′N 14°05′W.

Giving news of the sinking to the House of Commons the following day, Winston Churchill, the First Lord of the Admiralty, lost no time in directing attention to the provisions of international law, which placed submarines under the same obligations as surface warships when attacking merchant vessels:

> In particular, except in the case of persistent refusal to stop on being duly summoned or of active resistance to visit and search, a warship, whether surface or submarine, may not sink or render incapable of navigation a merchant ship without having first placed passengers, crew and ship's papers in a place of safety. For this purpose the ship's boats are *not* regarded as a place of safety unless the safety of the passengers and crew is assured, in the existing sea and weather conditions, or proximity of land, or the presence of another vessel which is in a position to take them on board.[1]

Churchill emphasised, 'That is the law',[2] and he went on to describe the sinking as an 'outrage' because 'under no circumstances can open boats 200 miles from land be regarded as a place of safety'.[3] Not to be outdone, the Labour Party spokesman, A. V. Alexander, forecast that the attack would arouse 'horror, disgust and indignation [in] all sections of the population'.[4] In response to a supplementary question from a Conservative backbencher, Churchill asserted that the *Athenia* had been 'torpedoed without the slightest warning, in circumstances which the whole opinion of the world after the late War ... stigmatised as inhumane'.[5]

British newspapers took up Churchill's theme with a will. The *Daily Mirror* alleged that, in sinking a ship carrying defenceless passengers, the Germans had resumed the barbaric conduct and 'frightfulness' of the First World War.[6] The *Manchester Guardian* declared: 'The solemn pledge of Germany's own freely given renunciation of such piracy was itself torpedoed, sunk without trace, within the first twelve hours of the war',[7] and by the week-end the *Observer* was using expressions like 'pitiless barbarity' and 'sea-murder'.[8]

The *Daily Telegraph* described the torpedoing as 'a stroke that at the same time outrages every human sentiment and breaks the pledged word of the German rulers',[9] and, in the next issue, under the head-line 'MURDER MOST FOUL', a leading article claimed that the German submarine had fired a shell to try to disable the *Athenia*'s radio:

> In that there could be only one purpose – the destruction of any possibility of aid reaching the hundreds of men, women and children who were taking to the boats 200 miles from land. The annals of the sea may be searched in vain for any such instance of cold-blooded murder, for murder and nought else was intended.[10]

Before long British public opinion had gained the impression, totally without foundation in international law, that in all circumstances attacks on their merchant ships must be illegal, barbaric, murderous and piratical.

After the First World War, Britain had hoped that the major naval powers could be persuaded to outlaw submarines altogether. The inclusion in the Treaty of Versailles of a complete prohibition against Germany owning any submarines was seen as merely the first step to a wider ban. At the 1921 Washington Conference, Lord Lee of Fareham had argued the British case that the submarine 'ought to be, abolished. It was a weapon of murder and piracy, involving the drowning of noncombatants ... Technically the submarine was so constructed that it could not be utilized to rescue even women and children from sinking ships.'[11]

Appreciating that these moral and humane considerations were being advanced, in part at least, to bolster the case for a policy which would be particularly advantageous to Britain on far wider economic and strategic grounds, the other powers at the conference (France, Italy, Japan and the USA), declined to accept a complete ban. They did agree, however, to a draft treaty laying down the principle that belligerent submarines were required to observe the same rules as surface warships. They also recognised 'the practical impossibility of using submarines as commerce destroyers without violating ... the requirements universally accepted by civilized nations for the protection of the lives of neutrals and noncombatants',[12] and they accepted a prohibition of such use as binding among themselves, inviting all other nations to accept it also.

A further attempt to limit the role of submarines in attacking merchant vessels was made in the London Naval Treaty of 1930. Again, wrangling about the precise wording in which the general principles were to be expressed delayed ratification until 6 November 1936, when they formed the basis of the London Submarine Agreement. It was that agreement which Churchill quoted in giving details of the *Athenia* sinking to the House of Commons.

In 1935, during the negotiations for the Anglo-German Naval Treaty by which Britain unilaterally agreed that Germany could begin building submarines once more, Germany had indicated a willingness to agree to some limitation on their use. She had, accordingly, become the first country not party to the Washington Conference of 1921 and the London Naval Treaty of 1930 to accede to the 1936 London Submarine Agreement. Churchill and the British press were, therefore, correct in claiming that *U–30*'s attack on the *Athenia* was in breach of international law with which Germany had freely agreed to comply. But international law is difficult to define and even more difficult to enforce, especially while a conflict rages.

As an outbreak of hostilities with Britain became increasingly probable, there had been some lively discussion within the German naval high command about the way their U-boats ought to be used in that eventuality. There was a good case for exploiting, as in 1917, their potential to inflict the maximum damage on Britain's merchant fleet before defensive armament could be mounted or convoys could be organised, and to that end the Commander-in-Chief, Admiral Erich Raeder, was in favour of announcing a zone around the British Isles within which an unrestricted campaign would be waged. But because of the predictable effect of such a campaign on neutral opinion, especially in the United States, there was also a good case for operating initially under the rules set out in the London Submarine Agreement of 1936, accepting the drastic limitation they imposed on the operational effectiveness of the U-boats. It would then be Britain that would incur the wrath of international public opinion as her economic blockade of Germany interfered with neutral ships and commerce; and, sooner rather than later, it would be possible for Germany to cite incidents with armed British merchant vessels as grounds for lifting the restrictions on the way the U-boats could attack them. This was the policy with which Germany entered the war.

Like the commanders of all the other German U-boats deployed across trade routes in the North Sea, and in the western approaches to the British Isles, Oberleutnant Lemp of *U–30* was under strict orders to operate according to a document known as the Prize Ordinance (*Prizenordnung*) which incorporated the limitations on action set out in the 1936 agreement. The Prize Ordinance did, however, leave him free to attack

> merchantmen proceeding under escort of enemy warships or aircraft ... merchant vessels which take part in any engagement or which resist when called upon to submit to inspection, [or] transports which are deemed to be on active service, to belong to the armed forces, and are therefore deemed to be warships.[13]

When Lemp encountered the *Athenia* on the evening of 3 September 1939 he may have been puzzled by her position and course well off the usual transatlantic liner routes, since she was following an evasive routeing specified by the Admiralty before she sailed. In deciding to make a submerged attack with torpedoes, and without any warning, he may have mistakenly identified the darkened ship as a transport or armed merchant cruiser, which would have been legitimate targets; or he may have been so eager to score a success and so afraid of losing such a tempting target as darkness approached that he threw caution to the winds. Whatever the explanation, his single torpedo-hit effectively wrecked not only the British liner but also the German government's carefully considered pose as a staunch upholder of international law when attacking merchant vessels. He must have realised this as soon as he surfaced, allegedly to open fire with his gun in an attempt to bring down the ship's radio aerials: then he could see the large number of passengers swarming onto the deck and beginning to abandon ship. Little wonder that he submerged again, left the scene, and kept radio silence about his success until *U–30* had returned to Germany at the end of September.

Reports, sometimes contradictory, of the experiences of survivors from the *Athenia* began to appear in the newspapers on 5 September, as survivors were brought ashore in Ireland and Scotland. From them general readers could appreciate something of the horror and suffering involved when a ship had to be abandoned. Of far greater practical significance, some early indications of the problems involved in survival could be gleaned by those in the Admiralty, Board of Trade and the shipping companies who, in the coming years, would have the task of trying to improve people's chances of survival when ships were sunk.

Those who found themselves deep below decks when a torpedo struck certainly seemed to be the most vulnerable. The great majority of the 112 dead and missing from the crew and passengers of the *Athenia* had either been working in the engine room and boiler room, both breached by the torpedo explosion, or dining in the third class and tourist dining rooms.[14] Some diners were reported to have been trapped and drowned when the explosion wrecked the staircase leading to the open deck.[15] Others had died in the passenger accommodation in the 'tween deck, although it is unclear whether their deaths were caused by blast effect from the torpedo, by a subsequent boiler explosion or by a shell-hit. 'There were many bodies lying about here: they were all completely blackened – clothes, faces, everything.'[16]

Although the *Athenia* did not sink immediately, *U–30* did not fire more torpedoes to finish her off. Indeed, the liner stayed afloat for almost fifteen hours. That was a stroke of good fortune for the approximately 1300 crew and passengers still struggling to survive. The time taken to grope their way along the ship's alleyways trying to find the cabins where they had left their lifejackets, and the desperate search for children, spouses or friends from whom they had become separated, would have cost many more lives if the ship had gone down, as many subsequently did, within a few minutes.

They were also fortunate that the ship did not take on a severe list. The well-drilled crew were able to launch all twenty-six lifeboats in about an hour, a remarkable feat considering that twenty-four of the boats were nested in pairs, that is two to each set of davits. The crew

> had to lower the top lifeboat first, recover the falls, haul in the davits, hook on the underneath boat, get the davits out and then lower the second ones. [They had] a lot of trouble with the second ones on the starboard side as, by [then], the ship had a list of 12°. Every boat was lowered without accident; only the last one on the starboard side was slightly damaged but was in no way made unseaworthy. There was no panic at all on board.[17]

Some of the passengers were less favourably impressed by the orderliness of the abandonment. They later spoke of having to jump a four foot gap to get into boats (no doubt an effect of the list), of having to climb down ropes, and of boats being dropped into the water (their fear probably exaggerating the effect of finally unhooking the falls). In great haste the boats seem to have been filled without too much regard to previously allocated lifeboat stations: one of them contained only women with just three or four of the crew as boat-handlers.

After all the boats had cleared the ship, there remained on board the captain and radio officers, who had been trying to contact other vessels to come to their rescue, the ship's deck officers and other crew members who had been tending the boat falls, and some stewards who been helping passengers into the boats. Ignoring the possibility of a renewed attack by the U-boat or their ship suddenly plunging to the bottom, they made a final search for survivors before summoning one of the motor boats to return alongside to take them off and distribute them among the other boats. As the war progressed this reluctance of captains to order the last crewmen to complete the abandonment of stricken ships would cost many lives.

For the people in the *Athenia*'s lifeboats, personal survival through the night of 3/4 September became a test of fortitude and endurance. American newspapers featured reports of survivors choking in oil scum, or bailing water with their shoes while teenage girls rowed until their hands were blistered.[18] The survivors were fortunate that their time in open boats was not prolonged. In the early hours of 4 September, rescue ships began to arrive on the scene in response to the *Athenia*'s SOS calls. The Norwegian *Knute Nelson*, the Swedish steam yacht *Southern Cross*, the US merchant ship *City of Flint*, and the British destroyers HMS *Escort* and HMS *Electra* picked up, in all, about 1300 survivors, a surprisingly high proportion of those who had sailed in the *Athenia*.

Survivors found that the arrival of rescue vessels was not necessarily an end to their danger. Transferring from an open boat in the open sea can be a difficult operation. One woman passenger described the problems of coming alongside and climbing the high side of the *Knute Nelson*.[19] A British seaman, probably from the same boat, said: 'Our boat got under her stern and was struck by the propeller, which knocked the bottom out ... Several of the people were killed. I drifted about in the water for three hours in my lifebelt before I was picked up by the yacht *Southern Cross*.'[20]

The survival of one woman passenger provides an example of how what some would call pure chance and others would call a miracle could, in the end, determine who would live and who would die when a ship was sunk. Long before the *U–30*'s attack, this woman had been injured and rendered unconscious by falling down a ladder. Patched up and sedated with morphine, she had known nothing of the torpedo hit or the scramble to abandon ship, and had remained in the sick bay aboard the deserted ship throughout the night. Checking on survivors aboard HMS *Electra* next morning, the chief officer of the *Athenia* discovered that two men he had ordered to get the injured woman out of the sick bay and into a boat had apparently failed to do so. He immediately asked for the loan of a boat and reboarded the liner with the bosun and a seaman. They found the woman still unconscious and quickly transferred her to the *Electra*. They had been just in time: had they been delayed by half an hour, the injured woman would have been carried to the bottom of the Atlantic in the *Athenia*'s final plunge.[21]

A final lesson to be learned from the first sinking of the war was that the privations of survivors were not automatically brought to an end when they were rescued. Some of the injured died after being picked up, including ten-year-old Margaret Hayworth of Hamilton, Ontario, who died from a brain injury as the *City of Flint* headed for Halifax, Nova Scotia. Most merchant vessels carried no doctors. Aboard the *Knute Nelson*, Dr Wilkes, a survivor whose wife and sons were thought to be missing, cared for the injured until two Irish doctors came out in a small boat to board the ship off the Aran Islands. Uninjured survivors slept on tarpaulins or bare decks, their inadequate clothing supplemented with blankets or clothing generously donated by the rescuing crews. On shore, arrangements for the reception and accommodation of large numbers of survivors had to be hastily improvised. At Galway, survivors landing from the *Knute Nelson* were greeted with hot food served on the dockside by a committee headed by the bishop.[22] When the British destroyers reached Greenock, many of the survivors were still clad in just their night clothes, with a sailor's great coat thrown over them. They were clothed and fed thanks to the spontaneous generosity of local people and businesses.[23] The injured woman rescued just before the *Athenia* sank died in Greenock hospital.

As soon as they learned of the *Athenia*'s sinking, the German Foreign Office and Navy realised that they had a potential public relations disaster on their hands. On 4 September, Ernst von Weizsaecker of the German Foreign Office was assuring the US Chargé d'Affaires that German forces were not involved. The German propaganda machine claimed that the ship must have been sunk by a floating British mine, or had been deliberately sabotaged on Churchill's orders to arouse

US hostility towards Germany. This theory even gained some credence for a time in the United States, and the Germans persisted with it even after *U–30* had returned to Germany and Lemp's misjudgement was known to the German authorities.[24] All German U-boat commanders were reminded that they were to conduct their operations in accordance with the Prize Ordinance, with an additional limitation dated 4 September: 'By order of the Fuehrer and until further orders no hostile action will be taken against passenger liners even when sailing under escort.'[25]

For a time the German commanders were meticulous in trying to operate in accordance with international law. When Kapitänleutnant Gunther Prien, commanding *U–47*, attacked the small freighter *Bosnia* on 5 September, he did not open fire with his gun until the British vessel's attempt to escape, in defiance of his order to heave to, provided a legal justification. As the freighter's crew began to abandon ship, their first lifeboat overturned because the ship still had way on her. Some decades later a survivor recalled:

> The submarine turned round and picked the men up out of the water; there was one man dead. When we got into our boat we went towards the submarine to pick these other men up; they all came into our boat. We saw them on top of this man and we thought they were hitting him, but they were trying to give him artificial respiration. He had a lifebelt on, but he was only in his singlet because he'd run up out of the stokehold. I think the cold water killed him ... The German captain was a smashing feller.[26]

Prien finished off the *Bosnia* with a torpedo, but assured himself that all the survivors would shortly be picked up by a Norwegian tanker.

The *Olivegrove* also tried to escape when approached by *U–33* on 7 September, but the master eventually hove to in response to a warning shot and signals from the U-boat, which waited until the two lifeboats were clear before torpedoing her. The master later reported that he had been taken aboard the German vessel while his ship's papers were examined. 'The U-boat commander said that he was very sorry that he had to sink my ship. He then said "Why does Mr Chamberlain want to make war on us?" I said that I did not want war any more than he did.'[27] The Germans gave him a course to take his lifeboats to Fastnet, 290 miles away. Concerned for their safety, the German commander even came back that evening and fired two Very lights to enable a neutral American liner to locate the boats in the darkness and pick up the thirty-three survivors.

Masters of British merchant ships were obviously determined to make a run for it and use their radio, rather than submit to the kind of stop and search procedure envisaged in the 1936 agreement. Indeed in 1938 the Admiralty had ordered: 'No British merchant vessel should ever tamely surrender to a submarine, but should do her utmost to escape. A vessel which makes a determined attempt to escape has an excellent chance of doing so.' [28] Masters were not, however, prepared to expose their crews to needless slaughter by persisting in an escape attempt when it was clearly hopeless. Reporting the sinking of the *Winkleigh* by *U–48* on 8 September, Captain Thomas Georgeson explained:

> Seeing that there was no chance of escape I stopped the engines and ordered my crew to the boats. Before leaving I sent out a radio message ... I went on board the submarine and he greeted me very cordially and said he was sorry he would have to sink my ship. He repeated that twice to me ... He gave me four loaves of bread; then he brought a bottle of Schnapps up, and taking out a packet of cigarettes, offered me one and put the remainder of the packet in my hand.[29]

After seven hours in their boats, the crew of the *Winkleigh* were picked up by a Dutch liner.

A similar pattern of events occurred when *U–48* sank the *Firby* on 11 September. Her master, Captain Thomas Prince, reported:

> I carried on zig-zagging until I thought we had gone far enough ... After about the fifth shot, I stopped and ordered the men to take to the boats. Every shot fired hit the ship. [The submarine commander] asked me to have a drink with him, so we both had a tumbler-full of whisky. He told me that he would send me an SOS out to Churchill and wished me the best of luck and hoped we would meet again after the war was over. He gave me four rolls of bandages and six loaves of bread for the wounded.[30]

After the submarine had left, one of the two lifeboats sank and all survivors had to crowd into the remaining boat, lying to a sea anchor until 0300 next morning when they were rescued by HMS *Fearless*.

Speaking in the House of Commons on 26 September, Winston Churchill publicly acknowledged that *U–48*'s commander had kept his promise to the master of the *Firby*:

> From time to time the German U-boat commanders have tried their best to behave with humanity. We have seen them give good warning and also endeavour to help the crews find their ways to port. One

German captain signalled to me personally the position of a British ship he had just sunk, and urged that rescue should be sent.[31]

Churchill then went on to claim: 'He is now in our hands and is treated with all consideration' (an error to which he had to confess in a written parliamentary answer a fortnight later).

To balance his tribute to the humane conduct of some German U-boat crews, Churchill also referred to cases like the *Athenia*, *Royal Sceptre* and *Hazelside* as examples of 'cruel and ruthless acts ... contrary to all the long acquired and accepted traditions of the sea [and] a violation of the laws of war'. Nothing had been heard of the *Royal Sceptre* since a radio signal on 5 September saying she was under attack 300 miles west of Ushant. No trace of her crew had been found by neutral vessels going to their rescue, and after three weeks it was presumed that the crew had not survived. The Ministry of Information seized the opportunity to reinforce, in face of other evidence, the propaganda picture of the inhuman German submariners in a press statement alleging: 'The crew of this ship were cast adrift in their boats without possible hope of reaching land, a foul act of piracy on the high seas on the part of the German Navy.'[32]

This crude attempt at propaganda was instantly disproved by the arrival of the survivors from the *Royal Sceptre* at Bahia, Brazil, aboard the British vessel *Browning* on 26 September. Chased in heavy seas by a U-boat, the master of the *Royal Sceptre* had persisted in his attempt to escape until his vessel had been hit by shells and his wireless aerial brought down. He was killed and some of his men were wounded as they prepared to abandon ship in two boats. In the scramble to leave, the radio officer had been forgotten. When he appeared on deck the U-boat's commander, once more the redoubtable Kapitänleutnant Herbert Schultze of *U–48*, stopped shelling and ordered one of the lifeboats to return to the ship to take him off. Schultze told the survivors he would send help, a promise which he kept by intercepting the British freighter *Browning* and sparing that ship on condition that they picked up the survivors from the *Royal Sceptre* and maintained radio silence until they reached Brazil.[33]

The evidence that, in the first month of the war, German U-boat commanders were genuinely trying to operate with humanity and restraint according to their orders is conclusive, given the large number of examples involving different U-boats. An Admiralty memorandum analysing the first thirty attacks concluded that, apart from the *Athenia* and one or two other cases, U-boats had made adequate provision for the crews of ships they had sunk, and that this had 'aroused a somewhat excessive enthusiasm in the crews concerned'.[34] A survivor from the *Pukkastan*, sunk by *U–34*, found her commander 'very courteous and very anxious that everybody was safely off the ship'.[35] The crew of the tanker *Inverliffey* were allowed to get away in lifeboats before *U–38* torpedoed her and, when the German commander saw that the immense flames were so intense as to endanger one of the boats 500 or 600 feet away, he took the survivors onto his U-boat's casing, then placed them in one of the other lifeboats for transfer to a neutral American tanker.[36] The master of the *Blairlogie* would have been amazed to learn that the German commander who allowed his men plenty of time to take to the boats, and then distributed gin and cigarettes to the survivors, was Fritz-Julius Lemp of *U–30* a week after his sinking of the *Athenia*.[37] When the benzine tanker *Cheyenne* was sunk by *U–53*, the Germans again allowed ample time for the vessel to be abandoned and offered to tow the boats towards the Irish coast, 160 miles away. That offer had to be reconsidered when a British destroyer announced its arrival by opening fire.[38]

In view of the need for U-boats to recharge their batteries on the surface at night, and the importance of the element of surprise when making their attacks, it seems almost incredible that some were pre-pared to reveal their position by firing rockets to attract rescuers to pick up survivors. Otto Schuhart of *U–29* did that after sinking the tanker *British Influence*;[39] and when Wilhelm Fröhlich of *U–36* discovered that the *Truro* had no wireless, he sent out an SOS call on her master's behalf, provided bottled beer for the men in the boats, towed them towards a possible rescue ship, and revealed his own position by firing red rockets to show where the survivors were. He could hardly be blamed for the rescue ship taking fright and disappearing into the darkness. The survivors eventually got on board two Belgian trawlers. Fröhlich introduced a novel feature in his dealings with survivors by requiring the master and two deck officers, as an alternative to being kept as prisoners of war, to sign an undertaking not to serve at sea again until the end of the war.[40]

These early sinkings caused relatively few deaths among British mer-chant seamen, and the presence of large numbers of neutral vessels ensured that survivors usually had to spend only a few hours in lifeboats. This began to make a favourable impression on world opinion, especi-ally in the United States,[41] but operating in strict accordance with the procedure laid down in international law inevitably required the U-boats to spend a dangerously long time on the surface. Their commanders had to identify their target as an enemy, order her to stop by lamp and flag signals (which merchant seamen complained were difficult to read), fire warning shots well clear of the target, then pursue the fleeing vessel until hits or near misses eventually forced her master to the conclusion that he had better comply with the U-boat's order and abandon ship to save sacrificing his crew in vain. In the winter months, with longer hours of darkness and worse weather, chases of this kind would become even more difficult, while the easily damaged pressure hull of the U-boat would be exposed to counter-fire as the British pushed on with mounting guns on the sterns of their merchant ships. Those guns might be of equal or superior calibre to those mounted on submarines and they would be operating from a higher and more stable platform. Already the British Ministry of Information was boasting that ships like the *Rothesay Castle*, *Baharistan* and *Baron Lovat* had successfully made good their escape when chased by submarines.[42]

Even when a merchant ship at length complied with the order to stop, the U-boat was required to wait for the boats to get away, interrogate the captain or a senior officer, and check the ship's papers before sinking her. The U-boat also had to ensure the safety of the survivors, usually by directing a neutral vessel to pick them up. Meanwhile, alerted by radio warnings which the merchant ship had transmitted, the British might be taking counter measures. In 1938 the Admiralty had advised masters of merchant vessels that 'such a [radio] report promptly made may be the means of saving not only the ship herself but many others; for it may give an opportunity for the destruction of her assailant by our warships and aircraft'.[43]

The speed with which British destroyers arrived in the positions where the *Athenia*, *Firby* and *Cheyenne* had been sunk illustrates the risk to which a surfaced U-boat might be exposed. Even more threatening was the possibility that a merchant ship's radio signals might bring aircraft to the scene so quickly that the U-boat would not have time to dive. The British attempted to exploit this possibility by deploying aircraft carriers in the southwest and northwest approaches. On 14 September they came close to what would have been a particularly welcome success. Lemp's *U–30* had stopped, and was in the process of sinking, the *Fanad Head* when the U-boat was attacked by Blackburn Skua aircraft from 803 Squadron, flying from HMS *Ark Royal*. Lemp managed to make good his escape because two of the aircraft, pressing home their attack from too low an altitude, were brought down by the blast of their own bombs. Lemp stopped to rescue two of the airmen.

Success again eluded the British three days later, when the *Kafiristan* was shelled by *U–53*. The master ensured that two radio signals were transmitted and rang the engine room telegraph to 'stop'. That produced no response: the engine room had already been abandoned in haste. One of his lifeboats was swamped through being launched prematurely without orders. The other boats could not be safely lowered until the ship's engines could be stopped, fifteen to twenty minutes later, by operating an emergency throttle gear on the boat deck. Only then could the order to abandon ship be finally given, some thirty minutes after the first shot had been fired.[44] While this was going on Kapitänleutnant Heinicke of *U–53* waited with as much patience as he could muster before launching a torpedo to sink the *Kafiristan*. Half an hour later he felt it necessary to finish her off with a second torpedo. He then spoke to the people in the boats and signalled their position to the US merchant ship *American Farmer*. He assured the survivors that, if the neutral vessel did not pick them up, his submarine would tow them towards the Irish coast. About two hours after the first shot had been fired, the American ship arrived on the scene. The *Kafiristan*'s master recalled:

> While I was manoeuvring towards the *American Farmer* I saw a plane flying towards the submarine from a direction roughly east. At this time the second officer's life boat was about two lengths away from the submarine and apparently on seeing the plane they began to pull away. The plane started to dive and the submarine crew dashed down the conning tower when the plane started to machine gun the submarine.[45]

This attack was, in fact, carried out by a Fairey Swordfish aircraft of 822 Squadron operating from HMS *Courageous*. The incident contained important lessons for both sides. The deaths of six British merchant seamen out of a crew of thirty-five underlined the danger of trying to launch boats prematurely while the vessel still had way on her. Despite the encouraging prospects for counter-attacking the U-boats, the experiment of operating large aircraft carriers in a trade defence role was proving risky. On 14 September, *U–39* narrowly failed to sink HMS *Ark Royal*, before herself being sunk by the escorting destroyers; and three days later, only some four-and-a-half hours after her aircraft had attacked *U–53*, HMS *Courageous* was sunk by *U–29*. The Admiralty promptly decided that the exposure of carriers in this way could no longer be justified.

For the Germans the wisdom of U-boats remaining on the surface, in order to fulfil all the requirements of the 1936 London Submarine

Agreement, was clearly called in question by the threat from the air. They were not to know that the aircraft carriers had been withdrawn. In any case, patrolling flying-boats or land-based aircraft still posed a serious threat. Another sharp reminder of the long arm of air power came on 18 September, when *U–32* stopped and sank the *Kensington Court*. As soon as the ship began to sink, the U-boat left the scene without spending any time approaching the lifeboats. Thus she missed the arrival shortly afterwards of RAF Sunderland flying boats in response to the ship's distress calls. Unable to find the U-boat, two of the flying boats landed on the sea to rescue the survivors.[46] This dramatic new rescue technique ensured that not a single member of the ship's crew lost his life, an early indication of the contribution aircraft would make in rescue work in the years to come.

For the German U-boat service, the lesson of this well-publicised incident was that, if *U–32* had followed the practice of so many of the other U-boats in remaining surfaced in the vicinity to ensure the welfare of survivors, her crew might well have paid a very high price indeed. To the head of the German U-boat Command (Rear-Admiral Karl Doenitz), to the Commander-in-Chief (Admiral Raeder), and to the German government there now appeared to be ample justification for removing some of the restrictions on U-boat warfare. This more ruthless approach, which they had always considered both inevitable and desirable, could be presented to the world as a policy forced on law-abiding Germany by British actions which had made the 1936 London Submarine Agreement unworkable in practice. On 24 September, with the approval of Hitler and Raeder, Doenitz's headquarters signalled to all U-boats: 'All merchant ships making use of radio on being stopped are to be either sunk or taken in prize. Efforts are to be made to save the crews.' [47]

On 30 September German radio stations broadcast an ominous warning that, in retaliation for several attacks on German U-boats by armed British merchant ships, Germany would have to treat every vessel of the British Merchant Navy as a warship.[48] The Admiralty advised all British ships of this broadcast and warned them to be prepared to meet an immediate change of policy in German submarine warfare. Meanwhile, Doenitz's staff were urging that permission should be given to sink all vessels sailing without lights, especially in areas where only British ships were to be expected. It was suggested that the order should not be put in writing but conveyed by word of mouth.[49] This measure was approved on 2 October, and the next monthly anti-submarine report of the British Admiralty's Trade Division was already drawing attention to a 'radical change' in U-boat tactics: 'No longer are courtesy and chivalry being shown towards merchant vessels. Torpedoing without warning has become a general habit.' [50]

Already two other methods of attack had begun to have an impact. Three merchant vessels had been sunk by German mines in September 1939, the *Goodwood* sinking only a mile from Flamborough Head on the 10th; and on the last day of the month the German pocket battleship *Admiral Graf Spee* began her brief career as a commerce raider by sinking the liner *Clement* in the South Atlantic. A further escalation came in December, when aircraft of the Luftwaffe began attacking British fishing vessels in the North Sea, and the small 487-ton coaster *Serenity* was bombed and sunk eight miles east-northeast of Whitby on the 17th. The *Manchester Guardian* alleged that these air attacks on fishing boats, and even on Trinity House vessels, were proof that German airmen were imbued with a 'spirit of savagery and lust to kill'.[51]

In the long run, however, the U-boats were to pose by far the biggest threat to British ships and British seamen as the restrictions laid down in international law were progressively discarded by the German navy. In November or early December, Doenitz issued his Order Number 154:

> Rescue no one and take no one with you. Have no care for the ships' boats. Weather conditions and the proximity of land are of no account. Care only for your own boat and strive to achieve the next success as soon as possible! We must be hard in this war.[52]

Clearly U-boat commanders were expected to end the consideration for survivors which they had been showing in September, but the order can be explained as a perfectly natural, if rather harshly expressed, response to the attacks by carrier-borne aircraft or destroyers which had endangered U-boats while they were trying to conform to the rules.

The order may also have been inspired by a feeling that some of his commanders were carrying chivalry towards survivors too far. After sinking the trawler *Cresswell* on 12 November off the Outer Hebrides, Gustav-Adolf Mugler of *U-41* picked up the seven survivors clinging to a raft. He kept them on board the submarine for six hours, gave them dry clothing and hot drinks, then put them on board another trawler with instructions to tell Churchill that German submariners were not heartless murderers.[53] Exactly a week later, Mugler torpedoed without warning the 1351-ton cargo ship *Darino* during the night. Eleven exhausted survivors, blown into the sea by the force of the explosion, were rescued by *U-41*. The senior survivor recalled:

We were taken below, our clothes were taken off, and we were put into bunks: some of the men on the submarine turned out of their own bunks for us to use. We had two meals on board – breakfast and lunch ... Whilst on board the submarine we were allowed to walk about and do what we liked and we talked to all the officers and quite a number of the crew, many of whom spoke English quite well.[54]

After ten hours in the U-boat, including a spell submerged while ships could be heard passing overhead, the survivors were released and placed on board a neutral ship. Doenitz and Raeder could hardly be expected to approve of actions such as this. It might have endangered one of the inadequate number of U-boats in service at a time when they were eager to unleash an all-out tonnage war calculated eventually to bring Britain to her knees.

The Germans were anxious to convince world opinion that Britain had forced them to move over to surprise attacks on merchant vessels. In February 1940, a statement from the German navy argued:

As it is not to be supposed that the English equip their ships with guns to shoot seals, it is obvious that these guns serve to offer armed resistance to search by German fighting forces. The international laws in question are therefore made inoperative ... Britain has destroyed the London Convention. German treatment of armed English merchantmen is, therefore, no longer bound by it.[55]

Admiral Raeder made a similar claim during a radio interview with an American reporter early in March, when he alleged that British fishing boats were naval auxiliaries and that the British waged war 'under the merchant flag'. He insisted that it was unreasonable to expect 'a warship to expose itself to the first shot an armed merchantman may fire'.[56]

The fine humanitarian sentiments and carefully honed phrases of the international jurists who had drawn up the 1936 London Submarine Agreement – and Hitler's pledges to abide by them – had managed to survive for only a few weeks when exposed to the harsh realities of poor visibility, rough weather, personal stress and the tactical imperatives faced by those who fought the war at sea, whatever flag they sailed under. British merchant seamen would have to face the consequences – a grim struggle for survival and a mounting death toll in 1940, 1941 and 1942.

In the spring and summer of 1940, the brilliantly executed campaigns which enabled the German army to overrun Denmark, Norway, Holland, Belgium and France transformed the strategic balance of the war at sea. At the beginning of the war German ships were normally restricted to the Baltic and the southeastern corner of the North Sea while the British Isles and British seapower lay athwart Germany's access to the Atlantic. Britain was ideally placed to throttle her enemy by imposing a comprehensive blockade on her imports and exports. After July 1940 Germany dominated the whole coastline of Western Europe. From ports in Norway and Western France she could effectively outflank Britain's efforts to dominate the access routes to the Atlantic, where a much greater area was brought within the operational range of the growing fleet of U-boats. Raeder and Doenitz could now launch the all-out tonnage war against Britain's merchant shipping which they had planned all along. It looked as if it was Britain, standing alone, that would have to endure a siege in such unfavourable circumstances. Churchill, for all his eloquence in voicing Britain's determination to fight on, harboured no illusions about the seriousness of the threat. Early in 1940, as he reminded a secret session of the House of Commons a year later, most defence experts would have advised that, in the face of an enemy controlling most of the west coast of Europe, the problems of bringing supplies across the Atlantic to the British Isles would become insoluble.[57]

2

Meeting the Threat

On the British side, pre-war planning had accepted that the successes achieved by the German U-boat campaign in the First World War would encourage them to mount a major effort against the British merchant fleet if hostilities were resumed. The British government had never relied exclusively on the flimsy protection of international law to guarantee the safety of ships and people sailing under the red ensign. By early 1939 the Civil Lord of the Admiralty, Colonel Llewellin, had been able to reveal that 6436 deck officers, that was approximately 43 per cent, had completed Part I of the Merchant Navy Defence Course, and 1121 had gone on to complete Part II. Courses for seamen were to begin shortly, there was 'a completely adequate supply' of anti-submarine weapons, and 'satisfactory progress [was] being made with anti-aircraft guns'.[1]

A month later, Geoffrey Shakespeare, the Parliamentary Under-Secretary to the Admiralty, gave an assurance 'that, as a result of over two years close co-operation between the Admiralty, the Board of Trade and the shipping industry, we shall be ready to institute a system of convoy soon after the outbreak of war on any route where it is considered necessary'.[2] He assured MPs that 2000 anti-submarine guns could be made available for merchant ships, with even larger numbers to be available shortly; by the end of the year about 1000 ships would have had their decks stiffened to mount the guns, a process which had been begun as early as 1937; and over 9000 officers of the Merchant Navy had already completed convoy and gunnery courses.[3]

The Admiralty's shipbuilding programme for 1939 recognised, rather belatedly, that far more small warships would be needed to meet the demand for convoy escorts. Fifty-six vessels were ordered in 1939, followed by a further 110 from British and Canadian yards after war had been declared. The design of these 'Flower' class corvettes, as they came to be called, was derived from a commercial whale-catcher. Only just over 200 feet long, they were armed with a single four-inch gun and depth charges. Capable of a top speed of sixteen knots, they rolled viciously in a seaway. They were small, cheap, inelegant: they were to prove invaluable.

In view of the crucial importance of shipping to the whole war effort, a contingency plan existed for creating, as in the First World War, a Ministry of Shipping to be based mainly on the Mercantile Marine Department of the Board of Trade, which was responsible for merchant shipping matters in peacetime. The new Ministry was brought into existence on 13 October 1939, with a staff of 822, including forty experts specially recruited from the shipping industry. The first Minister was Sir John Gilmour, a former Secretary of State for Scotland, Minister of Agriculture and Home Secretary. The parliamentary correspondent of *The Times* described his appointment as unexpected, and unlikely to please those who would have preferred a younger man with direct experience of merchant shipping. Their shipping correspondent thought that, while the industry would welcome the setting up of a separate Ministry, the Council of the Chamber of British Shipping had fully expected the Minister to be drawn from within the industry.[4] When Gilmour died on 30 March 1940, his successor R. S. Hudson held the post for less than two months before being replaced by Ronald Cross on 14 May. None of the Ministers could claim to be particularly knowledgeable about the shipping industry, although Cross had served as a Junior Minister at the Board of Trade from 1938 to 1939. The Ministry of Shipping was hardly distinguished by either the brilliance or continuity of ministerial direction in its early days.

The necessary specialist knowledge and continuity were provided by the team which was established just below ministerial level. The members of this team had all held senior appointments in the Ministry of Shipping during the previous war. Sir Arthur Salter, Parliamentary Secretary under all three Ministers, had served during the First World War in such posts as Assistant Director of Transports, Director of Ship Requisitioning and Chairman of the Allied Maritime Transport Executive. Sir Julian Foley, the Permanent Secretary, had served as Director of Military Transports and had been Under-Secretary in charge of the Mercantile Marine Department at the Board of Trade from 1929 to 1939. Sir Cyril Hurcomb, the Director-General, had been Deputy Director of the Ministry of Shipping, and then served ten years as Permanent Secretary of the Ministry of Transport. Brought in as Principal Shipping Adviser and Controller of Commercial Shipping was Sir Vernon Thomson, who had worked in the Ministry of Shipping in 1918, and had subsequently risen to be chairman of several shipping companies. He had also held office as Chairman of the Tramp Shipping Administrative Committee, Chairman of the Baltic Exchange, and President of the Chamber of Shipping, which gives some indication of his personal standing with shipowners. Clearly, with this formidable quartet of knights at his back, it might not matter very much if the Minister were a transient political figurehead.

A further input of practical expertise was provided in November 1939 by the setting up of an Advisory Council consisting of the Minister himself, Hurcomb, Thomson and Foley, plus representatives of the shipping companies (such as Cunard, P & O, Furness Withy, Ellerman, Court Line, and Coast Lines) and representatives of the various trades unions which served the Merchant Navy.[5] Throughout the war, the officials of the various seamen's and officers' unions co-operated willingly with government and shipowners on safety and other matters. At times their almost deferential attitude could cause annoyance to some of their more militant members, but they were right to speak plainly to their own members on safety matters. No one could really quarrel with the National Union of Seamen reminding the men: 'The life-saving waistcoat is intended for use and not for ornament', and, concerning the checking of lifeboat gear, 'Neglect of duty in such matters may have serious consequences for your comrades. Keep your mind on your job.' [6] Still less could anyone seek to defend disgruntled seamen, whatever their grievances, who resorted to slashing lifejackets,[7] or those who drunkenly endangered themselves and others by passing on information about convoys to Germans encountered in neutral ports.[8]

Despite the vast experience of its team of senior officials, the Ministry of Shipping faced considerable problems. Sir Arthur Salter, replying to an opposition censure motion criticising the ministry's lack of 'efficiency and foresight', explained:

> I should like the House ... to think what those ships mean under war conditions, from the point of ship management and direction: the assembly of the ships; their timing and selection, so that they shall not have to wait too long for a convoy, so that there shall not be excessive differences of speed in a convoy; all the consequent arrangements that result from the fact that they come not separately, but in bunches in a convoy; all the rearrangements that follow the fact that they are carrying Government cargoes, bought by the Government, selected by the Government, no longer imported under peace-time conditions. Above all, what follows from the fact that the demand for shipping considerably exceeds the supply.[9]

It is not really surprising that improving the survival chances of merchant seamen when their ships were sunk was well down the list of priorities for the officials at the Ministry of Shipping as they wrestled with the problems of making the most efficient use of the available tonnage to maintain the flow of essential imports. Shipping losses and casualties were not too heavy in the early months,[10] Britain still saw France as a powerful ally, and there was no immediately serious threat to national security, but the senior officials at the Ministry had no illusions about a quick end to hostilities. They were preparing for the brutal and long drawn-out assault on Britain's sea communications which they knew must come eventually. With that in mind, they could hardly afford to close their eyes entirely to the question of how crews might survive the inevitable sinkings.

In any case certain MPs, drawn from all shades of political opinion, were already using parliamentary questions to put pressure on the Ministry. During the first six months of war, from the Labour benches came enquiries about lifeboat davits (Ben Smith), clothing for survivors (Robert Gibson), lifejackets (Will Thorne), wireless transmitters for coasters (Emmanuel Shinwell), and motor lifeboats (Ellen Wilkinson); Conservatives asked about boat drills (Edward Keeling), life-rafts (Vice-Admiral Ernest Taylor), and notification of next-of-kin (Irene Ward); independent members wished to know about wireless operators (D. L. Lipson) and life-rafts, kapok waistcoats and steel helmets (Eleanor Rathbone).[11]

Detailed evidence of the need for improvement in survival equipment was also provided by the Admiralty. In addition to its enormous responsibilities for organising convoys and escorts, planning evasive routeing for independent sailings, and providing defensive armament for merchant vessels, the Admiralty had set up in August 1939 a casualty section within its Trade Division. At its head was Commander Norman Holbrook, a First World War submariner and holder of the Victoria Cross, who was called out of retirement. The casualty section was mainly concerned with gathering information about the sinkings of British merchant ships. As early as 15 September 1939 the Admiralty had made it a requirement that the senior survivor of vessels sunk by enemy action should, where possible, travel to London for debriefing.[12] The chief officer of the *Athenia* was one of the first to be interviewed. The interviews would almost invariably be carried out by Holbrook, who would subsequently circulate reports to relevant departments of the Admiralty, Ministry of Shipping and other interested departments. The casualty reports arising out of these interviews encompass a very large sample of British vessels sunk during the course of the war, and they form the basis of any study of the survival problems faced by British merchant seamen. It must be borne in mind, however, that they are only summaries of the main points raised at the debriefing: they are not verbatim transcripts, and their content was mainly determined by the questions posed, rather than by any more wide-ranging reminiscences of the survivors.

As the war developed the nature of the work of the casualty section changed, and so did the questions put by Holbrook to senior survivors. In the first months of the war the emphasis was on gathering information about the German U-boat service in order to build up a picture of the types of craft operating in particular areas, their patrol patterns, their commanders and crews, and the kind of torpedoes being used. During 1940 the emphasis began to shift towards how lives might be saved after vessels had been sunk. As a result of the interviews Holbrook was able to make a number of practical suggestions to the Admiralty and the shipping authorities. Unfortunately, the files which contained Holbrook's suggestions have disappeared after they were selected for preservation and transfer to the Public Record Office. These files, ADM 199/2156–2164, have shared the fate of so many good ships; they are simply listed as 'missing'. Undoubtedly Holbrook's work made an important contribution to the impetus for improvement in survival equipment, but its precise nature can now only be a matter of conjecture and inferences drawn from the original comments of survivors. The Admiralty also provided useful ideas through its Lifesaving at Sea Committee. Formed in December 1939 to examine the problem as it concerned the men of the Royal Navy, this committee's findings were readily made available for the benefit of merchant seamen also.

On 18 March 1940, less than two weeks before his death, Sir John Gilmour was able to tell the House of Commons of some of the first improvements brought in by his Ministry, although his preamble might have sounded rather complacent:

All our reports and all the losses suffered under war conditions have shown that within their limitations the [pre-war] provisions made have proved really satisfactory. The circumstances of modern war, however, require that additional steps should be taken ... We have now decided to make it compulsory for rafts to be carried on all ships going to sea in the danger area. That is now a definite order. These rafts carry lights which enable them to be seen by those who have been thrown into the sea and by rescuing vessels ... I shall be delighted [to show interested

MPs] some of the modern types of lights which have been invented, some of them by technical officials of the Ministry.

We have also pressed forward with the provision of life-saving waist-coats. Those who have had experience of wearing the ordinary lifebelt at sea know that it interferes in some measure with the wearer's freedom. The waistcoat, which was recently devised, is now being manufactured by some twenty different firms.[13]

He also announced that in future all new ships over 2000 tons built at the Government's expense would carry a motor lifeboat, and steps were being taken to speed up the training of radio officers so that a second operator could be carried on all vessels which, in the Admiralty's opinion, needed one.

The Ministry of Shipping was reluctant to ride roughshod over the sensitivities of the shipowners in matters concerning crew safety – after all, some of the key people in the Ministry were shipowners themselves, or had other close links with the industry. The introduction of new equipment was often tackled in three stages, over a period of a year or even longer. The first stage only applied to vessels owned by the Ministry or being built to its orders; then would follow a 'recommendation' or advisory notice which would probably be taken up by the wealthier or more socially responsible companies but which other, less enlightened, companies might in due course be shamed into following; finally the innovation would be made compulsory by Statutory Order. Another strategy might be to apply compulsion to ships above a certain size (or employed in a certain trade), and then extend it to smaller vessels (or those employed in other trades). Although this gradual introduction of new equipment laid the Ministry and the shipowners open to the charge of dragging their feet to save money at the expense of seamen's lives, it was probably the only realistic approach. It allowed for the design of equipment to be refined by what today would be called field trials, it allowed time for the necessary materials to be obtained and for manufacturers to become geared up to meet the demand, and it recognised that ships spread all over the world could not all be re-equipped at a stroke.

The task of ensuring that shipowners complied with changing government regulations fell to the marine surveyors, originally employed at the ports by the Board of Trade in peacetime. They routinely visited ships in harbour to check that survival equipment and other safety matters were in order. Surveyors operated under a set of very strict rules: *Instructions as to the Survey of Life Saving Appliances* (London, 1938).

They would be notified well in advance of any changes to the regulations, and their reports were closely monitored to see the effect of new measures.[14] On occasion, however, their safety role was undermined by the practicalities of wartime. If, because of production or other difficulties, the latest survival equipment could not be supplied to a ship about to sail in convoy, that ship could not be held back until the equipment became available. In the frequent changes of regulations, successive Ministers reserved the right to issue exemption notices. The hazards of war frequently meant that, with the full knowledge of the surveyor, ships sailed without complying in every detail with the letter of the law.

The ships themselves belonged to a very large number of private companies, ranging from large, prosperous concerns with such famous names as Cunard, P & O and Union Castle, owners of the great passenger liners, to obscure companies running just one or two rusty tramp steamers or coasters on a shoestring. Like any other commercial enterprises, the shipping companies existed to make profits for their shareholders, and they tended to view with suspicion any suggestion for additional safety equipment or for structural modifications which might affect the cargo-carrying or cargo-handling capability of their ships. They naturally wanted to know about the costs and who would have to foot the bill. They were also anxious to preserve from government interference as much as possible of their freedom to make their own decisions regarding their own ships, lest they should find themselves on a slippery slope which after the war might lead to yet more government direction – or even nationalisation. On the face of it, the division of responsibility between government departments and a large number of commercial companies, with all that entailed in the way of lengthy consultations, must have been an obstacle to the introduction of new safety measures.

The sheer variety of ships found in the British merchant fleet was another obstacle that called for great ingenuity if new safety measures were to be introduced. They ranged in age from vessels just completed to a very large number dating from the First World War, and to even more venerable ships such as the *Ulster Queen* (1904), *Wicklow* (1895) and *Gibel Kebir* (1887). In size they ranged from Cunard's *Queen Mary* and *Queen Elizabeth*, of over 80,000 gross tons, to small coasters of less than one hundred tons. The detailed design features, equipment and method of propulsion of each ship reflected in profuse variety the interaction between the fashion and technology when she was built, the foibles of her owners and the specialised requirements of the trade in which she was intended to be employed. There could, therefore, be no universal panacea for the problem of how all of these vessels should be equipped or how they might be safely abandoned in an emergency: solving their often unique problems called for flexibility and ingenuity. Thanks to the tension between central direction and the rights of individual shipping companies, a realistic pragmatic approach came to be adopted.

These merchant ships on which depended Britain's ability to supply the home islands and to operate her forces in other parts of the world did not require an inordinately large work force to provide crews. On 15 June 1938, vessels registered in the United Kingdom were manned by about 159,000 crew members, made up of about 107,000 British seamen, 7000 of foreign nationality, and 45,000 lascars, mainly Indian or Chinese seamen signed on Asian articles at lower rates of pay.[15] Possibly a further 25,000 British, 3000 of foreign nationality and 6000 lascars were on shore – on leave, waiting to sign on a ship, temporarily unemployed, ill, in gaol, on courses or otherwise engaged when the census was taken. Of the seamen classed as British, about 90 per cent were from the United Kingdom, 3.5 per cent from the Irish Free State, and the remaining 6.5 per cent came from all parts of the Empire.[16]

In the early months of the war the number of merchant seamen employed actually fell, as men transferred from the Mercantile Marine to the Royal Navy, either as members of the Royal Naval Reserve, naval reservists recalled to the colours, or enlisted on T124 agreements to man merchant vessels taken over by the Royal Navy for conversion into warships. Some seamen of foreign nationality were discharged as enemy aliens, others preferred to seek berths under less dangerous flags than the red ensign, while many seamen from catering departments found that, with the curtailment of passenger traffic and cruises, their services were no longer required. As civilians – sometimes quite elderly civilians – whose contracts of employment usually only lasted for the duration of a single voyage, merchant seamen were perfectly entitled at the beginning of the war to seek more congenial work ashore, although the younger ones then faced the threat of being conscripted into the armed forces. Overall, from all causes, the statistical adviser to the Ministry of War Transport calculated the reduction in the number of merchant seamen as about 10 per cent,[17] but, of course, crews did not have to be found for ships lost, undergoing lengthy repairs or taken into the Royal Navy.

There was, however, always the possibility of a crisis in the supply of suitable labour, as deaths among merchant seamen from enemy action and other causes began to mount. To that rate of attrition needed to be added those taken as prisoners-of-war, those who had to be discharged through illness, injury, age or infirmity, and those lost through desertion, imprisonment, transferral to other work, or dismissal for offences such as insubordination. As early as February 1940 the Labour MP Emmanuel Shinwell was directing the attention of the House of Commons to the effect of a shortage of seamen in delaying the sailing of some ships.[18]

To some extent the manning problem had been foreseen and steps had been taken to solve it. A Merchant Navy Reserve had been formed in 1938 to find experienced volunteers, willing to serve at sea in an emergency, from among men who had been driven to find work ashore, either by unemployment during the slump, or by personal disenchantment with the mariner's life. Almost 13,000 had signed up before war broke out and the number eventually rose to over 23,000.[19] There was also a steady stream of boys and young men eager to volunteer for a life of adventure on the high seas, despite their lack of seagoing experience.

Broadly speaking, the total pool of labour available for crewing British merchant vessels remained numerically adequate in 1939 and 1940, but the importance of enabling as many men as possible to survive when their ships were sunk, and to survive in a state fit to return to sea again, had a direct bearing on the qualitative aspect of the manning problem. New recruits, no matter how brave and enthusiastic, could not readily replace men who had spent a lifetime at sea acquiring the skills of navigation, seamanship, cargo handling and stowage, chartwork, safe operation of equipment, victualling, engineering, refrigeration, leadership, maritime law, man management, ship's accountancy, first aid, pilotage, meteorology, ship maintenance and the thousand and one other essential skills, attitudes and habits of the seaman's trade. Concern for the safety of survivors was, therefore, not only a matter of human sympathy for those whose lives were endangered, but also a matter of preserving as far as possible the supply of experienced and skilled labour without which Britain's merchant vessels could not be operated efficiently.

Beyond that lay the question of morale. During the evacuation of the British Expeditionary Force from France in late May and early June 1940 there had been a number of worrying instances of masters and crews of some of the ferry steamers having to be replaced because they had become so unnerved or exhausted by their experiences that they refused point-blank to make any more trips to Dunkirk. The crew of the *Ben-my-Chree*, attempting to rush ashore with their kit, had to be driven back on board their ship by Royal Navy seamen armed with rifles and fixed bayonets until a relief crew could be found.[20] Those responsible for organising Britain's merchant shipping must have wondered if these were untypical and isolated examples, or whether such problems would in time infect the whole Merchant Navy. If that were to happen the country's prospects would be very bleak indeed.

The ever-present danger while ships were at sea, the sight and sound of other vessels being sunk, the natural anxiety about their families in the blitzed ports, the strains of station-keeping in convoy, the deaths of former shipmates, the pitiful stories of some survivors, and the sadly mute evidence of the dead, all combined to place merchant seamen under considerable psychological strain. They were not some specially recruited elite force of 'gung ho' glory seekers avid for gallantry decorations and the excitement of combat: they were just ordinary men doing what they saw as an ordinary job in extraordinary circumstances. They included, perhaps, a fair number of social misfits, and certainly many of them had little cause to be particularly grateful to the country under whose flag they sailed. Their collective experience of social deprivation, orphanages, miserly shipowners, hard-driving mates, courts of summary jurisdiction, unemployment between voyages, abusive bullying of the weak, prejudice against coloured seamen, destitution in colonial territories and similar evils would hardly have been calculated to produce a flowering of patriotic virtues and self-sacrifice. The older men were, with good reason, often bitter about the way their efforts in the First World War had so soon been forgotten during the difficult economic conditions between the wars. Any real or imagined grievance could rouse their anger, and many of them were bitterly critical of the safety measures on which their lives depended. Yet on the readiness of merchant seamen to keep on sailing the ships year in, year out, whatever the dangers, depended Britain's ability to prosecute war at all.

In the national interest it was essential to build up and sustain their morale. They had to be shown that their lives would not be thrown away needlessly, and that every effort was being made to improve their chances of survival if their ships 'got the hammer', as they euphemistically called a sinking. From that point of view, the efforts of those concerned with improving survival chances would have been time and money well spent, even if they had made no impact whatsoever on the actual chances of survival: at least something was being done, and being seen to be done, and the seamen gained some comfort and reassurance in that knowledge. When survivors set sail on their next voyage they were living proof to their new shipmates that survival was possible, and they carried with them an additional expertise – in the arts of survival – which their new shipmates respected and valued highly.

Living with constant anxiety, seamen's families were keenly interested in news concerning matters of marine safety; and the state of their families' morale was reflected in the morale of their menfolk at sea. The general public also needed to know that something was being done. Even people living far inland could not close their eyes to the direct link between the sufferings of merchant seamen and the food rations they could collect from their butcher and grocer. Public opinion would have been outraged if those in power had seemed to be indifferent to the fate of the merchant seamen, and public opinion would not have been satisfied with the mere rhetorical flourishes with which politicians, admirals and business leaders routinely embellished their fulsome tributes to the seamen's bravery. No doubt the speeches were well meant, but hot air at official lunches could not warm men dying of exposure, and scraps of food from the (unrationed) menu at such functions could not feed men starving on rafts. Public opinion wanted to see really effective measures introduced to keep the men of their Merchant Navy alive.

That might be more easily demanded than achieved. The name 'Merchant Navy' was officially preferred to the more traditional 'Mercantile Marine' because it conveyed the impression of a coherent, well-organised and tightly controlled service comparable with the Royal Navy. That impression was misleading. Responsibility for the Merchant Navy did not lie with a single government department. The Ministry of Shipping was responsible for allocating ships and crews for particular purposes; the Admiralty controlled the operations needed to get them to their destinations; but other departments such as the Ministry of Labour, the Board of Trade, the Ministry of Health, and the Ministry of Agriculture and Fisheries were also concerned with such matters as employment and safety at sea.

Attempts to draw the right lessons from hard-won operational experience about matters of survival involved not only all these government Ministries, with their numerous internal sub-divisions, but also Members of Parliament, shipowners, maritime unions, researchers, inventors, the press, large and small businesses and interested individuals. Those who advocated changes in official policy had to be convinced, and be able to convince other interested parties, that their ideas genuinely would make a difference to Merchant Navy casualty rates. They also needed to be optimistic that the problems of disseminating information, and the difficulties of manufacturing new equipment and getting it installed in ships all over the world, could be overcome even under war conditions.

The motivation of many of the individuals involved was rooted in humanitarian concern for the suffering which merchant seamen had to endure, a suffering shared by the navy and army gunners who sailed with them and by the passengers they carried. One would have needed a heart of stone not to be moved by stories of men (and sometimes women and children) frozen to death in lifeboats, delirious and dying of thirst on rafts, incinerated alive in blazing oil, and a thousand other horrors. To many kind-hearted individuals, reducing the suffering and improving the chances of survival in circumstances such as these must have seemed worth any effort and expense, even if the number of extra people saved was unlikely to be particularly dramatic. In wartime, however, Ministers and senior officers, no matter what their personal humanitarian beliefs, also had to accept that human casualties were unavoidable, and sometimes the price might be very high indeed and entail unspeakable suffering. As far as possible, if war was to be waged at all, the casualties had to be weighed in a logical and unemotional way against the military, economic and political objectives achieved and against the erosion of scarce resources of manpower.

As a group, merchant seamen were not easily persuaded to accept central direction, especially in matters affecting their own safety. Most of them felt that they owed no special loyalty to the shipowners or the ship, their time-honoured motto being 'one hand for the ship and one for yourself'. Their civilian status meant that they were not subjected to a tight disciplinary régime like that found in the armed forces: masters of merchant vessels had only very limited powers to punish any breaches of discipline by derisory fines; and their authority did not extend beyond the end of a particular voyage. Merchant Navy officers had no authority over men from ships other than their own, and even on their own ship they seldom gave orders except to men in their own departments. Merchant seamen expected to think for themselves rather than give blind obedience. The master of every ship considered that, in an emergency, decisions about the safety of his vessel, crew and passengers belonged to him, and by tradition the safety of the people had priority over saving the vessel. Every mate had his own views about how safety equipment should be distributed and maintained; every engineer knew, and could make decisions about, the peculiar dangers in his own engine room; and every seaman had ideas about what he could – and would – do about his own safety. When a ship was attacked, this independent, freethinking outlook of merchant seamen was often a source of great strength, producing flexible, resourceful, intelligent responses and an ability to throw up men with impressive qualities of leadership, if need be from outside the ship's hierarchy. But a relaxed approach to discipline could also be a source of weakness and danger. Certainly some lives were lost through selfish irresponsibility, premature action without orders, uncoordinated responses and dissipation of effort.

For Britain, standing alone after the fall of France, these were truly desperate times. From June 1940 the Italian navy had been thrown into the struggle at Germany's side. In July, fearful that France might be forced to hand over her fleet to Germany as part of the armistice terms, Churchill felt that he had no alternative but to order the seizure of French vessels in British-controlled ports and to launch a pre-emptive attack on the French fleet at Mers-el-Kebir, near Oran. The Mediterranean Sea was no longer safe, even though an attack on Taranto by British carrier-borne aircraft in November crippled three of Italy's battleships. The much longer route round the Cape of Good Hope placed a considerable extra strain on the carrying capacity of Britain's merchant fleet.

Along the North Sea and Channel coasts of Britain the use of the major ports was much curtailed as shipping was brought under constant threat from fast E-boats, aircraft and mines. Contact mines, acoustic mines and magnetic mines sank over 330,000 tons of British shipping during 1940, although the minesweeping force had been greatly expanded to more than 1000 vessels and the 20,000 men who manned them were becoming more skilled and experienced in the variety of techniques required to tackle the more sophisticated types. Fortunately experts from the underwater weapons shore establishment at HMS *Vernon* had been able to recover a magnetic mine intact after it landed on mud flats in November 1939. Their analysis of its construction enabled government scientists to show that a ship could pass safely over such a mine if the magnetic field of her hull could be changed. To do that, by a process known as 'degaussing', an electric current had to be passed round the hull through a special cable. Like so many things in wartime, that cable was in short supply so that, although good progress was made, the programme of fitting ships with degaussing equipment had still not been completed by the end of 1940.

On the wider oceans, the Battle of the River Plate in December 1939 had seemed to show that the Royal Navy's long reach could snuff out the menace of the surface raider. Britain had been thrilled to see the *Admiral Graf Spee*, one of Germany's much vaunted pocket battleships, chased by three less powerful British cruisers into the neutral harbour of Montevideo outside which she ignominiously scuttled herself rather than renew the battle. The triumph was short lived. From the summer of 1940 Germany's disguised auxiliary cruisers, together with the heavy cruiser *Admiral Hipper* and the pocket battleship *Admiral Scheer*, seemed able to range far and wide seeking out Britain's merchant ships and defying her command of the sea with impunity, an unhappy portent of what might happen if the fast battlecruisers *Scharnhorst* and *Gneisenau* also penetrated into the Atlantic. Even more alarming was the threat posed by the powerful new battleship *Bismarck*, which was expected to be fully ready for action early in 1941 and would before long be joined by her equally powerful sister ship *Tirpitz*.

From August 1940, with U-boats operating from French ports on the Bay of Biscay, where they had a much shorter distance to travel in order to reach the convoy routes, and with the Luftwaffe flying from French airfields, convoys could no longer be routed through the south-western approaches and up the English Channel or St George's Channel. They all had to come through the northwestern approaches, offering the enemy a degree of predictability about the most promising areas to search for them. As early as July 1940 the Luftwaffe began flying four-engined Focke-Wulf Fw–200 Condor aircraft from an airfield near Bordeaux. This adaptation of a civil airliner could reconnoitre far out into the Atlantic beyond Gibraltar, the Azores and Iceland in search of Britain's merchant ships. Because of inadequate co-operation and a lack of joint training between the Luftwaffe and the Kriegsmarine, these reconnaissance flights rarely achieved their full operational potential for putting U-boats into contact with their targets, but the aircraft mounted a number of successful attacks on British ships, most notably setting the *Empress of Britain* on fire on 26 October 1940 and sinking the *Apapa* on 15 November.[21] This danger seemed likely to grow as more Condors became available.

From September 1940, on Admiral Doenitz's orders, and under his close direction by radio, the U-boats began to evolve the so-called wolf-pack tactics where as many boats as possible concentrated against a convoy once it had been located. They then attacked at night, prefer-ably on the surface where they enjoyed a considerable speed advantage over the merchant ships and even over many of the escorts. The low silhouette of a surfaced U-boat was difficult for ships' lookouts to spot visually and she was also invisible to the Asdic detection equipment on the escorts. The convoys were, in any case, inadequately escorted because so many destroyers had been lost in the Norwegian and French evacuations, and a large force of destroyers and other patrol craft had to be kept ready to repel a possible German invasion of the British Isles. The vulnerability of convoys to U-boats using wolf-pack tactics was rammed home by the loss of twenty-seven ships between 18 and 20 October from convoys SC7 and HX79 as they approached the safety of the North Channel. That constituted a serious blow, not only because of the loss of ships and men, but also the loss of vital cargoes, many purchased in the United States where Britain's financial resources for making such purchases under US 'Cash and Carry' legislation would soon become completely exhausted. Admiral Sir Martin Dunbar-Nasmith, the Commander-in-Chief Western Approaches based in Plymouth, told the Admiralty sadly: 'Our escorts have been too limited in number and ill-equipped to withstand the enemy's new method of attacking on the surface at night, particularly when the convoy is straggling and the visibility poor.'[22]

Much had been hoped from an agreement reached on 2 September 1940 by which the United States handed over to Britain fifty obsolete destroyers of First World War vintage in exchange for the lease of bases in British possessions in the Western Hemisphere. The agreement was a significant symbol of American support and a great boost to the morale of the British people and their political leaders, but the destroyers could make very little immediate impact on the convoy battles until they had been overhauled and their equipment brought up to date. In fact, even by the end of 1940, forty of the American destroyers were still in no fit state to be sent into action, and twenty of them had still not been brought up to an acceptable standard by the middle of 1941.

Losses of merchant ships became so serious that details of the vessels sunk and casualties among their crews had to be concealed, as much to avoid depressing the British public as to deny valuable intelligence to the enemy. In fact, the average monthly loss of British tonnage to enemy action rose from just under 105,000 gross tons in 1939 to over 203,000 gross tons in 1940,[23] while the average monthly number killed from their crews, including DEMS gunners, rose from almost 125 in 1939 to almost 470.[24] It is significant that, while the average monthly loss of tonnage almost doubled between 1939 and 1940, the loss of men almost quadrupled. Even more worrying was the seemingly inexorable increase in the tonnage lost each month. In each of the last seven months of 1940 the British merchant fleet lost over 265,000 tons, and for September, October and November the figure was over 300,000 tons.[25] To those alarming statistics had to be added the substantial losses suffered by allied countries, such as Norway and Holland, now

under enemy occupation, the sinking of neutral vessels still willing to
ship cargoes to British ports, the damaged ships lying idle until they
could be repaired and the lengthening delays before ships could discharge their cargoes at the overburdened west coast ports, where air
attacks and the blackout compounded the problems. Inevitably, by the
autumn of 1940, there was a dramatic fall in imports until they were
running at only two-thirds of the level which had been achieved in the
spring of that year.

Recalling those times in his postwar memoirs, Churchill confessed
that the U-boat menace had been the only thing which had really
frightened him during the whole war. The steady accumulation of coldly
impersonal statistics, and their visual representation by lines on charts
and graphs, emphasised the potential danger of national strangulation.
The national will to struggle on against the odds would be of no avail
if essential food and war supplies could not reach the British Isles.[26]

3

The Battle for National Survival

In the first half of 1941, Britain's ability to carry supplies to the home islands and to her forces all over the world was being eroded at an ever more alarming rate. After a relatively 'moderate' loss of almost 210,000 gross tons of shipping during January's bad weather, the British Merchant Navy lost over 316,000 tons in February, over 360,000 tons in both March and April, and over 385,000 tons in May, while the June figure of almost 270,000 tons was only slightly less appalling. In that same sixmonth period, over 825,000 tons of Allied merchant shipping and over 100,000 tons of neutral shipping were also sunk.[1] At that stage Germany seemed to be well on the way to winning the tonnage war and giving substance to Hitler's prophecy that intensified U-boat operations during 1941 might 'lead before long to the collapse of British resistance'.[2] It was abundantly clear to intelligence analysts on both sides that merchant ships were being sunk far more quickly than they could be replaced by new building, at a time when there was no opportunity to make good the shortfall by buying up surplus second-hand tonnage from other countries, a policy which had enabled Britain to make good at least part of her losses in the first year of the war. No wonder Churchill would have preferred to face the intense but stimulating perils of a German invasion, which he was confident could be defeated, to the remorseless pressure of lost ships and lost cargoes.[3]

Within the shipping industry, there appears to have been some concern that the Admiralty Trade Division's casualty section was neither liaising with the shipowners as effectively as it might nor taking their role and views sufficiently into account. In February 1941 this concern was spelled out in a memorandum from J. R. Hobhouse, a partner in the Alfred Holt shipping company and Vice-Chairman of the Liverpool Steamship Owners' Association, to Sir Thomas Brocklebank, another Liverpool shipowner. Hobhouse complained:

While most shipowners still hold enquiries into accidents arising from normal marine perils, it is almost impossible for them to conduct proper enquiries into losses due to war risks ... Usually what happens is that the Admiralty have a private and personal interview with the senior surviving officer of the merchant ship ... But there is very seldom any exchange of information between the Admiralty and the owners on such matters and certainly not any effort at collaboration to profit and learn by mistakes and thus avoid and prevent a repetition of such accidents.[4]

There is some evidence to suggest that subsequently closer collaboration was achieved, with shipping companies sending reports of their own debriefing of survivors to the casualty section at the Admiralty.

On the German side, new U-boats were being built and commissioned much faster than they were being lost, the Focke-Wulf Condors continued their successes, and the *Scharnhorst* and *Gneisenau* succeeded in breaking out into the Atlantic in February for a two-month cruise in which they sank 115,000 tons of shipping, a figure which would undoubtedly have been higher if they had not been forced to sheer away from two intercepted convoys on finding that the escort for each included a British battleship. From the end of March the German battlecruisers were based in Brest, where they posed a continuing strategic threat, while the *Admiral Scheer* had eluded the British hunters and returned safely to Germany at the beginning of April.

Now that all convoys had to be routed north of Ireland, Plymouth was no longer the best place from which to direct convoy operations. Churchill suggested that a more appropriate location would be on the River Clyde but the Admiralty chose Derby House, Liverpool, instead. A new headquarters for the Western Approaches Command was set up there on 17 February 1941 with Admiral Sir Percy Noble as Commander-in-Chief. To facilitate closer inter-service co-operation this became a joint headquarters shared with RAF Coastal Command's No. 15 Group, which was placed under the Admiralty's operational control from April 15.

On 6 March Churchill, in his capacity as Minister of Defence, issued a directive proclaiming that the 'Battle of the Atlantic' had begun.[5] Of course, the battle had actually begun some eighteen months earlier with the sinking of the *Athenia*, and since that day it had been an ever-present matter of life and death for those who went to sea. They had no need of a ministerial directive, but Churchill wanted to bring home to everyone concerned the crucial importance of keeping open the sealanes from the United States and Canada if Britain was not to share the fate of the rest of Europe. The continuous and unglamorous maritime struggle, conducted far from public view and with many details withheld from the press, could too easily fall, along with the blackout, rationing and conscription, into the category of things people had come to accept with tired resignation. The Prime Minister wanted to galvanise them into action, innovation and improvisation with a real sense of urgency. In conferring the name 'Battle of the Atlantic' he was seeking to inject a greater sense of purpose and to give the issue a greater dramatic impact. By choosing a name which echoed the earlier 'Battle of Britain' he was reminding people that, even against the odds, battles can be won.

Churchill's directive ordered that the Battle of the Atlantic was to be lifted onto the highest level of priority in such matters as equipping ports with anti-aircraft defences, giving ships more anti-aircraft weapons, speeding up ship repairs and cargo-handling at the ports, and finding means of providing air cover and stronger surface escorts for convoys. His thinking was not, however, entirely defensive; he also emphasised the importance of taking the offensive against the Focke-Wulf Condors and the U-boats at sea, in their bases and where they were built. To ensure that these matters should be kept under constant review he established, under his own chairmanship, the Battle of the Atlantic Committee of relevant Ministers and service chiefs which began regular meetings from 19 March.

Most of the work of the Battle of the Atlantic Committee was, in fact, concerned not so much with the actual cut and thrust of naval and air operations as with import procurement, the allocation of shipping space and the distribution of imported goods. This emphasis arose from events in the United States, where Britain's financial reserves to purchase weapons, food and raw materials had just about run out. Faced with the prospect that American supplies would dry up when Britain could no longer satisfy the stringent 'cash and carry' terms which US law imposed on all trade with belligerent nations, Churchill had broadcast on 9 February his famous plea: 'Give us the tools and we will finish the job', an offer which, at that period of the war, was inspired more by defiant desperation than cold realism. Recognising that encouraging Britain's continued resistance was in the best interests of the USA, the US Congress proceeded to pass President Roosevelt's Lend-Lease Bill which became law with the President's final assent on 11 March 1941. Britain could now order what she needed from the USA without having to worry about paying cash before it could be shipped, but American neutrality legislation still prohibited US merchant ships from carrying goods to any belligerent country, including Britain. Churchill felt relieved that American supplies would be available in abundance, but the problems of getting them across the Atlantic still had to be faced.[6] Given the rate at which merchant shipping was being sunk, it would be no easy task. America might well be prepared to act as the 'arsenal of democracy' – and act as a generous banker as well – but it would all be in vain if the goods themselves ended up rusting or rotting on the seabed a thousand miles from their intended destination.

Important naval successes offered Britain some encouragement during this anxious time. In March, three of Germany's most successful U-boat 'aces' were lost while attacking convoys. Günther Prien of *U–47* and Joachim Schepke of *U–100* were killed when their boats were sunk, while Otto Kretschmer was taken prisoner after *U–99* had taken her final plunge. Bold and experienced commanders such as these could not easily be replaced, and their loss was a warning to others in the U-boat service that even the most famous, charismatic and skilled might eventually run out of luck. On 28 March the British Mediterranean Fleet sank three Italian heavy cruisers and two destroyers at the Battle of Matapan. Finally, in May 1941, the new battleship *Bismarck* and the cruiser *Prinz Eugen* made their long expected break out into the Atlantic. Although, after passing through the Denmark Strait, the raiders sank the battlecruiser *Hood*, the British Home Fleet managed to hunt down and sink the *Bismarck* on the 27th before she had any opportunity to maul the Atlantic convoys which were her real target. The *Prinz Eugen* joined the *Scharnhorst* and *Gneisenau* in Brest where all three were subjected to frequent, but not very effective, air attacks for the remainder of 1941.

Determined to see every aspect of the Battle of the Atlantic conducted with greater urgency and efficiency, Churchill undertook a drastic reorganisation of ministerial responsibility for the Merchant Navy from 1 May 1941. The Conservative MP for Southend, Henry 'Chips' Channon, recorded in his diary some Westminster gossip about a new Ministry of Communications being set up under a political outsider, an 'unknown' called Leathers who had been given a peerage and appointed a Privy Councillor.[7] Winston Churchill remembered it differently. Before the war, while he was still out of office, he had held the directorship of a small shipping company, and had formed a high opinion of the competence of its Chairman, Frederick Leathers. Casting around for ways of improving Britain's chances of surviving the Battle of the Atlantic, Churchill became convinced that the nation's entire transport system would have to be managed with maximum efficiency.

That task extended from merchant shipping to speedy cargo-handling in the hard-pressed west coast ports and the use of rail and road transport to distribute cargoes before enemy bombers could destroy them in dockside warehouses. He decided that Leathers was the right man, in both experience and personal qualities, to organise this integrated national transport service, which would be placed under a new Ministry of War Transport, combining the functions of the former Ministries of Transport and Shipping. As Minister of War Transport, a post he held until 1945, Leathers was given a peerage so that he could concentrate on his job without the distraction of having to fight a by-election and sit in the House of Commons. He fully justified Churchill's confidence.[8]

Leathers seems to have been the perfect man for the job. His shipping credentials were impressive – he had been Deputy Chairman of William Cory and Sons, the collier company; he had been a Director of many shipping companies; he was a member of both the Institute of Shipbrokers and the Council of the Chamber of Shipping. From the old Ministry of Shipping, Hurcomb became the Director-General of the new Ministry of War Transport, and Foley became one of three Deputy Directors-General. Sir Arthur Salter continued as Parliamentary Secretary, and an additional Parliamentary Secretary was appointed; Colonel J. J. Llewellin, a pre-war Civil Lord of the Admiralty. With Leathers in the House of Lords, these Junior Ministers would have to carry the burden in the Commons. Initially the responsibility for answering questions concerning the safety and welfare of Merchant Navy survivors seems to have been in Llewellin's hands until his appointment as President of the Board of Trade in February 1942, when he was replaced by Philip Noel-Baker, a Labour Member of Parliament.

One of the first problems to worry the new Ministry was the likelihood of a crisis in the manning of merchant ships. Intelligence estimates based on the heavy casualties suffered in the first half of 1941 projected that, with many additional U-boats expected to come into operational service in the later months, total losses for the year might reach something like 7,000,000 tons. The writer of the official war history of merchant shipping calculated that by June of that year the number of British merchant seamen (excluding lascars) was probably as low as 108,000, 'just, but only just, enough men to go round'.[9] To meet the manning problem the Ministry of Labour and National Service imposed in May the Essential Work (Merchant Navy) Order to prevent merchant seamen from seeking jobs ashore, to provide them with continuous employment in the Merchant Navy Reserve Pool in between voyages, and to compel former seamen between eighteen and sixty to register for possible re-employment at sea if they had served in the Merchant Navy at any time since 1936.[10] In this way 53,000 former seamen were identified. Of course, many of them were unsuitable for further sea service on age or health grounds, and many others were engaged in key jobs ashore from which they could not be spared, but the Essential Work (Merchant Navy) Order produced 6000 experienced men for the Merchant Navy in the second half of 1941 and almost 5300 in 1942.[11] Other stop-gap measures adopted during the war included the retraining of surplus stewards as deckhands or firemen, allowing some volunteers for whom the Royal Navy had no immediate employment to transfer to the Merchant Navy in preference to being drafted into the army, and encouraging boys from various youth organisations, especially the Sea Cadets, to volunteer for the Merchant Navy from the age of sixteen, when they would have been considered too young to join His Majesty's Forces.

If they could have continued to inflict the same heavy rate of sinkings over the whole of 1941, the Germans might well have forced Britain out of the war. The official history of British wartime intelligence concluded that the U-boat campaign came very close indeed to achieving a decisive result in that year.[12] In the second half of the year, however, the number of British merchant ships sunk as a result of enemy action was significantly reduced. In both July and August the losses amounted to less than 100,000 gross tons and, while the September figure rose to 215,000 tons, in October the figure fell to just over 150,000 tons and there was a further fall to just over 90,000 tons in November. In December the figure would have been below 80,000 tons, but by then the entry of Japan into the war resulted in an additional 194,000 tons being lost by sinking or seizure in the Far East.[13] Broadly speaking, Allied and neutral losses fluctuated in much the same pattern.

The reasons why success eluded the Germans in the second half of 1941 were both varied and complex. Of prime importance was the developing policy of the United States which, having recognised that Britain's continued resistance amounted to an invaluable outer bastion of America's own defences, felt obliged to involve herself more and more in the Battle of the Atlantic. Gradually Doenitz found himself facing a new opponent, while also being forbidden by Hitler to strike back. In April 1941 Roosevelt had announced that the Pan-American Security Zone would be extended to cover the whole Western Atlantic as far from America's shores as longitude 26°W. American warships, some transferred from the Pacific, engaged in aggressive patrolling inside that zone to discourage German activity and they reported to the British the position of any German vessels they encountered. British warships and merchant vessels were being built or repaired in US shipyards under the Lend-Lease Agreement. On 7 July US forces took up garrison duties in Iceland to free the British garrison, which had been stationed there since 1940, for duties elsewhere; and on 5 September the USS *Greer* narrowly avoided a torpedo attack after becoming involved in an action between a German U-boat and a British aircraft. An indignant Roosevelt ordered the US Navy to protect all merchant shipping inside his unilaterally declared security zone and to attack on sight U-boats which might threaten the merchant ships. In agreement with Britain, the United States Navy began escorting British convoys as far as Iceland, releasing some British escorts for other duties. These decidedly un-neutral acts would have supplied Germany with ample grounds for declaring war, but Hitler declined to approve such a step while he was engaged in a land campaign in Russia. Nevertheless, U-boat commanders could hardly be expected to establish beyond doubt the nationality of escorts glimpsed briefly during darkness or bad weather. As a result the USS *Kearney* was badly damaged by torpedo on 17 October while escorting convoy SC48 and, two weeks later, *U–552* sank the USS *Reuben James* while she was escorting convoy HX156. One hundred and fifteen American sailors from her crew lost their lives in a war which neither Germany nor the USA was prepared to declare openly. That step was finally taken by Germany on 11 December 1941, after the Japanese attack on Pearl Harbour.

Hitler's decision to invade Russia on 22 June 1941 was another important influence on the Battle of the Atlantic. German air power was mainly directed to supporting the army on the Eastern Front when it might have been flying reconnaissance missions in support of the U-boat wolf-packs in the Atlantic or bombing Britain's seaports and convoys. Steel, which might have expanded the U boat building programme even faster, went into tank production for the army's drive on Moscow, Leningrad and the Ukraine. Instead of contributing to Doenitz's efforts to strike a knock-out blow in the Atlantic, mines and U-boats were diverted to the Eastern Baltic and the Arctic to bottle up the Russian fleet.

From September 1941 the Germans also began to withdraw U-boats from the Atlantic campaign in order to transfer them to the Mediterranean where they could support Italy.[14] In November they scored two important successes by sinking the aircraft carrier HMS *Ark Royal* near

Gibraltar and the battleship HMS *Barham* off the Egyptian coast. As Commander-in-Chief of the German Navy, Admiral Raeder seems to have come to the conclusion that 'submarine warfare on British imports in the Atlantic [would have to be] greatly reduced for a time ... as tasks in the Arctic Ocean and the Mediterranean Sea [were] more urgent'.[15] By December thirty-six U-boats were either in the Mediterranean or on passage there, and the intention was to increase the force to fifty U-boats.[16] This diversion of effort away from the battleground where the U-boats had the possibility of victory within their grasp seems contrary to the basic principles of naval strategy. During 1941 Germany's U-boat force grew from 89 boats to 249, yet it has been calculated that the daily average of boats actually engaged at sea on the Atlantic convoy routes only rose from twelve in the first quarter to sixteen or seventeen later in the year.[17] Of course, some boats would always be on passage to or from their patrol areas, others had to spend time in port for victualling or repairs, and a large number were training new crews in the Baltic; but it is surprising that the Germans did not make a bigger effort to find more boats for Doenitz in what could have been the decisive theatre.

On the British side, more newly-built corvettes were coming into service and there was no longer a pressing need to guard against the imminent threat of a cross-Channel invasion. Convoy escorts could be strengthened and more attention devoted to improving the training of the commanding officers and their crews. By using a refuelling base in Iceland and the co-operation of the growing Royal Canadian Navy, it became possible from July 1941 to provide some kind of escort for convoys all the way across the Atlantic. The effectiveness of escorts in detecting surfaced U-boats in night battles around the convoys was greatly improved by the use of radar, especially when the new centimetric Type 271 set began to be introduced from mid-1941 in place of the older Type 286, which had first appeared towards the end of 1940. From October 1941 escorts also began to receive another detection device – HF/DF, a high frequency direction finder which would indicate the bearing of the numerous brief radio signals made by U-boats when they were shadowing convoys, concentrating the wolf-packs and passing information to U-boat Headquarters. During the autumn of 1941 a new illuminant flare known as 'Snowflake' was developed for escorts to use, in place of the unsatisfactory star shell, when attacking surfaced U-boats at night. 'Snowflake' was also issued to merchant vessels but could be something of a mixed blessing, if used with more enthusiasm than discretion, since it might well illuminate the U-boat's target instead of the U-boat itself.

Aircraft of RAF Coastal Command were at last being equipped with efficient ASV radar sets, while more extensive patrols by long-range aircraft, such as the Sunderland, Catalina and Liberator over the Bay of Biscay, the northwestern approaches, south of Iceland and east of Newfoundland made it riskier for U-boats to operate on the surface except in a 300-mile zone in mid-Atlantic which was still beyond the reach of shore-based aircraft. The work of Coastal Command was, however, constantly hampered by the difficulty of obtaining sufficient four-engined aircraft with the endurance required for long-range flights over the sea. Bomber Command's insistence that the air offensive against Germany gave them prior claim on such aircraft seemed to carry more weight with those in charge of the higher direction of Britain's war effort. Despite Churchill's proclaimed intention of giving priority to the Battle of the Atlantic, Bomber Command were always reluctant to mount major raids on targets such as the German surface warships in Brest, the concrete U-boat shelters under construction in the Biscay ports, or the U-boat training centres on the Baltic coast. They argued that their campaign to destroy Germany's industrial centres and cripple German civilian morale would utimately diminish Germany's assaults on Britain's shipping.

Urged on by Churchill's demands for innovation and improvisation, progress had been made in providing convoys with their own air protection by mounting fighter aircraft on catapults, initially on Royal Navy ships such as HMS *Pegasus* and Navy-manned former merchant ships such as HMS *Springbank* and HMS *Ariguani* but subsequently on ordinary merchant ships, such as oil-tankers, carrying their normal cargoes. Although they achieved reasonable success in driving off the Focke-Wulf Condors, the catapult ships were a measure of desperation because, unless they were within range of land, the fighter pilot eventually had to abandon his aircraft, parachute into the sea and hope to be picked up. For the longer term, the introduction in September 1941 of the light escort carrier HMS *Audacity*, with a simple flight deck for take-off and landing mounted on a merchant ship hull, offered much greater potential, not only for fighter protection but also for flying anti-U-boat patrols in the vicinity of a convoy. The *Audacity* had only a short, eventful career before she was torpedoed and sunk by *U–751* on 21 December, but by then she had amply proved the validity of the escort carrier concept.

The German Navy's *Beobachtungsdienst* (*B-Dienst*) or Signals Intelligence Service deserved part of the credit for the success of Doenitz's U-boat campaigns. Since 1940 they had been able to break into some of the codes used for British convoy radio signals. Although the amount which could be read and the speed with which it could be read varied when the codes were changed from time to time, information gleaned in this way had given Doenitz the incalculable advantage, on some occasions, of being almost as well-informed about his opponents' dispositions and intentions as someone with free access to the Western Approaches Command operations room.

Kriegsmarine signals traffic, passing through the ingenious Enigma machines on transmission and reception, had for a long time defied the best efforts of the British Government Code and Cypher School at Bletchley Park, but that was all changed very dramatically during 1941. The code-breakers at Bletchley Park gradually built up an understanding of the operating procedures and construction of the Enigma machines from papers or equipment taken from the German armed trawler *Krebs* during a commando raid in March, from the intercepted German weather ship *München* and from Kapitänleutnant Lemp's *U–110* before she sank in May. Further seizures were made from the weather ship *Lauenburg* in June and from *U–570* which surrendered to a British aircraft in August.

From June 1941 the Bletchley Park experts began reading the German Home Waters Enigma signals. The speed at which they could accomplish this task varied, but it was usually within little more than twenty-four hours and sometimes very much less. Western Approaches Headquarters became very adept at using this information, together with radio direction fixes on U-boat transmissions, to order convoys to change course away from areas where U-boats were known to be concentrated and to send reinforcements to the escort of any threatened convoy. It is significant that in September, the month of heaviest sinkings in the second half of 1941, Doenitz temporarily baffled Bletchley Park by changing the encoding procedures and curtailing the use of radio signals. The German naval historian Jürgen Rohwer has estimated that the use of information provided by Bletchley Park saved 1,500,000 tons of shipping which would otherwise have gone to the bottom of the Atlantic in the second half of 1941.[18] At the casualty rates then prevailing in merchant ships sunk by U-boats, the information probably saved the lives of five thousand merchant seamen and DEMS gunners.[19]

Despite this reduction in shipping losses in the second half of the year, the average monthly loss of British ships for 1941 as a whole rose to just over 235,000 gross tons,[20] while the average monthly number killed among the crews, including DEMS gunners, rose to over 650.[21] Even though statistics such as these were now treated as top secret, the serious nature of the losses could not be hushed up completely, especially in the major seaports where so many families of merchant seamen lived, and to which survivors returned after being rescued. The horror of some of the sensational reports allowed through the censorship during 1940 and 1941 generated considerable public disquiet.

In particular, a book was published in 1941 about the sinking of the cargo steamer *Anglo Saxon* by the German auxiliary cruiser *Widder* on 21 August 1940. Under the title *Two Survived*, it told how seven survivors from the crew of forty had managed to reach a lifeboat after their ship had been shelled and torpedoed without warning in the Atlantic, and how just two of the men had survived the seventy days which elapsed before their boat was washed up on Eleuthera Island in the Bahamas. Some details of their ordeal appeared in various publications,[22] but the book gave a much fuller account. The author expressed the hope that the story might

> direct public attention to the criminal neglect of ordinary common-sense provisioning of lifeboats carried on cargo vessels ... The British tramp goes to sea with the same old clinker built wooden boat of Elizabethan days. [As to provisions], the breaker, holding six gallons of water, was only half-full ... There were a few cans of mutton and condensed milk, both of which produce thirst.[23]

In view of its powerful indictment of the Ministry of Shipping, it seems surprising at first glance that the official censor passed the book for publication, but he was probably influenced by the fact that it was also being published by Random House in New York.

Public anxiety about stories such as this was reflected in pressure from certain Labour Members of Parliament during 1941. David Kirkwood demanded more frequent inspection of the provisioning and seaworthiness of ship's boats, and suggested the provision of blankets to prevent deaths from exposure;[24] Glenvil Hall urged the Ministry 'to ensure that all ships' boats shall be fitted with effective signalling apparatus';[25] and David Adams wanted to see 'measures for securing greater safety and comfort to occupants of lifeboats and rafts'.[26]

To reassure Members of Parliament and the general public that they were not callously neglecting safety issues, the Ministry of War Transport, assisted by the Ministry of Information, launched a public relations offensive. In June 1941 the Crown Film Unit released the film *Merchant Seamen*, featuring genuine seamen as actors and with a plot centred on a sinking, a rescue and a survivor returning to sea to sink an enemy submarine with his new ship's gun.[27] In July the BBC began broadcasting

a magazine programme called *The Blue Peter* to provide merchant
seamen and their families with a mixture of 'news, views and humour'.[28]
Also in July, Lord Leathers himself launched the first of six touring
exhibitions of photographs illustrating the risk and dangers faced by
merchant seamen.[29] A special exhibition of drawings, models and actual
lifesaving equipment was staged in October for Members of Parliament
so that they could see for themselves the latest developments which the
Ministry was introducing. In November, the Merchant Navy featured
in two striking posters, one of them bearing the inscription 'Heroes
All' and the lapel badge worn in lieu of a uniform by the seamen.[30]
The parade for Birmingham's Warship Week featured two lorries from
the Austin Motor Company carrying a fully rigged lifeboat and
examples of the company's lifeboat engines, together with a banner
inscribed 'Save Our Seamen' which emphasised the SOS of the initial
letters.[31]

In December 1941, encouraged by the success of the exhibition
staged for Members of Parliament, the Ministry of War Transport set
up even bigger exhibitions for the general public in London, Newcastle,
Hull, Southampton, Cardiff, Liverpool, Glasgow and Belfast, with Edinburgh added in the following month. Staged at Charing Cross
Underground Station, the London exhibition was designed 'as a tribute
to the men of the Merchant Navy' and to 'bring comfort ... to all who
have relatives at sea'. It covered 'every scene in the life-saving drama
of the sea, from the moment the captain gives the order "abandon
ship" until the rescue ship or plane comes in sight'. The central exhibit
was a lifeboat from the *Lapwing*, sunk on 26 September 1941 while
she had stopped to pick up survivors from two other vessels. Nineteen
survivors, drawn from all three ships, had sailed the boat several
hundred miles to Ireland. In opening the exhibition, Lord Leathers
assured his audience that life-saving was a matter of daily concern.

> The spreading of the war at sea to all parts of the globe ... made it
> more important than ever that those who man our ships should be fully
> protected against wartime hazards ... The Ministry were now taking
> practical steps to see that [ships] carried the best equipment available
> [and] they would persevere until provision had been made against every
> conceivable danger of the sea.[32]

To be fair, considerable improvements had been made or were in
the process of being introduced, and no doubt Lord Leathers was
sincere in what he had to say. But the realities of the merchant seamen's
war had been, and would continue to be, a far cry from the world of

Ministers, shipowners, Members of Parliament, committees and exhibitions. In any contest between 'every conceivable danger of the sea'
and the 'daily concern' of the Ministry that seamen should be 'fully
protected', few merchant seamen would have been prepared to bet their
war risk money (or even the price of a pint of beer) on the Ministry of
War Transport.

By the end of 1941, as Lord Leathers emphasised, the war had ceased
to be a European affair; the involvement of the Soviet Union, the United
States and Japan had transformed it into a global conflict. British
merchant ships were at risk of being sunk not only in the Atlantic and
the Mediterranean but also in the Arctic Ocean, the Caribbean, off the
Cape of Good Hope, in the Indian Ocean, the South China Sea and
the Pacific Ocean. Wherever sinkings occurred they were still, in essence,
part of the Battle of the Atlantic. Lines drawn on maps by geographers
cannot be treated as if they define the limits of maritime conflict like
sportsfield touchlines. A tanker set alight in the Caribbean was one ship
less in a convoy passing through the North Channel three weeks later,
and its cargo of aviation spirit would not reach the fuel tanks of the
long-range aircraft trying to drive U-boats away from subsequent
Atlantic convoys. A cargo ship sent to the bottom of the Mozambique
Channel would not steam past Liverpool pierhead fifty days later, and
her cargo of tea would not cheer the night-shift workers at the Rolls-
Royce works in Derby as they built the aero engines to power the RAF's
bombers. A passenger liner sunk by Japanese aircraft in the Straits of
Malacca would not be available to ferry American troops across the
Atlantic for the North African or Normandy invasions. For the enemy,
also, a decision to send U-boats to the Indian Ocean meant fewer
U-boats around the Atlantic convoys which, in turn, were then deprived
of the protection of the surface escorts and aircraft drawn off to protect
shipping in distant waters.

Conflict in the wider oceans, involving many ships sailing independently rather than in convoy, had important implications for
survivors. No one might know of their plight, they might be exposed
to greater extremes of climate, and their chances of being picked up by
a passing ship were diminished. Distances were far greater, requiring
more very long voyages in lifeboats and on rafts, and survivors might
come ashore in some out of the way places where medical and welfare
arrangements for their reception were inadequate or non-existent. On
the credit side, the development of very long range reconnaissance
aircraft improved the survivors' chances of being spotted from the air,
but each new extension of the enemy's war on merchant shipping

produced fresh challenges to the ingenuity of those who were trying to improve survival equipment, arrange for its manufacture and installation, and ensure that it was used effectively.

The problem of how to improve the odds in favour of the merchant seamen's survival did not, of course, depend entirely on someone's ability to push safety innovations through the complicated technical, organisational and human labyrinths which made up the British Merchant Navy. The enemy, by the modes of attack they adopted, by the geographical areas they selected for operations, and by their conduct towards the survivors from ships which had been sunk, could significantly change the odds both for and against survival.

For example, attacks by major surface warships or disguised auxiliary cruisers rarely led to heavy casualties, since most merchantmen realised the hopelessness of prolonged resistance. Large numbers of survivors were rescued and taken back to enemy held territory as prisoners-of-war, because the surface ships had space on board to accommodate prisoners who could later be transferred to a network of supply ships and blockade runners. Commerce raiding by the auxiliary cruisers, having achieved its greatest successes in 1940 and 1941, petered out during 1942. Raiding operations into the Atlantic by Germany's major surface warships had virtually come to an end in 1941. Obsessed with the possibility of an Allied invasion of Norway, Hitler chose to station some U-boats and most of his remaining major surface units, including the *Tirpitz*, where they could guard against that anticipated danger. From their bases in the fiords, when conditions were thought to be favourable, they might still make a lunge at the Arctic convoys to Russia and they could still seem to threaten a further incursion into the Atlantic. The escape of the *Scharnhorst*, *Gneisenau* and *Prinz Eugen* from Brest on 11 February 1942 and their immediate return to Germany by a bold dash up the English Channel was seen at the time as a terrible humiliation for British seapower, but it was really a strategic defeat for Germany. Hitler and his admirals had been forced to withdraw the ships for a defensive purpose because growing British air power had made it too dangerous for them to remain where they had seemed so favourably poised to threaten the convoys.

Losses of merchant ships to mine warfare, also at its most dangerous between 1939 and 1941, were confined to relatively shallow seas where survivors might well be able to reach land in their own boats, or they could be rescued by boats from the shore. But the mine was an indiscriminate weapon, as likely to strike by night as by day. Crews on quite small vessels which were blown to pieces by detonating enough explosive to sink far larger craft, or men left floundering in the water during darkness, had a poor chance of survival. On the other hand, aircraft attacks, most frequent in 1940 to 1943, were usually made in daylight, and merchant ships were able to fight back with at least some hope of success. Survivors from ships sunk by mines or aircraft attacks could very seldom look to the enemy for rescue.

Attacks by enemy submarines, predominantly the German U-boats, accounted for almost 68 per cent of the British merchant ship tonnage lost over the whole war, as compared with 14 per cent by air attacks, just over 7 per cent by mine and just under 7 per cent by surface raiders.[33] Changes in U-boat tactics, and improvements in the torpedoes themselves as the war progressed, increased the danger for the crews of the merchant vessels that were attacked. Sometimes submarines might take one or two senior survivors as prisoners-of-war, but they did not have space to accommodate the rest.

The reduction in British shipping losses which had looked so promising in the second half of 1941 did not continue into 1942. In the early months of the year, as heavy losses in the Far East continued, German U-boats found easy targets along the ill-defended shipping lanes off the east coast of the United States and in the Caribbean. In January 1942 Britain lost, from all types of enemy action, over 145,000 gross tons of merchant shipping, and thereafter the losses became even heavier, with December's 226,000 tons being the next lowest figure. February and August both saw losses of over 340,000 tons, while October's alarming figure of 409,000 tons was immediately overtaken by the sinking of almost 470,000 tons in November. In all Britain lost about 3,470,000 tons of merchant shipping that year, while Allied countries, including the United States, lost a further 4,000,000 tons.[34]

These very heavy shipping losses can be partly explained by the four or five months taken by the Americans to set up a convoy system for shipping along their east coast and in the Caribbean. For a time the situation was so desperate that in some areas anti-U-boat searches were entrusted to amateur yachtsmen in their pleasure cruisers and amateur pilots flying their own light aircraft. A convoy system for the US east coast was not fully in place until May 1942 and the Caribbean, with its valuable oil tanker traffic, was not fully covered until July. Even then the captains of American escorts and merchant ships took time to acquire the skills and disciplines of convoy work. Some British escort vessels were sent to pass on the benefit of their hard-won experience.

Another costly aspect of the war at sea in 1942 was the necessity of running supply convoys to Malta and to the Russian ports of Murmansk and Archangel. On these routes, where there was little room for manoeuvre, the enemy enjoyed air superiority and, with their heavy warships based close at hand, there was always the threat that they might establish local surface superiority also. The heavy losses incurred in fighting these convoys through were considered justified by the strategic importance of Malta for the land battles in North Africa and the critical importance of enabling Russia to resist the German offensive.

Doenitz showed great skill in shifting the focus of his U-boat campaign to probe the weaknesses in his opponents' defensive measures. He seemed able to find profitable targets for his new and efficient magnetic pistol torpedoes wherever he chose: from the US east coast, to the Caribbean and Gulf of Mexico, then to the convoys in the mid-Atlantic air gap, to the coast of Brazil and Trinidad, off West Africa and the Gulf of Guinea, and as far afield as South Africa and the Mozambique Channel. There was no shortage of targets because additional shipping movements were needed to reinforce Britain's threatened position in India and Ceylon, to build up the 8th Army in Egypt for its offensive against Rommel in October and to launch the Anglo-American invasion of French North Africa in November. To operate in these more distant waters Doenitz could call on U-boats with a far greater endurance. The Type IXD for example, with twenty-two torpedoes, had a range of 23,700 miles on the surface at twelve knots compared with the Type VIIC's 6500 miles with fourteen torpedoes.[35] In the middle of 1942 the Germans introduced the Type XIV U-boat tankers from which other boats could refuel on their way to or from the more distant areas.

Of all the advantages enjoyed by Doenitz, the most important lay in the field of signals intelligence. While the German *B-Dienst* was able to read much of the British naval cypher and the inter-Allied Atlantic convoy signals quickly enough for the information to be used in directing operations, the British Government Code and Cypher School at Bletchley Park had lost the ability to read the U-boat Enigma signals. Changes in the coding procedures and the introduction of a fourth rotor for the Enigma machines in February 1942 vastly increased the number of letter permutations to the dismay and bafflement of the British code-breakers. The Commander-in-Chief Western Approaches could no longer confidently divert convoys away from concentrations of U-boats of whose location he was as well informed as Admiral Doenitz himself. The Germans were also beginning to reap the benefits of their U-boat building and training programme. The average daily number of boats engaged operationally in the Atlantic, which had been only in single figures in 1940 and about fifteen during 1941 and the first half of 1942, rose to twenty-five in the third quarter and forty in the last quarter of that year.[36]

On the British side improvements continued to be made in equipment to fight the U-boats. From the middle of 1942 most escort vessels were fitted with Type 271 radar sets, while the aircraft of Coastal Command began to surprise U-boats on the surface by using a combination of ASV radar and the Leigh searchlight until the Germans countered with a radar detector known as the 'Biscay Cross'. By the end of the year most British escort vessels had also been fitted with HF/DF apparatus to pinpoint the position of any U-boat using its radio in the vicinity of a convoy, and escorts were also getting radio telephones which enabled them to co-ordinate collaborative anti-U-boat strikes more effectively. A very promising new weapon called 'Hedgehog' was being fitted on escort vessels. This could fire twenty-four contact-fused bombs from a multi-barrelled spigot mortar. Its great advantage was that it could fire ahead of the escort while she still had a contact accurately pinpointed by Asdic, whereas traditional depthcharging required the escort to run over the U-boat, a manouevre in which the Asdic contact was inevitably lost in the noise of the escort's own propellers and the disturbance caused by the exploding depth charges.

Most encouraging of all was the tremendous expansion of the American shipbuilding industry. The first of the 'Liberty Ships', the *Patrick Henry*, took only six months to build when she was launched in September 1941. That remarkable achievement was soon excelled as the use of prefabricated sections and welded construction brought the building time down to about two months in mid-1942; and that in turn was outshone by the building of the *Robert E. Peary* by the Kaiser Corporation in under five days in November. In all US shipyards turned out almost five and a half million gross tons of new merchant ships to share with Britain during 1942, as compared with only 815,000 tons the previous year. Even with over 1,800,000 tons of new ships from British Empire shipyards, however, 1942 showed a net shipping loss for the Anglo-American alliance. American shipyards might well be on their way to building enough ships to replace losses, but it seemed doubtful whether all the lost cargoes could be replaced and whether the new ships could be adequately manned, given the heavy casualties among experienced merchant seamen. From the crews of British merchant ships sunk in 1942 almost 10,000 merchant seamen and DEMS gunners lost their lives, while some who survived were in no condition to return to sea.[37]

The distinguished military historian Correlli Barnett has claimed that the shipping losses inflicted by the U-boat campaign during 1942 were so serious that Britain seemed to be heading for a crushing defeat and economic breakdown.[38] In his view, the evidence available to Churchill's government at that time indicated that there was no chance of the bombing offensive bringing Germany to her to her knees quickly enough to avert disaster for Britain at the hands of the U-boats in the Atlantic.[39]

In January 1943 Doenitz was appointed Commander-in-Chief of the German Navy in place of the long-serving Admiral Raeder, who had become discredited in Hitler's eyes by the failure of the *Hipper* and *Lützow* to sweep aside the British destroyer escort and massacre convoy JW51B to Murmansk in December 1942. As Commander-in-Chief Doenitz hoped to use his influence to ensure that greater priority would be given to the U-boat offensive against merchant ships. In addition to his wider responsibilities, he retained the U-boat command, although the day to day control of operations was left to his chief of staff, Rear-Admiral Godt.

Doenitz was now faced with a new opponent, Admiral Sir Max Horton, a vastly experienced submariner, who had replaced Admiral Noble as Commander-in-Chief Western Approaches in November 1942. It was fortunate for Admiral Horton and for Britain that from 13 December 1942 Bletchley Park once more began to read some of the U-boat Enigma traffic thanks to material recovered from *U–559*, which had been sunk off the Egyptian coast. By the beginning of 1943 Western Approaches Command were once more achieving some success in the evasive routeing of convoys by using information gleaned from German signals. Coincidental changes in the British cyphers were, for the time being, making life more difficult for the code-breakers of the German *B-Dienst*. Nevertheless, with a daily average of fifty U-boats operating in the Atlantic it could not be expected that evasion would be as successful as it had been in the second half of 1941. British shipping losses were still heavy, but on nothing like the scale of 1942. In the first six months of 1943 losses from all types of enemy action were below 100,000 gross tons in January and June, and between 145,000 and 195,000 tons in February, April and May. Only in March, with the loss of almost 385,000 tons, did it look as though the destruction might match the 1942 figures.[40] In that month two large eastbound convoys, SC122 and HX229, lost twenty-two merchant ships in a four-day battle with large wolf-packs.[41]

Three months later, although no one could have realised it at the time, the outcome of the Battle of the Atlantic had virtually been decided; the German threat to Britain's survival had been defeated. In each of the last five months of 1943 the loss of British merchant shipping to enemy action of all kinds fell to about 60,000 gross tons, while the figure for the complete year, at just over 1,500,000 tons, was less than half the 3,470,000 lost in the previous year. In 1944 the total loss was below 500,000 tons and in 1945 below 200,000 tons.[42] In contrast to those figures, the American shipyards, supplemented by the shipyards of the British Empire, built a prodigious surplus of almost eleven million gross tons of new shipping over and above the total world-wide losses of the Allies in 1943 and almost twelve million tons more than the Allies lost in 1944. Doenitz had lost the tonnage war, although he continued to play what proved to be a losing hand with considerable cunning and determination. The number of German U-boats sunk rose from a mere twenty-four in 1940 to thirty-five in 1941, eighty-seven in 1942, 237 in 1943 and 242 in 1944, with a further 151 in 1945.[43] Those figures illustrate the impact of better weapons, improved technology, assiduous intelligence gathering, more numerous surface escorts, better air defence of convoys and the bombing campaign against U-boat bases and transit routes. In face of appalling casualties the U-boats continued to seek out their prey until the *Avondale Park* became the last British merchant ship lost in the Second World War when she was torpedoed by *U–2336*, in the Firth of Forth, on 7 May 1945.

Of Germany's remaining surface warships, the *Gneisenau* was crippled by bombs on 27 February 1942 while she was having mine damage repaired in Kiel. She was never again fit to venture outside the Baltic. The *Scharnhorst* was driven away from an Arctic convoy by British cruisers and sunk by HMS *Duke of York* on 26 December 1943. The *Tirpitz*, a potential threat even while lurking ignominiously in Norwegian fiords, was damaged in a midget submarine attack on 22 September 1943, further damaged by Fleet Air Arm aircraft on 3 April 1944, and damaged yet again in other air attacks before being finally sunk by RAF Lancasters using six-ton 'Tallboy' bombs on 12 November 1944.

In part the Battle of the Atlantic was won by the application of airpower. The dreadful losses of March 1943 at last convinced those directing the British and American strategy that very long range aircraft, mostly Liberators, had to be found to close the mid-Atlantic gap in the air cover for convoys. Closing the air gap was greatly facilitated by persuading Portugal, in October 1943, to allow the use of airfields in the Azores. At the same time more and more convoys were protected by light escort carriers or merchant aircraft carriers, such as the *Empire MacAlpine*, with Merchant Navy masters and crews, which continued in their commercial role despite being encumbered with a primitive flight deck. Both land-based and sea-based aircraft were invaluable in locating U-boats as they approached a convoy. Once they had been forced to submerge, the U-boats' slower speed made it more difficult for them to maintain contact and manoeuvre into a favourable firing position. Whether in the vicinity of convoys or on passage to and from their bases, U-boats became increasingly vulnerable in the later years of the war to aircraft equipped with sophisticated radar sets, Leigh lights, rockets and more efficient bombs and depth charges, while their bases and the U-boat building yards were targeted by the bomber offensive.

In part the battle was won by providing convoys with more and faster escort vessels, 300-foot long frigates capable of twenty knots. They were more heavily armed, more comfortable in heavy seas and had greater endurance than the corvettes. Progress was made in equipping escorts with better radar, HF/DF and radio telephone sets; and, with experience, they became adept in using the 'Hedgehog' weapon, and the similarly forward-firing 'Squid' to deadly effect. Escorts were regularly refuelled at sea, and it became possible to keep the same group of ships together so that team work and confidence in one another were fostered. Training of commanding officers and crews was stepped up, and the lessons learned from experience were widely disseminated. Besides the immediate convoy escorts, support groups were formed to go to the aid of any threatened convoy. Freed from the chore of close escort, the support groups were able to pursue U-boats spotted from the air at some distance from the convoy and to harry a detected U-boat to destruction, even if the chase took two or three days and led them far from the merchant ships.

The Bletchley Park code-breakers continued to read, after varying periods of delay, the German signals traffic. A very valuable outcome of this was the tracking and destruction of the 'milch cow' tanker U-boats by identifying their refuelling rendezvous positions and waylaying them there.

It should not, however, be thought that in 1943 or 1944 it was by any means certain that Germany had finally lost the Battle of the Atlantic. There was always the risk that shipping losses might begin to rise again as they had after the misleading fall in the second half of 1941. The Germans had not given up the struggle by any means. From time to time their scientists came up with promising devices to warn U-boats when they had been detected by radar, only to see their inventiveness nullified by subsequent improvements in the radar sets. They produced devices that a U-boat under attack could release to mislead the attackers into believing that a 'kill' had been achieved when, in fact, the U-boat was trying to steal silently away. They produced improved versions of two torpedoes successfully brought into service in 1943: the *Federapparat* (FAT), which would zigzag backwards and forwards across the track of a convoy even if it missed the vessel at which it had been aimed, and the *Zaunkönig* which was attracted towards a target's propeller noise and detonated acoustically. The latter was particularly successful against escorts travelling at high speed, but it was found that it could be distracted by towing a noise-making device some distance astern. In February 1944 the first U-boat equipped with *Schnorkel* apparatus was sent on patrol, and by the end of that year all U-boats had been equipped with this special tube through which sufficient air to run the diesel engines could be sucked down into the boat while at periscope depth where she was undetectable by radar.

Even as late as 1945 British naval intelligence was warning against the possibility of another major U-boat offensive liable to inflict losses comparable with those of early 1943.[44] During 1944, despite the Allied bombing, the invasion of France and the Russian advance, the German Armaments Minister, Albert Speer, had managed to organise the building of two completely new types of U-boat. Driven by batteries of far larger capacity, their electric motors could achieve much higher submerged speeds than conventional U-boats. The larger Type XXI was designed to achieve bursts as high as 17.25 knots submerged, while the smaller Type XXIII was designed for 12.5 knots.[45] At those submerged speeds they could have outpaced a convoy and outrun many of the escorts. Eventually over one hundred of Type XXI and over sixty of Type XXIII were completed, but only a few of the smaller type were ready for operations before the Allied armies overran Germany. Instead of directing a new offensive in the Atlantic, Admiral Doenitz found himself, as Hitler's designated successor, authorising the final surrender of the Third Reich.

Admiral Doenitz was in no doubt why Germany had lost the Battle of the Atlantic:

> In Britain, for the government, for the various service chiefs and for the nation as a whole, the Battle of the Atlantic was a conception which they could all readily visualise, and a fact, the supreme significance of which they all readily appreciated. In Germany this was not so. Our gaze was fixed on the continental land battles. By winning those battles,

it was thought, we could at the same time defeat British sea power. That out there in the Atlantic a handful of U-boats was being called upon to fight a battle that would decide the war was something that the continentally-minded German Government and High Command of the German Armed Forces were both, unfortunately, quite incapable of grasping.[46]

4

From Fire and Foe

The Battle of the Atlantic was fought out at many different levels. Heads of State, Ministers and Chiefs of Staff struggled to define the priorities which would outwit and overwhelm their rivals on the other side. Commanders-in-Chief juggled with arrows and symbols and lines on giant maps to thwart their own immediate opponents. Bletchley Park and the German *B-Dienst* racked their brains to build up an accurate picture from enemy radio traffic. Intelligence officers competed to gather the tiniest fragments of information which might enable them to complete a complicated and constantly changing jigsaw puzzle. Shipbuilders laboured night and day to build ships faster than their enemies could sink them. Scientists and manufacturers strove to invent, develop and produce weapons and other equipment that would give their own side a significant advantage or baffle and frustrate their opposite numbers. Farmers and tightly-rationed housewives made their expert contribution to reducing the demand for food from abroad, while schoolchildren bought National Savings Certificates in special campaigns to finance the building of new warships. Ultimately, however, everything depended on thousands of men whose lives were directly at risk on, over or under the sea. Out there, grand strategy and the concept of the tonnage war came down to the determination of frightened men to survive and their willingness to continue the battle. Without their bravery, their resilience and their fortitude in the face of all hardships, the Battle of the Atlantic could not have been sustained.[1] Neither side had a monopoly of those qualities. They were demonstrated throughout the entire war by men from many different countries and different services, and demonstrated by none more abundantly than by the British merchant seamen whose ships were sunk.

Throughout the war, whatever improvements to lifesaving equipment were introduced, a merchant seaman's greatest chance of being killed lay in the period before he could get away from a sinking ship. A post-war survey by the Medical Research Council found that, on average, approximately 26 per cent of the crew of a sinking ship would lose their lives before they could reach the relative safety of a lifeboat or raft.[2] Analysis of the reports and reminiscences of survivors shows that these deaths were caused in five main ways:

1. Direct fire of the enemy

2. Being trapped below decks

3. Hazardous cargoes

4. Delaying the abandonment too long

5. Accidents in launching lifeboats and rafts

   Apart from such general measures as regular minesweeping, sea and air escorts for convoys, degaussing against magnetic mines, and flying barrage balloons or kites to deter aircraft attacks – all measures intended primarily to protect the whole vessel and cargo – there was little that anyone could do to protect seamen once they were exposed to the various means of direct attack. The sides and decks of merchant vessels were not armour plated, and they offered little resistance to the explosive impact of bombs, mines or shells. Machine-gunning from aircraft was, however, a different matter. Something could be done to encourage men to stay at their posts on the ship's bridge or firing whatever anti-aircraft weapons had been provided. It was obviously unsatisfactory that the second mate of the small 1013-ton *Upminster*, sunk by air attack on 10 January 1940, should have to report: 'The planes kept circling round with machine-guns firing. We kept running behind the funnel as they came in front and then to the other side as they moved round.'[3]

   In February 1940 the Protection of Exposed Personnel (Merchant Ships) Order gave the Admiralty an 'open-ended' authority to require British shipowners to provide such protection against machine-gun attacks as it might see fit to specify from time to time.[4] At first this protection consisted of nothing more sophisticated than a few steel helmets for the men on the bridge and manning guns, plus sandbag protection for the wheelhouse and radio room. Later, as time, labour and materials could be found, the rapidly disintegrating sandbags were replaced by concrete slabs, and anti-aircraft guns were mounted in steel-plated weapons tubs. August 1940 saw the first trials of plastic armour, a mixture of stone chippings and asphalt, which could serve the same purpose. This material was invented and perfected by an unlikely collaboration between Edward Terrell, a barrister serving as an acting lieutenant at the anti-aircraft weapons and devices section of the Admiralty, and William Glanville, an engineer employed as Director of Road Research for the Department of Scientific and Industrial Research. Their plastic armour proved to offer better protection than concrete; it was eventually fitted to over 10,000 British and Allied vessels of all kinds. It was so highly regarded that in 1948 the inventors were permitted to register a patent for it. In 1949 they received an award from the Royal Commission on Awards to Inventors.[5]

The importance of protecting crews against aerial straffing is indicated by the fact that, in the first twelve months after the publication of the Protection of Exposed Personnel Order, over 160 British merchant ships and fishing vessels damaged at sea by aircraft attacks were successfully kept afloat and brought into port.[6] On 5 March 1941 the First Lord of the Admiralty, A. V. Alexander, was able to make the claim: 'Up to the present twenty-seven enemy aeroplanes attempting to bomb merchant-men have been brought down by the merchantmen's guns, and fifteen others have also probably been destroyed.'[7] Clearly, if the men could be protected during an air attack, there was a fighting chance of saving the ship and inflicting losses on the enemy, but a damaged ship brought into port might still, of course, have some of its crew dead or wounded, either from machine-gun and cannon fire or from exploding bombs.

A merchant ship offered little protection from the bombs themselves – explosion, flying splinters or blast could all be deadly, and even near misses could kill. When Japanese aircraft bombed the 6121-ton freighter *Pinna* in the entrance to Rhio Strait, near Singapore, on 3 February 1942, a single bomb which hit the fo'c'sle killed the majority of the engine-room ratings and some of the deck crew, twenty-two Chinese in all; and when the bombers returned next day to finish the ship off, several men sheltering under the lee of the bridge were injured by receiving the direct blast of two bombs which struck No. 2 hold.[8] Of course, much depended on which part of a ship was hit and where the crew were at the time. After receiving a bomb from 7000 feet directly into a hold containing 300 tons of cordite, during the disaster of Convoy PQ17 to Murmansk in July 1942, the master of the *Bolton Castle* reported: 'Wreckage and debris were blown about by the explosion but nobody was hurt.'[9]

Some seamen must have been born under a particularly lucky star. When the freighter *Pacific Grove* was struck by a bomb on 23 September 1940 there was no explosion. Volunteers from the crew, led by the third officer, the chief cook and the Danish bosun, cleared a path through the wreckage, located the unexploded bomb and, manhandling it on pillows and blankets, took it out on deck before rolling it overboard.[10] Seven weeks later, the second engineer of the 932-ton coaster *Pitwines* was not so lucky: he was killed when a small bomb exploded as he was trying to throw it overboard from the gun platform.[11]

Even very large vessels were easily penetrated by bombs. On board the 42,348-ton passenger liner *Empress of Britain*, after she had been struck by bombs from a Focke-Wulf Condor aircraft on 26 October 1940, 'an injured woman lay screwed up in a corner. She was bloody, her clothes had been partially ripped off by the bomb blast and she was screaming for help. By her side lay a soldier, his body grotesquely twisted, either unconscious or dead.'[12] In another part of the ship 'the lights were out ... the air, heavy with smoke, reeked of explosive. Women and children were screaming and the groans of the injured came ... as though from a deep black well.'[13]

Horrific scenes such as these could also be produced by gunfire. Fortunately for their crews, many masters of merchant vessels were quick to recognise the futility of trying to outrun or outfight a major enemy surface unit or a heavily armed modern merchant vessel operating as an auxiliary cruiser. For their part, captains of German surface ships operating far from home were usually content to hold or check fire while waiting for a ship to be abandoned, as long as she stopped using her radio. In that way they conserved ammunition and might later put a prize crew on board to see whether the ship could serve as a scout or supply ship, or be worth trying to run back through the British blockade to a German-occupied French port. In these encounters there would usually be only light casualties among the British merchant seamen. In September to December 1939, for example, the pocket battleship *Admiral Graf Spee* sank nine British vessels without a single fatal casualty among the crews.

There was little point in a tramp steamer, which might manage ten knots at best, trying to outrun a major warship that could steam three times as fast. A member of the crew of the *Stanpark* vividly recalled her encounter with the pocket battleship *Admiral Scheer* in the South Atlantic on 20 January 1941:

> She ... ordered us by signals not to use radio or she would shell us instantly. Then she gave the order to heave to and stop. Resisting this order would have been suicidal as she would have blown us out of the water. And Captain Lewis, our master, acted with cool courage and diplomacy in carrying this order out, with the result that no member of the crew was lost. That was a big achievement when one saw other crews coming in half of them lost, through German brutality and ruthlessness

in attacking our ships. In the camp where I was afterwards interned there were very few ships that could boast full crews.[14]

Masters of British merchant ships usually showed more determination to make a run for it, at least until they had obeyed the Admiralty's instructions about transmitting a raider warning, when confronted by one of the German auxiliary cruisers. As converted merchant ships these raiders did not have much of a speed advantage over some of their prey, and they might even be susceptible to a lucky shot from a merchant ship's anti-submarine gun. In the Tasman Sea on 20 August 1940, the *Turakina* made a very determined effort to escape from the German auxiliary cruiser *Orion*. Despite repeated hits from 5.9 inch shells and smaller weapons setting his vessel on fire, Captain Laird of the *Turakina* persisted in flight, while her gun crew served their weapon until the breech was under water, but thirty-five of the crew, including Laird himself, were killed. Captain Weyher, the German commander, risked the safety of his own ship by spending five hours searching for and picking up survivors in the darkness.[15]

As the German raiders became more apprehensive about the potential dangers to themselves if their position was revealed by the target's use of radio, they became more inclined to open fire without warning, in the hope that a display of overwhelming force would discourage any resistance. In this way the auxiliary cruiser *Komet* attacked the freighter *Australind* on 14 August 1941 near the Galapagos Islands. Interviewed almost three years later, on his return from captivity, the third officer of the British vessel recalled:

I put on my lifejacket, steel helmet, etc., and hurried on to the main deck ... By now several shells had struck the ship ... I was about to go on the lower bridge when a further shell struck the master's accommodation. I ran onto the bridge, and saw the captain lying face down at the foot of the lower bridge ladder, covered by a heap of debris. I turned him over, saw that he had been shot through the head and neck, and was dead.[16]

One of the engineer officers was also killed; another engineer officer later died of wounds on board the raider.

It is hardly surprising that most ships attacked in this way quickly stopped their engines and ceased transmitting, their crews passing into captivity with only light casualties or none at all. True, the Blue Funnel liner *Menelaus*, by pushing her engines to 15½ knots, managed to get away from the German auxiliary cruiser *Michel* in the South Atlantic on 1 May 1942 – but that was the only successful escape. The *Michel* made no mistake in attacking the *Gloucester Castle* on the night of 15/16 July 1942. Ten minutes of intense shelling from main armament, secondary armament and automatic weapons destroyed the radio room, killed both radio officers and reduced the old Union Castle liner to a listing and sinking wreck. Only fifty-seven crew and four passengers (two women and two children) were rescued by the raider; eighty-two crew, six women and two children were lost.[17] The *Michel*'s captain, Helmuth von Ruckteschell, had adopted the technique of shelling his targets into submission during an earlier cruise in command of the raider *Widder* in 1940, during which he sank the British vessels *British Petrol*, *King John*, *Anglo Saxon*, and *Cymbeline*.

Sometimes submarines could also inflict terrible casualties by gunfire. The Japanese submarine *I–10* shelled the cargo ship *Congella* at night on 24 October 1943 near the Maldive Islands. The first three shots hit the bridge, the captain's cabin and the radio room. The second officer later estimated that the Japanese scored hits with about forty-five out of fifty shots. If so, it was quite remarkable shooting in a rough sea with wind force 5/6.

> The chief officer, third officer and an apprentice had been killed when the bridge was hit, and the master, S. W. Folster, mortally wounded. The master's arm and a leg were blown off and there was a large, gaping wound in his stomach. The chief engineer had also reached the bridge by this time, to whom the master said 'I'm finished chief. Stop the engines and abandon ship.' [He was given] ten tablets of morphia to ease the pain.[18]

The second officer estimated that about twenty-two other members of the crew were also killed by the Japanese shells.

Although bombs or shells might penetrate a ship's engine room, the risk of being killed by direct enemy fire during surface gun attacks or bombing and straffing from aircraft was greatest for those merchant seamen and DEMS gunners whose duties were on the upper decks. This applied particularly to those on the bridge, in the radio room or manning the defensive armament, since the enemy would be trying to knock out those facilities; but it could also apply to all the crew at the time of abandoning ship if the enemy did not cease firing soon enough. This sometimes led to accusations that there was a deliberate intention to kill as many of the crew as possible. It seems likely, however, that in poor visibility from weather, smoke or darkness, and with survivors trying to abandon from the far side of the vessel or running around at sixes and sevens, most of these cases involved nothing more sinister than a failure to realise soon enough that the crew were beginning to abandon ship.

When ships were sunk by mines or torpedoes the seamen at greatest risk of being killed by the direct impact of the explosives were those working deep inside the ship. This most often meant the people on watch in the engine room and, in steamships, the boiler room. It needed a very special kind of courage to stand a watch for eight hours each day below the waterline when, under the impact of a mine or torpedo, the thin steel plates might burst open at any moment, the sea come pouring in, and the familiar workplace be reduced to a torture chamber of superheated steam, burning oil, choking coal dust and torn metal.

That happened to the engine room and boiler room staffs of the *Athenia* on the first day of the war, and it went on happening right up to the end of the war. In report after report, survivors had the same stories to tell of torpedo hits in the engine room, and of engine rooms 'wrecked', or 'flooded immediately', or 'filled with steam' or 'on fire'.

Possibly because most of the reports collected by Commander Holbrook's casualty section at the Admiralty consist of information supplied by masters or deck officers, or because no one on watch in the engine room survived, they frequently lack detail about what happened in the engine room. Occasionally, however, the veil is drawn aside:

> The third engineer, sixth engineer and ninth engineer were in the engine room at the time of the explosion. The sixth engineer luckily found himself swimming near the top of the engine room and managed to get out but he saw nothing of the third or ninth engineer. Two greasers were either drowned or killed in the engine room.[19] (*Otaio*, torpedoed on 28 August 1941)

> The second engineer and four firemen are missing ... I think the boilers must have burst ... The engine room and cross bunkers were flooded.[20] (*Allende*, torpedoed on 17 March 1942)

> The torpedo ... struck on the starboard side of the engine room. There was a terrific explosion, and I saw a flame shoot out of the engine room skylight to a height of approximately one hundred feet. The engine room flooded immediately, and within one minute the water had covered the cylinder tops. [The second, fourth and two junior engineers were among the missing.][21] (*Hopetarn*, torpedoed on 29 May 1943)

> [The] senior fourth engineer, who was on watch at the time ... was, apparently, killed ... Subsequent to the vessel being hit [he] was not

seen by anybody, not even by the senior second engineer, who was also in the engine room at the time, but on the middle platform, and who escaped although being scalded and burned before getting out.[22] (*Athelduke*, torpedoed on 16 April 1945)

Obviously, as long as the war had to be fought at all, there was no way in which any amount of sincere humane concern, research groups, joint committees of shipowners and unions, or anyone else, could really hope to find effective measures to diminish the effect when a torpedo or mine explosion breached a ship's engine room and boiler spaces. Given the ever-present danger, one can easily understand why, occasionally, a torpedo hit elsewhere on their ship would lead men to abandon their posts in the engine room, without orders, in a scramble to reach the open deck. The master of the *Kafiristan* complained that his engine-room watch had left their positions and tried to launch a boat prematurely;[23] the master of the *Ross* could not understand why he got no response to the engine-room telegraph until he discovered that the engineers were already on deck;[24] the engine-room watch on the *Oakbank* rushed on deck, but after a minute or two they returned to their posts to stop the engines. They kept the lighting and power going until the master eventually gave the order to abandon ship.[25] There were other examples, some involving Chinese or Indian engine-room ratings. The premature evacuation of an engine room which was as yet undamaged certainly represented danger for the rest of the crew if the engines were left running. With the ship still forging ahead, boats would probably be swamped on launching; or they might be filled by water from the main discharge; or boats, rafts and swimmers might be struck by the still rotating propeller blades. In fairness, it must be said that many of the survivors' reports pay handsome tribute to the gallant engineer officers who, at great personal risk, ignored the possibility of a further torpedo or sudden foundering to go down into a deserted engine room to stop the engines, or who managed to achieve the same result using a remote control mechanism on the boat deck.

For those brought up on romanticised stories of selfless heroism and daring deeds it is, perhaps, too easy to categorise men who left their posts, whether in the engine room or elsewhere, as cowards. Such a facile judgement ignores the very real problems of communication in many old merchant ships. At the start of the war there were still plenty of vessels relying on just the voice pipes and engine-room telegraphs, both of which could be put out of action by the shock of a torpedo, mine, shell or bomb explosion. Telephones, introduced primarily to facilitate the precise adjustment of engine revolutions necessary for station keeping in convoy, provided improved communication with the bridge but there was no guarantee that they were shock proof. For frightened men stuck deep in the bowels of a ship, perhaps in darkness, assailed by all kinds of alarming noises, without any information whatsoever about what was happening or what they were expected to do, the most natural thing in the world would be to dash topsides to find out. Indeed, later in the war, as experience built up of the short time which elapsed before many ships sank and it came to be realised how few ships, apart from empty tankers, were capable of surviving a torpedo, some masters issued a standing order for the engines to be stopped, without waiting for orders from the bridge, as soon as the ship was hit.[26] Everyone could then muster for abandoning ship and, in the unlikely event of a decision to get the ship under way again, it would not take long to re-enter the engine room and restart the engines.

Because of the unpredictable nature of blast damage, underwater explosions could also inflict casualties far beyond the engine room. The master of the *Sampa*, mined on 27 February 1945, was blown from his bridge into the sea. He was fortunate to be picked up by another vessel. The first officer found himself in command and the bridge wrecked:

> I organised a party to take the injured on deck and all who were alive were taken out of the saloon, bridge etc. The bodies of the second officer and fourth engineer were identified and there were at least two more bodies which were unrecognisable. In the gunners' mess ... were at least two more dead bodies. It is impossible to state categorically how many dead were in these two places as pieces of bodies were lying in various positions. One member of the crew was found in the port alleyway on captain's deck, smashed to pieces ... No signs were seen of the third engineer or O'Neill the fireman, both of whom were on watch at the time of the explosion.[27]

In addition to direct risks from the explosion of various types of enemy ordnance, merchant seamen faced the further terrifying possibility of being trapped and carried down with the sinking ship. Men could become trapped anywhere on the vessel: ladders might collapse, alleyways catch fire, closed doors jam fast, debris engulf men, or injuries render them immobile. Against risks of this kind some precautions could be taken, and everyone involved could make some contribution. Even if some shipowners were initially reluctant to supply them, individual seamen could, without great expense, set themselves up with a whistle, a knife and a small torch; and they could familiarise themselves

with the geography of their ship so that they knew alternative routes
for use in an emergency. This was more easily said than done because
the casual nature of most seamen's employment before May 1941, and
the allocation of men from what was known as the Merchant Navy
Reserve Pool after that date, meant that most men would sail from the
United Kingdom on an unfamiliar ship and be at risk from the moment
the ship sailed – or even earlier if the port were blitzed from the air
before sailing day. In bigger ships many, possibly most, seamen only
really knew their way around the areas of the ship for which their own
department was responsible.

The master or mate of an individual ship could ensure that a few
tools such as axes, sledge-hammers and crowbars were handily placed
in certain key locations, and a rope ladder or length of rope kept ready
for use as an emergency exit from the engine room. Shipowners, suitably
encouraged or compelled by the Ministry of Shipping (later War Transport), could supply improved fire-fighting equipment, battery-operated
emergency lighting in alleyways, and special stretchers in which an
injured man could be securely strapped. They could also undertake
some not very costly modifications to the structure of ships. Hooks on
cabin doors allowed them to be secured in a slightly open position
where they could not become jammed if the frame warped in an
explosion; some doors were fitted with crash panels which could easily
be kicked out by trapped men; handles could be welded outside port-
holes so that it was easier for men to pull themselves through; and a
few large ventilators might be turned into emergency exits by welding
a few rungs inside them. While the Ministry could advise on matters
such as these, the great variations in the design of ships meant that
work of this kind could only be undertaken pragmatically with surveyors,
company marine superintendents, ships' officers and installers sorting
out on the spot the practical applications for any individual ship.

Whether seamen became trapped during an attack depended on a
complicated interaction between their precise location at the time, the
unpredictable effects of blast and the stresses on the ship's construction
and machinery. Finding themselves trapped often brought out the best
qualities of self-reliance and resourcefulness in the men as they ingeniously organised their own escape. For example, men from the
stokehold of the *Langleeford*, torpedoed on 14 February 1940, 'found
that the upper ladders had collapsed, so they climbed up the wire of
the ash ejector'.[28] A man trapped on the rapidly sinking *Empire Hudson*
emerged with injured face and hands after succeeding in his third
attempt to force his way out of a hole blown in the ship's side.[29] The

purser of the *Dahomian*, with the deck collapsing under his feet and his cabin door jammed, climbed out through the porthole, while the second officer, struck by a ventilator and buried under a pile of cargo and debris on deck, managed without help to dig himself out unhurt.[30]

There can have been few luckier men than Second Officer V. P. Wills-Rust of the tiny 694-ton *Abukir*, torpedoed on the night of 28 May 1940 by what he thought was a surfaced submarine but which was, in reality, an E-boat. Wills-Rust gave a matter-of-fact description of his ordeal:

> There was a terrific smash and everything was pandemonium on deck. The wheel house collapsed on top of me and I was trapped by the concrete slabs which had fallen on me and pinned me to the deck. I think the ship sank in about thirty seconds, after breaking in two ...
>
> Although I was trapped, I could see everything over my head. The stern burst into flames and I saw flames forward. I could see the water coming up and coming over my head. The ship hit the bottom and turned over, the debris was thrown off me and I was released and I came to the surface.[31]

It was ironic that the concrete slabs recently installed as protection against air attack should so nearly have cost him his life, but he was extremely fortunate that his ship, fleeing precipitately from Ostend to escape the advancing German army, was sunk in quite shallow water near the West Hinder light vessel.

Men who seemed inextricably trapped were left confronting an appalling death, as they knew their ship might sink at any minute – while their shipmates were left with the agonising dilemma of deciding how long they could afford to spend searching for the trapped men, or trying to free them, without jeopardising their own chances of survival. Such crises could inspire men to show immense courage in the face of fear. Normally rough, unsentimental men could show great tenderness in the face of pain; and men from all ranks could suddenly be fired by a bloody minded determination not to be beaten by either the enemy or the sea.

Mere words cannot convey adequately what these incidents meant to those involved. The facts speak for themselves. The second officer and two able seamen swam back to the *Goodwood*, mined off Flamborough Head a week after war was declared, to free the master who was trapped under wreckage with both his legs broken. The chief officer of the *Ahamo*, mined off the Norfolk coast, went below, despite escaping ammonia fumes, to free four men trapped behind timber. The second officer of the *Empire Cromwell* lost his life trying to save men who had fallen into a hold from which the hatch covers had been blown off. The chief engineer, doctor, purser, refrigerating engineer and third officer of the *Clan MacArthur* sacrificed their chance to leave in a lifeboat in order to release injured men trapped in the fo'c'sle. The first three lost their lives in the attempt.

This type of gallantry was not confined to ships' officers. The cook of the *Empire Eve* forced open the jammed door of a cabin to rescue an unconscious officer. Elizabeth May Owen, a stewardess of the *St Patrick*, sunk by aircraft in St George's Channel, forced open doors on the lowest deck to release trapped women passengers, and guided them to the upper deck where she fitted them with lifebelts even though she had none for herself. Her bravery serves as a salutary reminder that some women were included in the ranks of the Merchant Navy.[32]

One could cite lots of other examples. Many more unsuccessful ones must have passed unobserved into oblivion with a ship's final plunge. The remarkable thing about many of these attempts to rescue trapped men is that they were often performed out of a sense of duty or out of respect for the tradition of seafarers, rather than from any close bonds of friendship or affection between rescuer and rescued. Officers might risk their lives for subordinates they would normally have considered insufferable nuisances, while subordinates might risk their lives for officers they had cordially detested.

The danger of people being trapped below decks in sinking passenger vessels and troopships was, of course, considerable. To some extent such ships were protected by their relatively high speed and by the strong escort under which they usually sailed, especially in the later years of the war, but if their protection proved inadequate the number of fatalities could be very high indeed. Virtually untrained in abandon ship procedures, crowded together in an unfamiliar environment and perhaps debilitated by humidity or the effects of seasickness, passengers were unlikely to cope well with the disorientation caused by smoke, darkness, collapsed ladders, obstructed alleyways or a pronounced list.

While she was evacuating troops and a few civilians from St Nazaire, the Cunard liner *Lancastria* received a direct hit from a bomb, rolled over after about twenty minutes and sank off that French port on 17 June 1940. Because she was close to the shore, other craft were quickly on the scene to rescue almost 2500 survivors. Given the great haste in which the ship had been loaded, there is no really reliable figure for how many lives were lost but the Association of *Lancastria* Survivors believes that the death toll was probably far in excess of the estimate of around three thousand, including sixty-six crew, which is usually quoted.[33] Even if one accepts the figure of three thousand, this was the largest number of fatalities from the sinking of a single British vessel during the Second World War, but if a really huge liner such as the *Queen Mary* or *Queen Elizabeth* had been sunk the number of deaths might have been four or five times greater.

Other troopships were also sunk with considerable loss of life. On 26 November 1943, off the Algerian coast, the British India Line's *Rohna* was set on fire by a direct hit from a German glider bomb. Although she took ninety minutes to sink, only about half of the people on board were rescued, while 1105 American servicemen being carried as passengers and 133 crew lost their lives.[34] From the troopship *Khedive Ismail*, torpedoed and sunk in two minutes by the Japanese submarine *I–27* near the Maldive Islands on 12 February 1944, there were only 214 survivors out of a total of more than 1511 people who were on board. Among the 1297 dead were 675 East African soldiers, 178 British soldiers (including four DEMS gunners), 209 men of the Royal Navy (including seven DEMS gunners), seventeen Women's Royal Naval Service, fifty-one army nurses, eight from the Women's Territorial Service, a war correspondent, a mother with her five-month-old son, and 156 members of the crew.[35]

Examples of smaller, but still tragic, passenger ship fatalities are provided by such cases as the Booth Line's *Anselm*, torpedoed north of the Azores on 5 July 1941, when 250 troops were lost from over 1200 being carried; and the Henderson Line's *Yoma*, torpedoed off the coast of Cyrenaica on 17 June 1943 with the loss of 451 of the 1670 troops on board. Occasionally a ship was lost leaving no survivors at all. That was the fate of the Blue Star Line's *Almeda Star* whose 194 passengers, 137 crew and twenty-nine gunners all perished when she was torpedoed by *U–96* near Rockall on 17 January 1941.[36]

It seemed that the Shaw Savill liner *Ceramic* was also a case of a ship being lost with all on board. She was carrying 378 passengers, mainly servicemen, 264 crew and fourteen DEMS gunners when she was torpedoed by *U–515* in mid-Atlantic west of the Azores on 6 December 1942. In fact there was a solitary survivor, Sapper Eric Munday of the Royal Engineers. He was travelling as a passenger and became a prisoner-of-war when he was subsequently picked up by the U-boat. Repatriated at the end of the war, he was able to give an account of the *Ceramic*'s sinking to an Admiralty interviewer:

[When the vessel was hit] I was in the lounge and at once made my way to my boat station on the port side. There was a little panic, probably owing to our having women and children on board, but it was nothing serious, and quite understandable as it was so very dark that slight confusion was inevitable ... Probably the starboard boats were damaged, as there were many more people in my boat than were allocated to it ... There were over fifty people in the boat, which was obviously too many for safety. [A number of boats and rafts got away from the ship.] As there were mostly military personnel in the boat nobody knew very much about handling it. By daylight a Northerly gale had sprung up, with storms of rain and sleet, with high confused seas. Huge waves were breaking over the boat, we bailed furiously, but it was impossible to free the boat of water before another wave crashed over, swamping it so that it capsized and we were all thrown into the water.[37]

They were unable to right the boat, and he swam for four hours before the U-boat commander, looking to pick up the captain of the *Ceramic* and unable to find him, picked up the very lucky Sapper Munday and made him prisoner instead. No other survivor was ever found, those who did manage to get away from the ship having presumably perished in the appalling weather conditions

In contrast to cases such as these, it has to be said that some heavily laden passenger ships and troopships were abandoned with surprisingly light casualties. From the Orient liner *Orcades*, torpedoed in the South Atlantic by *U–172* on 10 October 1942, 322 of the crew of 352 were picked up from lifeboats by the Polish ship *Narwick*, along with 694 of the 712 passengers. Only six of the crew and five passengers were lost when the P & O liner *Strathallan* was torpedoed by *U–562* north of Oran on 21 December 1942. Although on fire, the ship remained afloat until next morning. Even so, it was a remarkable achievement that over 4400 troops, about 250 nurses and other passengers, and 425 crew survived her loss. Three months later, also in the western Mediterraneanan, an even lighter death toll attended the loss of the Union Castle Line's *Windsor Castle* when she was sunk in convoy by aircraft torpedo on 23 March 1943. She, too, remained afloat for several hours, permitting other vessels to rescue every one of the 2690 troops who were on board and all but one of her crew of 290.[38]

When passenger ships were being used to transport large numbers of enemy civilians and prisoners-of-war the problems of abandoning ship were compounded by the impossibility of holding regular lifeboat drills for them and by the need to ensure that they were kept closely confined until it was absolutely certain that the ship would have to be abandoned. Then the inevitable haste, fear, confusion and panic were not helped by language barriers and national animosities between crew, guards and prisoners who might themselves be of mixed nationality. On 2 July 1940, almost 1200 German and Italian civilian internees and prisoners-of-war, about 200 guards and 174 crew were on their way to Canada on the Blue Star Line's *Arandora Star* when she was torpedoed by *U–47* seventy-five miles west of Ireland. Although the ship remained afloat for about an hour, perfectly understandable panic among the prisoners prevented the boats being got away in good order. Press reports seized on the propaganda opportunity to highlight the way Germans and Italians had fought one another for a place in the boats. It is thought that more than 700 of the internees and prisoners, thirty-seven guards and fifty-five members of the crew lost their lives. *The Times*, for the benefit of its more affluent readers, reported that the pre-war managers of the Piccadilly Hotel, the Hungaria Restaurant and the Café Anglais, the restaurant manager of the Ritz and the banqueting manager of the Savoy were among the internees missing, while among those saved were the partners in the Monseigneur Restaurant, and the chefs at Quaglino's and the Café Royal. At the time of the attack, the *Arandora Star* had been sailing unescorted. The death toll would have been even higher if a patrolling Sunderland flying-boat had not spotted the survivors in the water and guided a Canadian destroyer to their rescue.[39]

The unescorted Cunarder *Laconia* was carrying almost 1800 Italian prisoners-of-war, a contingent of Polish troops to guard the prisoners, and some British passengers, when *U–156* torpedoed her 250 miles northeast of Ascension Island on 12 September 1942. All told, over 2700 crew and passengers were on board. Eventually between 1100 and 1200 survivors were rescued, but over 1600 had perished, including about 1350 of the Italians.[40] This disaster, and the epic rescue which followed, have featured prominently in subsequent debates about the way the war at sea was conducted.[41]

Some ten weeks after the *Laconia* disaster, *U–177* torpedoed the *Nova Scotia* in the Mozambique Channel on 28 November 1942 while the Furness Warren liner was carrying 780 Italian prisoners-of-war, 130 South African troops to guard them, a few other passengers and 127 crew. She sank rapidly, leaving fewer than 200 survivors. All but sixteen of her crew perished, along with about 650 of the Italian prisoners and eighty-eight of their guards.[42]

Yet another sinking inflicting casualties on Italian prisoners-of-war was the loss of the unescorted Canadian Pacific liner *Empress of Canada*, torpedoed by the Italian submarine *Leonardo da Vinci* in the South Atlantic on 13 March 1943. With a crew of 362, including her forty-four

DEMS gunners, she was carrying over 1500 passengers. Among the passengers were many Greeks and Poles, as well as 500 Italian prisoners-of-war guarded by a Royal Navy contingent. The stricken ship remained afloat for over an hour, while nine lifeboats equipped with Welin davits and three equipped with Wylie davits were successfully lowered and filled to capacity. In his subsequent report to the Admiralty, the master was bitterly critical of the difficulty of using the Wylie boat gear once a ship had taken a heavy list. He was also critical of the panicky behaviour of his Greek and Polish passengers. He pointedly directed attention to the fact that all of the Greek officers and most of the Polish officers had survived. The Italian prisoners, by way of rather invidious comparison, were reported to have behaved without any sign of panic, although they were (perhaps understandably) slow and reluctant when getting into the boats or taking to the water. The Royal Navy guard contingent behaved impeccably in shepherding their charges on deck and over the side. A second torpedo, fired about an hour after the first, overturned a lifeboat as it was being loaded alongside and killed a number of prisoners and their guards. The submarine rescued an Italian doctor who was with the prisoners. The main work of rescue was undertaken by HM Corvettes *Boreas*, *Petunia* and *Crocus* and the Armed Merchant Cruiser HMS *Corinthian*, but fifty-two of the *Empress of Canada*'s crew (including eight DEMS gunners) and 340 passengers were lost. It is unclear how many Italian prisoners were among the dead passengers.[43]

In disasters of this kind, there is no way of distinguishing how many died trapped below decks and how many from other causes. As to the conditions below decks, there are a few eye-witness accounts. Doris Hawkins recalled trying to carry a baby to her boat station on the *Laconia*:

> We made our way upstairs. We were carried on a surging wave of people, some with their emergency outfits, many without, for they had been unable to reach their cabins. As we went the lights failed. All this time the ship had been taking on an increasingly heavy list, and by now it was very difficult going with my precious burden. We stumbled over fallen doors, broken woodwork, and shattered glass to our lifeboat station. There we waited.[44]

There was no waiting around on the *Khedive Ismail*, for she sank less than two minutes after being torpedoed, leaving little chance for those below decks. The second officer reported:

> Many were killed when the troop deck and accommodation ladders

collapsed. At the time of the incident many troops were in the saloon listening to a concert given by the Nursing Sisters; I learned later from a man who was in this saloon and managed to escape through a porthole, that, as the ship heeled over, the grand piano slid across the floor, pinning a number of people against the ship's side.[45]

For men serving on cargo vessels chances of survival could be determined by the nature of the cargo being carried. Where a cargo lacked inherent buoyancy, the vessel might sink very quickly indeed if the enemy's mines, bombs or torpedoes caused a catastrophic impairment of her water-tight integrity. Two vessels in Convoy SL34 illustrate this 'cargo factor' very clearly. Both were torpedoed by *U–16* within eight minutes of one another on 12 June 1940. The *Barbara Marie*, with a cargo of iron ore, was reported to have sunk in forty-eight seconds, leaving just five survivors from her crew to be plucked from the water. By contrast, the *Willowbank* soon sank lower in the water when first hit, but eventually took over an hour to sink because she was carrying almost 9000 tons of maize which slowed the inflow of seawater. In her master's opinion, 'this fact was no doubt the cause of the whole crew being saved'.[46]

Another example of how quickly a cargo could carry a ship down was provided by the *Empire Hurst*, sunk by a bomb from a Focke-Wulf Condor aircraft on 11 August 1941. Of the thirty-five men on board only nine survived. Bosun S. J. Bramich told the interviewer from the Shipping Casualties Section of the Admiralty:

> I jumped over the starboard quarter just as she was going and saw the propeller rising out of the water, still turning. From the time I heard the alarm to until when I was in the water was no longer than a minute; we had no watertight bulkheads, just one long hold, and we were carrying iron ore ... All the men who were saved had to jump for it.[47]

Again and again one comes across similar examples, where survival depended on the pure luck of who happened to be in a position to jump or be washed into the sea as the vessel foundered – just two survivors from the crew of forty-five on the iron ore ship *Grelhead*; twenty lucky survivors from the crew of thirty-eight on the *Baron Newlands*, sunk with her cargo of manganese ore in thirty seconds; fifteen survivors from the crew of eighty-one on the *Observer*, sunk with 3000 tons of chrome ore in less than a minute.[48]

A different danger was presented by cargoes such as petroleum products or ammunition, both absolutely essential to the prosecution

of the war. With these cargoes a bomb or torpedo hit might trigger a
tremendous explosion from which few, if any, crew members could
hope to escape. On 29 November 1941 Kapitänleutnant Wolfgang Lüth
of *U–43* saw his torpedoes set off the ammunition cargo of the *Thornlie-
bank*, sending smoke, flames and debris hundreds of feet into the air,
and producing a blast wave which rocked the U-boat. When in command
of *U–181*, Lüth attacked the 193-ton *Harrier*, also carrying explosives,
on 6 June 1943. He described in his log how his torpedo set off a huge
column of flame and pieces of debris were thrown far and wide. After
that nothing remained of the target except small fragments and the
stench of gasoline.[49]

In certain circumstances, a ship's crew could lose their lives because
of the explosion of a neighbouring vessel's cargo. An attack by German
aircraft on the Italian port of Bari on 2 December 1943 caused the
American ammunition ships *John Harvey*, *John L. Motley* and *Joseph
Wheeler* to explode with such force that many of the other ships in port
were also lost, including the British *Testbank*, *Fort Athabaska*, *Devon Coast*
and *Lars Kruse*. All the seventy-five crew of the *Testbank* were killed,
except five men who happened to be on shore; from the *Fort Athabaska*'s
crew of fifty-six there were only ten survivors; and, while the *Devon
Coast* lost only one man, her twenty-two survivors suffered temporary
blindness through coming in contact in the water with mustard gas
which had been part of the cargo of the *John Harvey*.[50]

Even if there was no explosion, a cargo of petroleum products could
easily catch fire. On 23 March 1942 the *Empire Steel* was bound for
Halifax with 6100 tons of aviation spirit and 4150 tons of kerosene
from Baton Rouge. 'A torpedo struck the ship in No. 7 tank on the
starboard side, which was filled with aviation spirit. A huge column of
oil was thrown up which descended on the bridge, saturating everything,
and within a matter of seconds the ship was ablaze from stem to stern.'[51]
There were only eight survivors from the crew of forty-seven. Many
other tankers suffered the same terrifying fate, and there can have been
few merchant seamen who really looked forward to a voyage on a
tanker. Yet the division of the hull into separate tanks and their powerful
pumps meant that these ships were capable of withstanding a torpedo
hit, if they were empty or if they were carrying heavy oil which was less
likely to explode or catch fire. During 1942 no fewer than twenty-four
tankers over 6000 gross tons were brought into port after being torpedoed.[52]

It is hardly surprising that so many merchant seamen never really
had a chance to abandon ship, when one considers the dangers which

could suddenly arise at any hour of the day or night – from direct explosion of the enemy's mines, torpedoes and bombs; from becoming entrapped in a rapidly sinking ship; or from the propensity of certain cargoes to sink a ship in seconds, blow it sky high or turn it into an inferno. How merchant seamen viewed these risks depended on their different temperaments. Some adopted a stoic fatalism that it all depended on 'whether your number was up'; others professed a 'devil may care' belief in their own luck; some were afflicted by strange superstitions about what could bring bad luck or were filled with gloomy premonitions of eventual doom; perhaps most of them just accepted the risks as part of the job they had chosen to do. Neither the government nor the shipowners could do much, if anything, to protect the seamen from risks of this kind, but a great deal could be done to improve the survival chances of those seamen who were in a position to set about abandoning their ship.

Morale-boosting poster featuring Merchant Navy 'Lewis' gunners. The small metal badge (bottom right), two centimetres across and designed for the lapel of a civilian jacket, was the only form of recognition worn by most merchant seamen when ashore. (*Imperial War Museum*)

5

Abandon Ship!

Once his ship had been struck by bomb, torpedo, mine or shells, every merchant seamen must have asked himself how long she was likely to remain afloat. The answer depended on such factors as the extent of the damage, the construction of the ship, the type of cargo, the sea and weather conditions at the time and whether the enemy inflicted further damage. A post-war analysis of the time taken to sink, from all causes, by a sample of 296 ships where survivors had given clear information on this point found that 69.6 per cent sank in the first quarter of an hour after being hit, 9.5 per cent in the second quarter of an hour, and a further 9.8 per cent before an hour had elapsed. Only 11.1 per cent remained afloat for more than an hour.[1] A different study of 110 British ships sunk by torpedoes from submarines between 1940 and 1943 found 47.7 per cent sank in the first quarter of an hour, 12.6 per cent in the second quarter of an hour, and a further 11.7 per cent before an hour had elapsed. Some 27.9 per cent remained afloat for more than an hour,[2] of which one or two did not sink for several days. Where ships stayed afloat for several hours, the final plunge might occur very rapidly indeed if it were brought about by a second torpedo or the collapse of a vital internal bulkhead.

Figures such as these need to be treated with considerable caution. Given the stress of abandoning ship and the delay before they could be interviewed, no doubt survivors' estimates of time were of variable reliability. They might also vary in their personal definition of the precise moment when a vessel could be considered to have finally sunk. The figures do not include some important categories – for example, ships which were damaged but not sunk. If this category could be added to the figure for ships still afloat after one hour they would show that sinking was not necessarily as imminent as the quoted figures suggest. On the other hand, if one added the ships which sank leaving no one left alive to interview, one might reasonably expect the figures for rapid sinking to be boosted. Other ships excluded are those where the senior survivor did not give any indication of the time taken to sink. If the figures would hardly satisfy a sophisticated statistician, they still indicate that the prudent course for merchant seamen whose ship was damaged was to assume the worst and get ready to abandon her immediately.

In any case, one urgent task was to let others, both at sea and on shore, know that the ship was in trouble. Lives would depend on how quickly help could arrive. If other vessels were in sight, as in convoy for example, signals could be passed by flags or lamp. In the early days of the war, many ships lacked an adequate signal lamp, and many deck officers lacked confidence in their ability to send or read morse at any speed, but soon the supply of the ubiquitous Aldis lamp brought a considerable improvement. At night the ship's plight could be indicated by displaying a red light above the bridge, provided that the damage sustained had not already knocked out the power supply, broken the bulb or brought down the triatic stay on which the light had to be hoisted.

Perhaps the most dramatic and attention-grabbing distress signal was the firing of rockets. Many survivors owed their lives to the fact that even the least alert lookouts were unlikely to miss seeing them, especially at night. But they could be exasperating devices to operate. To take three examples from August 1941: rockets on the *Cape Rodney* could not be set off because the blue lights used to light them were too damp to ignite;[3] the master of the *Ciscar* bluntly told the Admiralty interviewer that the rockets were 'inadequate and useless, as they take so long to light';[4] and on the *Otaio*, torpedoed in daylight, rockets were successfully fired, but they still had recourse to the ancient distress signal of flying the ensign upside down.[5]

No doubt the problem with the rockets throughout the war years lay in their deterioration over time. The more they were kept handy for rapid use, the more they were exposed to the ravages of weather or careless handling. Even where, as on the *Baron Pentland*, care had been taken to protect them with a metal shield and a canvas cover, after ten days in a North Atlantic convoy the master found that he could not ignite them when his ship was torpedoed on 10 September 1941.[6] When the *San Florentino* was torpedoed, on the night of 1/2 October 1941, rockets stored in the chartroom to ensure that they were kept dry still refused to take off, even after the fuses had been lit successfully.[7]

The Ministry of War Transport was slow to respond to this kind of evidence; they continued to claim that the rockets were perfectly satis- factory. No doubt they were impressed by the many reports which mentioned the sighting of rockets fired at night by ships in trouble on the far side of a convoy. The Trade Division at the Admiralty had, however, formed the opinion from interviews with survivors that too many rockets failed in an emergency. They therefore offered to provide technical assistance in developing a waterproof rocket with a more reliable method of firing. By the end of 1941 the Ministry of War Transport, having come round to the Admiralty point of view, agreed to tackle the problem as a matter of urgency.[8] In April 1942 a simple watertight rocket firing five stars was ready for trials,[9] but the inevitable problems of arranging for their production in quantity and distributing them to ships meant that many months elapsed before the older rockets were finally withdrawn. Improved designs of rocket could never eliminate the problem entirely under service conditions, and no amount of research could solve the difficulty encountered by the master of the *Empire Antelope* who found that a torpedo explosion on 2 November 1942 made such a mess on his bridge that he could not even find the rockets.[10] In a few cases shipmasters refused to fire rockets for fear of starting a fire on their own ship or endangering survivors from another ship when the sea was covered in petrol.

Where ships were not in visual contact with other vessels, the only hope of communicating with the outside world lay in using the radio, although they were expected to maintain radio silence except in dire emergency. Before the war, vessels under 1600 gross tons were not required by law to carry a radio transmitter (some shipowners, however, installed one voluntarily), and most radio-equipped cargo ships employed only one radio operator who kept a listening watch at certain internationally agreed times. Obviously, in wartime there was a strong case for equipping the smaller vessels with transmitters. By 23 January 1940 Sir Arthur Salter was able to claim that 'a very considerable proportion of coasting ships are fitted with wireless telegraphy or telephone apparatus'.[11] Even so, over a year later, the journal of the Navigators' and Engineer Officers' Union was complaining that small vessels were still not compelled to carry a transmitter, which crews had a right to expect to ensure 'that they will have at least a "sporting chance" should their ships be sunk as a result of enemy action'.[12]

It was also necessary to increase the number of radio officers on ocean-going cargo vessels so that a listening watch could be kept over a longer period each day. On this point the interests of merchant seamen and the Admiralty happily coincided. The seamen's chances of getting off a distress message and having a potential rescuer hear it could be improved, while the Admiralty's need for the fullest possible intelligence about the enemy's activities and for a means of diverting

ships away from danger areas could be met. Initially the aim of the
Ministry of Shipping was by stages to provide a second radio officer
on each ship. They were chivvied along by the Independent MP for
Cheltenham, D. L. Lipson. In February 1940 he alleged that some
shipping companies were trying to avoid employing a second operator,[13]
and the following month he suggested that second operators could not
be found because there simply were not enough trained men. The
Minister of Shipping, Sir John Gilmour, assured him:

> All former sea-going wireless operators have been invited to take up
> employment again in the merchant navy; and the time taken to train
> wireless operators has been reduced by the introduction of more intensive
> courses of training. These measures have contributed largely to the
> much improved position ... Between the 6th November last and the
> 16th February, 518 ships have had a second wireless operator.[14]

Under the Wireless Operators and Watches (Merchant Ships) Order
of March 1940 the Admiralty was given the power to require any ship
to carry a second operator. The training programme was so successful that by September 1940 Gilmour's successor, Ronald Cross, was
able to announce that discussions were taking place about providing
a third radio officer so that twenty-four-hour listening watches could
be mounted.[15] In 1941 and 1942 this enhanced manning became
increasingly common.

On the ships themselves additional equipment was added as it became
available. An extra emergency aerial, rigged separately from the main
aerial, was added on many ships early in the war on the recommendation of the Ministry of Shipping. Costing very little and easily
improvised, they were made compulsory under the Wireless Telegraphy
Receiving Apparatus and Watches (Merchant Ships) Order of 1941.[16]
A telephone link between the radio room and the bridge was also
added. Later, an extra transmitter was introduced as back-up to the
main transmitter in an emergency. More and more ships had this
emergency transmitter housed in a separate radio room, often specially
constructed and well away from the main transmitter, to reduce the
chances of both being knocked out in an attack.

In the first weeks of the war, as in such cases as the *Athenia* and the
Kensington Court, distress calls transmitted by ships had been reasonably
successful in bringing rescuers, and sometimes possible avengers, to
the position of sinkings. Newspaper reports in Britain and the United
States showed that the signals were regularly picked up by shore stations
such as Valencia in Ireland and Mackay Radio in the USA. As the rate

1. An unidentified standard fast cargo ship of late 1944. The lifeboats and the rafts on their inclined launch-ways are ready for instant use. Note the defensive armament on bow, bridge, boat deck and poop. (*Imperial War Museum*)

2. HMS *Vetch*, a 'Flower' Class corvette, at Liverpool, 9 August 1942. She sports a disruptive camouflage pattern. Mainstay of the convoy escorts, over 250 corvettes were built in British and Canadian shipyards during the war. (*Imperial War Museum*)

3. A bomb falls astern of the *Glenorchy* on 12 August 1942 during the 'Operation Pedestal' convoy to Malta. Her escape was short-lived: she was sunk by an E-boat on the following day. (*Imperial War Museum*)

4. HMS *Spey*, a 'River' Class frigate on the 2nd Escort Group, with convoy in early 1944. (*Imperial War Museum*)

5. *U–109*, a type IXB U-boat, at Lorient in May 1941. (*Bundesarchiv*)

6. The sinking of an unidentified merchantman, probably taken from the conning tower of *U–107*. (*Bundesarchiv*)

7. A lookout on the conning tower of Korvettkapitän Erich Topp's *U–552* watches the British freighter *Beacon Grange* break in two after being torpedoed on 27 April 1941 in the North Atlantic. (*Bundesarchiv*)

8. Square-ended 'Chipchase' liferafts show their capabilities under oars or sail. The wartime caption says this shows a genuine rescue, but is it a propaganda fake? (*Imperial War Museum*)

9. British merchant seamen being rescued from a raft by a vessel of the United States Coastguard. The rescuers have lowered a scrambling net for the survivors to climb up. (*Imperial War Museum*)

10. Covered in oil, an exhausted survivor from a torpedoed British tanker sits in the scuppers of the ship which rescued him. (*Imperial War Museum*)

11. A boatload of survivors approaches *U–107*, commanded by Kapitänleutnant Gunther Hessler, the son-in-law of Admiral Doeritz. (*Bundesarchiv*)

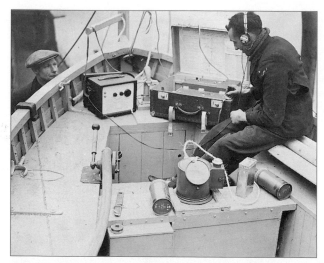

12. This posed photograph from March 1942 shows the lifeboat radio transmitter and small receiver. Other equipment includes the large galvanised water tank under the thwart, semi-rotary handpump (on left), smoke flares and magnetic compass (which should face towards the tiller instead of away from it). (*Imperial War Museum*)

13. Specially posed photograph of March 1942. It shows improvements in survival equipment: kapok lifejacket with red light; yellow survival suit; tins of milk tablets; pemmican and chocolate in galvanised tank below thwart; canvas hood with side screens; tins of massage oil; distress flares etc. (*Imperial War Museum*)

14. Photographed from the RAF aircraft which guided her to the spot, a rescue ship manoeuvres to pick up a party of survivors from a raft. (*Imperial War Museum*)

15. A typical wooden lifeboat, with only two men at the oars, struggles to come alongside a rescuing warship. Note the line, becketed round the boat's gunwale, to assist swimmers trying to climb out of the water. (*Imperial War Museum*)

16. After thirteen hours adrift, survivors are hauled on board one of the former US four-funnel destroyers transferred to Britain in 1940. A bare-footed lascar is suffering from frozen feet. (*Imperial War Museum*)

17. A rescued crew, relieved to be safe on shore after being picked up, 200 miles out to sea, by a Sunderland flying boat of RAF Coastal Command. A DEMS gunner from the Royal Marines is in the centre of the back row, and three lascars are to the right of the front row. (*Imperial War Museum*)

of sinkings increased, however, and as the war spread to more distant waters, the proportion of successful distress calls seems to have diminished, despite the extra operators and improved equipment. One explanation for this is that enemy surface ships, or U-boats making gun attacks, became increasingly adept at using their more powerful transmitters to jam the merchant ship's weaker signal. Disguised auxiliary cruisers opened devastating fire without warning, intending to knock out the radio room. Even after a ship had surrendered, her attacker would resume firing at the slightest sign of any radio transmission. Some of these auxiliary cruisers even carried a small Arado seaplane which would use a grapnel on the end of a wire to tear down the target's radio aerial during an attack in daylight.

When a ship was torpedoed, the shock of the explosion often caused enough damage to prevent any distress call being transmitted. Typical examples of survivors' reports from 1942 include: 'The explosion wrecked the ... main wireless transmitter and badly damaged the auxiliary transmitter' (*Melpomene*);[17] The radio room was 'in darkness and full of smoke' (*George H. Jones*);[18] 'The wireless set was completely shattered by the explosion' (*Empire Arnold*);[19] 'The main aerial was destroyed, and with my torch I saw that the emergency aerial was foul, and therefore useless' (*Teesbank*).[20]

Where the wireless room itself had been destroyed, or the delicate wiring circuits and valves damaged beyond repair, there was little the radio officers could do. The more common problem of the aerials being brought down could be tackled if the ship remained afloat long enough for the radio officer to rig some kind of jury aerial. When Japanese aircraft sank the *Pinna*, on 4 February 1942, 'Radio Officer Simpkins climbed up the mast and rigged up another aerial without any assistance in order to send out an SOS'.[21] The *Trevalgan*, torpedoed on 30 November 1942, provides another example of a jury aerial being successfully erected.[22]

If the radio installation was left apparently undamaged in the attack, the radio officer might have to wait for an order from the bridge and details of the ship's position before breaking radio silence, always with the possibility that the officers who could provide that authority and information might be incapacitated or preoccupied with other matters. Some masters, appreciating the speed at which vessels could sink and the possibility that a usable radio might not remain that way for long, wisely authorised their radio officers to act on their own initiative. Reporting on the torpedoing of the *Benmohr*, on 5 March 1942, the master explained:

A wireless distress message was sent off immediately and an answer was received. The wireless officer was given our position every half hour and he sent off the message without further instructions, as I had given him previous orders to do this immediately in a case of emergency.[23]

There were numerous examples of radio officers receiving prompt instructions from the bridge and getting off a message almost as smoothly as if they were working a peacetime schedule. How reassuring it must have been when they could pick up an acknowledgement from some distant shore station or from a neutral vessel able to come to the rescue. But many radio officers, tapping out their morse as the vessel settled beneath them, were denied the satisfaction of receiving any acknowledgement. They had to hope that their signal was being picked up by other vessels who were maintaining radio silence or that the fault lay in their receiver rather than the transmitter; and as time began to run out they had to fight the dispiriting suspicion that they were probably labouring in vain, defeated by a damaged aerial or transmitter, inadequate power or unfavourable atmospheric conditions. Even when a distress message was successfully transmitted, there might not be any ships or aircraft which could be diverted from other operations to search for survivors. In 1941 and 1942 there were simply too many calls for help.

While these attempts were being made to contact the outside world, a decision had to be made about such matters as whether the ship would float long enough for an orderly abandonment, whether she could still survive by getting under way again, whether to fight back or whether to surrender. Decisions of this kind properly belonged to the master or senior surviving officer, and it was usually they who finally gave the order if the ship had to be abandoned. Sometimes (and possibly more often than they cared to admit in subsequent interviews) the decision might be taken out of their hands. If the ship sank more or less immediately individual crew members simply had to make their own decision about when to jump overboard without waiting for orders. In some cases the fact that the vessel was mortally stricken was so obvious to all hands that abandonment was more a matter of an unspoken commonsense consensus rather than formally issued orders, while in other cases the order might be given by some other officer using his own judgement. After a torpedo attack on 19 October 1941, the chief engineer of the tanker *Inverlee* had to face up to a problem of this kind:

The bridge caught fire. I tried to get in communication with the bridge but neither the telegraph nor telephones were working ... The vessel was out of control. I decided to stop the engines and abandon the ship without orders from the bridge, as the flames were increasing and made us an easy target for another attack.[24]

Occasionally the crew of a damaged ship might be ordered to leave her by one of the convoy escorts who could no longer remain standing by when they were urgently required to screen the rest of the convoy. This usurpation of his prerogative was unlikely to be well received by the master. Still afloat over four hours after being torpedoed on 24 February 1941, one complained:

> I was more or less sure that the *British Gunner* could have been got in if a tug had been available ... I was busy getting out towing springs when we were suddenly ordered to abandon my ship by HMS *Petunia*. I was very surprised at this.[25]

Masters had to decide whether to give the order to abandon ship soon after the first attack or wait to make a considered decision after receiving assessments of the damage from the chief engineer, chief officer, bosun and carpenter. At whatever point the decision was taken, communicating the order to the crew could prove difficult. The ship's whistle, alarm bells, telegraphs and telephones were all liable to be rendered mute through damage; hand whistles or shouted words of command might be drowned by the roar of flames and escaping steam – or even by the wind. Over fifty years after the *Empire Tourist* was torpedoed east of Bear Island, a survivor could still recall that the noise from escaping steam was so loud that her master had to give the order to abandon ship by hand signals and by silently mouthing the words.[26]

Even when a formal order to abandon ship had been given, some of the crew might only learn of it from what others told them, possibly in garbled form, or by drawing inferences from the way they saw other crew members acting. This could easily lead to confusion, especially where a master chose, as a precautionary measure, to order his crew to go to their boat stations and clear away the boats ready for launching while the damage to the vessel was assessed. This preparatory stage could acquire a momentum of its own and precipitate a premature abandonment fuelled by the men's fear and uncertainty.

The master of the *Deucalion*, sunk on 12 August 1942 during the 'Operation Pedestal' convoy to Malta, had to face this problem when his ship received the first, but not then fatal, damage from aircraft torpedo and bombs:

I stopped the ship to assess the damage and ordered the boats to be cleared and lowered to deck level ... The chief officer and carpenter sounded the holds and wells ... Whilst this examination was going on, some greasers took it upon themselves to lower Nos 3 and 6 lifeboats and pull away from the ship. Shortly afterwards, HMS *Brahman*, a destroyer, appeared on the scene, and I ordered these men to return to the ship at once, as I had decided to carry on. They refused at first, but eventually they came back and climbed on board.[27]

After the *Fort Chilcotin* was torpedoed by U-boat on 24 July 1943 'the crew ... quickly mustered at their boat stations. No order was given to abandon ship. The after port and two forward starboard boats were lowered.'[28]

When the *Birchbank* was sunk by glider bomb on 11 November 1943, her irate and indignant master reported: 'On going along to the boat deck, I found that some of the crew had not awaited my instructions, and were lowering the two remaining port lifeboats ... As I was actually talking to them, someone in No. 4 lifeboat cut the painter and the boat drifted astern.'[29]

In contrast to these examples, one occasionally finds vessels being abandoned with the master controlling each step with text-book precision. Captain R. Brown described how it could be done in his report of the torpedoing of the *Glenshiel* by the Japanese submarine *I–7* in the Indian Ocean at 0233 on 3 April 1942:

I immediately ordered the lashings to be cast off and the boats to be swung out ready but gave special orders that no one was to get into the lifeboats until I gave the order ...

[While a radio signal was transmitted, confidential papers dumped, and damage investigated], the ship was still carrying way and I waited until I judged she was stopped before ordering the boats to be lowered into the water with orders to keep alongside ...

[After the engineers had been ordered out of the engine room], the ship was settling slowly by the stern and I therefore ordered the crew and passengers to abandon ship and pull away clear. A final distress signal was sent out ... The crew and passengers left the ship without any signs of panic. Everyone had time to go to their cabins and collect their valuable possessions ...

[With one boat remaining alongside for the final party], I ordered everyone to abandon ship ... I collected a folio of charts, a chronometer and sextant with sailing directions and put them in the boat along with the ship's papers, articles, official log and register, and everybody was out of the ship by 0351. I was the last to leave the ship, taking my bathrobe and topee with me as I anticipated being very hot in the boat.[30]

All seventy-nine crew, nine DEMS gunners and twelve passengers abandoned ship without a single casualty. Undoubtedly fortune smiled on them: a torpedo hit well aft, a cargo of cotton piece goods which would resist the inflow of water, well over an hour in which to leave the ship, no second torpedo until they were clear, fine weather, very good visibility and a calm sea. Even so, it was a very creditable achievement by a well-drilled crew under firm and confident leadership.

The pre-war regulations of the Board of Trade required every British merchant vessel to carry sufficient lifeboats to accommodate all the people on board, and the boats' construction and equipment were specified in great detail. The master, on pain of a penalty of £50, was required to see that everyone on board had a lifeboat station, to hold regular lifeboat drills and to enter the details in the ship's log,[31] but a popular textbook used in the training of deck officers throughout the war complained that crews were inexperienced in 'real boatwork at sea, their only practice being an occasional boat station and the lowering of boats for inspection purposes in harbour'.[32] Events during the first few months of the war led the Ministry of Shipping to issue advisory notices at the beginning of 1940 stressing the importance of regular practice and clear instructions about their duties for crews on both fishing vessels and ocean-going ships.[33]

In April 1940 the Ministry began to consider moving away from the policy of persuasion towards compulsion. That did not suit the Chamber of Shipping, an owners' organisation, which argued strongly in favour of allowing flexibility in the matter,[34] but the Ministry insisted on introducing tighter regulations in July.[35] So far as training was concerned, this amounted to little more than requiring that lifeboat drill in cargo ships should be increased from once a fortnight to at least once a week, with one drill to be held before the ship left port. Even this last, seemingly obvious, requirement could be dispensed with if the master could claim that the complete crew had already received proper lifeboat training in that vessel and were familiar with their various duties.

In many cargo ships, lifeboat drills often consisted of men mustering on the boat deck at the sounding of the 'Abandon Ship!' signal, the officers checking the lifebelts and boat equipment, and everyone standing by the falls, hooks, plugs, tiller or whatever piece of equipment they would be responsible for in a real emergency. Once in a while a mast might be stepped and the sail hoisted, more with a view to drying it out than giving practical training in its use, and occasionally boats might be lowered to the water in port to check that they did not leak too badly. In some ships the log might be falsified to record drills which never took place, or the drills might be mere token efforts, but even in very well run companies like Elder Dempster or Blue Funnel one finds masters' reports containing revealing comments such as: 'the crew themselves do not get into the boats'; 'I did not order the passengers actually into the boats as the operation sometimes involves some slight accidents'; 'lifeboats were swung out [in port] but not lowered'; or '[in Liverpool] lifeboats were swung out and secured but not entered by the crew, except by those whose duty it was to attend to the lashings and so on'.[36] Some, however, might attempt a more realistic exercise. Before the *Stentor*, for instance, sailed from Freetown in October 1942 a drill was held with passengers and crew sent away from the ship in their boats. Three passengers who refused to take part were peremptorily turned off the ship.[37] But no government regulations, no artificial drills, no leisurely spell at the oars in Freetown harbour or Liverpool's Gladstone Dock, could hope to prepare merchant seamen for the hellish reality of trying to launch lifeboats from a sinking ship in the open sea – perhaps in darkness, perhaps against a severe list, perhaps on fire, perhaps in bad weather.

The first great problem which had to be faced was that all of the lifeboats were unlikely to be available. When she was torpedoed, on 8 August 1940, the *Upwey Grange* was lacking one boat which had not been returned after it had been lent for the Dunkirk evacuation. In a few cases boats might already have suffered weather damage, but the most common cause was enemy action. Many of the survivors' reports contain such comments as: 'the starboard lifeboat had been blown away'; 'the port lifeboat was blown to pieces'; 'the starboard after lifeboat was completely blown away'; 'the port lifeboats had been blown away by the explosion'.[38] Other reports mention boats on fire, or filled with debris, or held by twisted davits or riddled with machine-gun bullets. In addition, men could be prevented from reaching their assigned boats by injury, fire, damage to the ship or speed of sinking, and there was a very natural reluctance to abandon ship on the side from which further torpedoes, shells or bullets might come. Of necessity, therefore, many ships had to be abandoned without much regard to the roles set out in the notice of lifeboat stations and practised in the weekly drills: men just scrambled to launch whichever boat they could reach and tackled whichever jobs seemed to need doing, even though they might be uninstructed about how they ought to be done.

The second great difficulty lay in the mechanism for getting the boats launched. Lifeboats on ocean-going ships needed to be large and strongly constructed, which also made them heavy and clumsy. They were suspended from pairs of davits which provided a means of swinging the boat out over the ship's side. They could then be lowered into the water by means of rope or wire falls rigged through a system of pulley blocks. The most modern passenger liners and some modern cargo ships were fitted with gravity davits which could be controlled by one man. By using a brake lever he could utilise the boat's own weight to run it to the outboard launching position, stop it at deck level for boarding, and then lower it into the sea. In tests before Board of Trade inspectors it had been demonstrated that, with Welin-Maclachlan gravity davits, a boat could be put into the water in twenty to thirty seconds, though that was certainly an optimistic figure under active service conditions. Desirable though it might have been, there was never any chance that the many older vessels could be re-equipped with davits of this type: that would have involved taking ships out of service for a major reconstruction. The ships could not be spared, and the money, men and materials could not have been found.

Older ships, and even many constructed in wartime, were fitted with either quadrant davits, where men had to wind handles which canted the davits outboard to bring the boats into the launching position, a task which might take three or four minutes, or the even older radial, or gooseneck, davits, where each davit in turn had to be manually rotated through 180 degrees while the boat was manoeuvred between them. This could be quite a performance for ten or a dozen men in daylight and without the need to hurry. On radial davits a pre-war textbook written by a master mariner commented: 'The system has little to commend it as it is cumbersome, slow and awkward to work, especially when the boats are housed inboard.' [39] In view of these difficulties, the usual wartime practice was to have these older davits rigged with the boats in the outboard position ready for immediate lowering, but prevented from swinging about by being bowsed in against padded booms lashed to the davits. The wire gripes which held boats securely in this position were fitted with a quick release device known as a senhouse slip. The disadvantage of carrying boats in this way was that they were more exposed to damage from the weather or from exploding torpedoes. A minority of shipmasters also disliked the arrangement 'because when they are swung out they are likely to become warped and leak when put into the water. When inboard they would rest in their chocks and not be so liable to warp as when hanging in the falls.' [40]

Some attempts were made to find better ways of utilising these older types of davit,[41] and some survivors suggested that boats should be fitted with a patent quick release gear to ensure that both ends of the boat were unhooked simultaneously when it reached the water, but the simplest equipment and practice remained the standard. Indeed, a committee called together to consider the whole question of ships' lifeboats and their equipment in 1943 was firmly of the opinion that on merchant ships the launching gear had to be kept simple in view of the 'unskilled' nature of the personnel.[42] In the same year the Council of the Merchant Navy Officers' Federation admitted: 'The ideal ship's lifeboat and launching gear has yet to be designed. It may well be that there is a complete solution to this problem, but in the view of the Council it has yet to be found.'[43] With the older types of davit, the problems were truly beyond solution. So much depended on a properly coordinated sequence of releasing the gripes; ensuring the boat was connected to the ship with painter or boatrope; lowering away on the falls steadily, evenly and simultaneously; fending the boat off from the ship's side as it was lowered; unhooking the boat from the falls when it reached the sea; holding it alongside and manning the boat via manropes or pilot ladder. Given the conditions under which many ships were abandoned, it is not surprising that this complicated procedure often broke down.

On some ships the training and discipline collapsed altogether. When the *Clan MacPhee* was torpedoed on 16 August 1940 the chief officer found one boat overcrowded with men originally assigned to a boat which had been blown away. He ordered some to move to other boats but failed to persuade them even at the point of a gun. Then he began to pull them out physically.[44] He discovered later that, their own boat having been lost, they feared that they would not be allowed to get in any other boat – but, on a ship sinking in eight minutes, no one could really afford this kind of confrontation. On the *Bulysses*, torpedoed on 10 September 1941, a boat had been successfully launched, and was being manoeuvred to take in men from one which had been smashed, when 'about thirty of the Chinese crew jumped into the boat. They had apparently panicked and were jumping over one another to get into the boat.'[45] Lascars on the *Trentbank*, sunk in an air attack on 24 November 1942, instead of lowering the boats, simply sat in them and waited for the British officers and gunners to do the job. They then sheered off leaving the men tending the falls to jump for it.[46]

Panic under stress could break out with crews of any nationality, but there were also examples of fine discipline and competence from crews of all nationalities. The *Clan MacPherson* had a lascar crew with British officers and gunners. Reporting on her sinking, on 1 May 1943, her master said: 'All my men lined up like soldiers, no one attempted to do anything without orders, and within ten minutes the five lifeboats and the one small boat were clear of the ship.'[47] In all 140 men got away smoothly and efficiently, and none was lost. Next morning the master reboarded the ship with men from five of the boats, but, after an unsuccessful attempt to steam and tow the ship to port, they abandoned her again with just two minutes to spare before she sank. On that occasion four of the engineers did not manage to get out of the engine room in time.

While some ships were able to get all of their boats away within a few minutes, survivors' reports contain horrifying examples of the various things which could go wrong.

> While lowering the captain's boat ... the forward davit broke, causing the boat to fall into the water.[48]

> Lowering the boat was very difficult as the falls were covered in oil and very difficult to hold.[49]

> In attempting to push this boat away from the ship's side, many of the oars were broken.[50]

> In spite of the port boat being 250 feet away from the ship it was filled with burning benzine, and being a metal boat it soon melted. The occupants must have perished immediately.[51]

> I found some of the crew had released the falls which had jammed and the boat had fallen into the slings. We could not lift it.[52]

> The small starboard boat was let go with a run and the two men in it were thrown into the water.'[53]

> The port boat was in the water, but as it had not been unhooked, it was dragged down as the ship sank.[54]

> As the ship's stern swung round, the propeller which was still turning fouled this lifeboat.[55]

> The after fall carried away, causing the boat to fall into the water on top of No. 5 lifeboat which was already in the water with a number of the crew in it.[56]

> Heavy sea lifted boat clear of ship unhooking falls, crew unable to gain boat.[57]

There was some delay in lowering this boat, as the forward fall became jammed, and one of the sailors who was trying to release it got his hand in the block. The second officer ... assisted by the crew, eventually managed to lift the boat and released the man's hand.[58]

They had difficulty in clearing the falls, and before they could pull clear the vessel sank rapidly by the head ... dragging the boat and its occupants with it.[59]

Probably the commonest problem was letting one or both of the falls run out too quickly, so that the boat became hung up, or swamped or capsized with men thrown into the sea. Such boats were not necessarily rendered unusable; they were often boarded and bailed out, and sometimes capsized boats were righted. Nevertheless, if one adds the boats which were burned, swept away or carried down by the sinking ship to those destroyed by enemy action or weather damage, it is clear that survivors were unlikely to get away in a full complement of lifeboats. A post-war analysis of a sample of 209 vessels found that they managed to launch a total of 492 lifeboats, only 52.8 per cent of the boats with which they were equipped. Within that sample, 144 ships which sank in 0–15 minutes launched 48 per cent of their boats, with eighteen launching no boats at all. For twenty-three ships which sank in 16–30 minutes successful launches rose to 62.2 per cent, and for ships which sank in 31–59 minutes it rose to 71.7 per cent. Rather strangely, ships which remained afloat for more than an hour only managed to launch just under 57 per cent of their lifeboats,[60] but some of them may have been hastened on their way by a second torpedo attack or the sudden collapse of a bulkhead.

Survivors were not, however, totally dependent on their lifeboats. Rafts which could be quickly thrown overboard or which would float free when the ship sank provided an obvious, simple and robust alternative place of refuge. In fact the government had first advised shipowners to provide rafts as early as August 1939, just before the outbreak of war, but at that stage they were not made compulsory. The term raft might encompass a great variety of craft: oval Carley floats similar to those used by the Royal Navy, a kind of buoyant flat mat called a Flotanet, the type of buoyancy aid which doubled as deck-seating on passenger craft, and all kinds of individualistic designs by ships' carpenters. They carried little, if anything, in the way of supplies, and they merely offered something for men in the water to cling to. Their provision created two contrasting approaches. Some put their faith in having many small rafts, widely distributed about the ship and easily thrown overboard, but rather flimsy in construction; others preferred fewer, bigger and heavier rafts which would support more men and be more easily spotted by rescuers.

The Ministry of Shipping's policy on rafts soon encountered considerable criticism. The advocates of bigger rafts began to point to the superiority of the rafts being developed for use on neutral ships. For example, *Motor Boat and Yachting* featured a description of a twenty-four-man raft, developed by a firm in Amsterdam. The article was accompanied by photographs, one showing a score of Dutchmen comfortably seated on the raft, which floated on twenty-four barrels.[61] The proprietor of the Tyne Gangway Company, James Linklater, claimed that rafts which met the pre-war Board of Trade requirements were too small for wartime conditions. In his view, a piece of buoyant apparatus currently certified for twenty-two men would support only two or three if they tried to climb on top of it. He advocated a double-sided raft capable of carrying fifteen to twenty men on top, and equipped with oars and rowlocks.[62] To meet this kind of criticism the Ministry of Shipping drew up an advisory specification for a more substantial square raft constructed of timber and enclosing drums as flotation chambers.[63] To ensure speedy provision, combined with minimum cost, the design was well within the competence of a ship's carpenter.

A second line of attack on the Ministry came from those who did not consider that a voluntary, do-it-yourself approach was an adequate response to the problem. Miss Bridget Talbot, a granddaughter of the eighteenth Earl of Shrewsbury, was tireless in badgering Members of Parliament and the government on all aspects of safety for merchant seamen. She was an unusual and formidable advocate. Having won the Italian Military Cross as a nurse in the First World War, and sailed as a member of the crew of the Finnish barque *Pamir* through a ninety mph gale, she was not easily fobbed off by civil servants. Following a powerful letter to *The Times*, she visited the Ministry of Shipping on 17 January 1940 to argue forcefully that liferafts should be made compulsory.[64] In the House of Commons, Vice-Admiral E. A. Taylor, Unionist MP for South Paddington, pleaded that this was a matter of urgency, and was assured by Sir Arthur Salter that shipowners were taking active steps 'but my Right Honourable Friend [i.e. the Minister] will have no hesitation whatever if we find that these rafts are not being provided as quickly as possible, in using compulsion'.[65] In February, Emmanuel Shinwell, Labour MP for Seaham, took a deputation from the seamen's unions and other interested organisations to the Admiralty to argue for compulsory public provision of rafts.[66] The sympathetic First Lord, Winston Churchill, then pressed the Ministry of Shipping and intimated that rafts in Admiralty stores might be provided if supply was the problem.

Supply had indeed been the fundamental influence on the Ministry's approach. There was no serious shortage of raw materials, but it was thought unlikely that the dockside companies which manufactured liferafts would be able to cope with a sudden increase in demand. The gradual approach also had the advantage of not antagonising the shipowners by imposing new and expensive requirements. The success of the voluntary principle was demonstrated when a special survey, carried out by the senior surveyors at the major ports in late January 1940, revealed that with few exceptions shipowners were providing rafts. Now compulsion could be considered to bring into line the recalcitrant minority of shipowners who had not responded to persuasion.[67] On 27 February 1940 Sir John Gilmour, the Minister of Shipping, was able to tell Eleanor Rathbone, Independent MP for Combined English Universities, that he intended to make compulsory the provision of rafts on all ships operating in dangerous waters.[68] A week later, he assured her that he intended to see that there should be sufficient rafts to accommodate all on board, and that they should be supplied with self-igniting lights, as already required for lifeboats.[69] These requirements were embodied in the Merchant Shipping (Additional Life-Saving Appliances) Rules issued on 7 March 1940. Rafts also had to be equipped with a lifebuoy and line, at least two paddles, a painter, at least one gallon of fresh water, condensed milk or similar food, and distress signals. On tankers and motorships the self-igniting lights had to be powered by electric batteries, since the older calcium flares might ignite petrol or oil on the surface of the sea. Some indication of the difficulty of enforcing regulations such as these is provided by the fact that survivors from the *Ciscar* and the *Grelhead*, torpedoed in August and December 1941 respectively, reported that their rafts were not equipped with the self-igniting lights, but whether they had been stolen or never supplied is not stated.[70]

A number of commercial firms, sometimes two or three in a single port, were interested in supplying rafts. Since the beginning of the year Cocks Reinforced Hatchcovers of Cardiff and London had been manufacturing a ten-man raft to the Ministry's specifications. They asserted in their advertisements that anything larger would be 'cumbersome and heavy, taking up too much deck space, and too difficult to launch'.[71] This raft was 8ft 6in long, 6ft 3½in wide and 2ft 8½in deep. Although it was widely adopted, it was criticised on the grounds that its square shape made it difficult to paddle or tow, and there were still influential voices raised in favour of an even bigger craft.

A solution to the raft-launching problem was provided by R. S. Chipchase, Managing Director of the Tyne Dock Engineering Company, who invented an inclined steel frame which could be fixed outboard of the shrouds supporting ships' masts. On this the raft was mounted in a position where it took up no deck space and where, in an emergency, it could simply be left to float off or be deliberately launched by merely knocking off a senhouse slip quick-release device which would allow it to slide overboard. It was claimed that a raft could be launched by a boy in a second. With the support of the Ministry, Chipchase generously offered his invention as a gift to the shipping industry. He declined to claim any royalties and placed no restrictions on its manufacture.[72]

This simple and practical launching device cleared the way for the advocates of larger rafts. The enthusiasm of the proprietor of the Tyne Gangway Company led to a fifteen-man raft measuring 10ft by 7ft 6in by 2ft 6½in.[73] By the spring of 1942 they were supplying rafts measuring 12ft 8¾in by 7ft 6in by 2ft 7in which could be rowed, sailed or towed. It was claimed that, with eight buoyancy chambers distributed along their entire length, they also offered greater thwartship and longitudinal stability than the various modifications to earlier designs, many of which by that time had adopted pointed bows and sterns. These modifications improved the manoeuvrability of the rafts but might have an adverse effect on the longitudinal stability if they projected beyond the buoyancy tanks.[74]

Lifeboats remained the preferred means of abandoning ship, but rafts provided a very worthwhile back-up system because getting them into the water required very little time or skill. When ships sank very quickly, or when men were tipped into the sea from incompetently launched lifeboats, rafts offered an alternative means of survival; and, even if all survivors were accommodated in the lifeboats, the equipment and provisions from rafts could be salvaged to supplement what was carried in the boats. Like lifeboats, rafts were prone to being blown overboard in a torpedo attack but, since they were intended to be tumbled unceremoniously into the water, they often survived intact. On 3 March 1942, all six rafts from the *Helenus* were lost in this way, but all floated perfectly well allowing their stores to be recovered.[75] Sometimes a torpedo explosion might prevent a raft from being launched by twisting the frame on which it was carried, but rafts jammed in this way often floated off when the vessel sank.

The torpedoing of the *Empire Antelope* in Convoy SC107 on 2 November 1942 showed both the value and some of the problems of rafts. Two lifeboats were successfully launched, but could not be held against the ship's side long enough for all the crew to climb down into them. The master described how the remaining twenty-six men abandoned ship:

> We released a raft and about eighteen men floated off on it, in charge of the chief officer. Then some of the gunners, who had stood by until the last, informed me that the large raft on the port side was jammed and they could not clear it. I got an axe, managed to cut the raft away, and the remaining eight of us left the ship on it. We then found that the bridle lashing on the raft had become foul, making it impossible to push the raft from the ship's side. I realised that someone would have to reboard the vessel to cut the raft clear, and as I was the only one who knew anything about it, I waited until the raft lifted on the swell and scrambled back on deck. I chopped the raft clear, shouting to the men to keep as close alongside as possible, then jumped for it, but missed the raft and fell into the water. I was wearing my lifejacket, however, with the red light attached, and was quickly pulled on to the raft without further mishap. This being the weather side we had great difficulty in getting the raft away from the vessel.[76]

Survivors from the *Empire Antelope* were fortunate in being able to board the rafts directly from the ship. Like that ship's master, many survivors from other ships only managed to reach the rafts after a spell in the water, and others who were unable to reach boat or raft simply had to swim or drift and hope to come across some piece of buoyant debris to which they could cling. Some found themselves floating when their ship sank beneath them; some jumped overboard, some were blown overboard by explosions; and some were tipped into the sea by lifeboats upending in the falls or capsizing in the sea. Among them, in some cases, would be key members of the crew who had deliberately delayed their own attempt to reach safety.

Some radio officers stayed behind trying to rig a jury aerial or get an acknowledgement of their distress calls. Concentrating on that task with their earphones on, they might not even know that the order to abandon ship had been given. As early as the second month of the war, the Radio Officers' Union had written to the Ministry of Shipping about this problem, citing the sinking of the *Italian Prince* and *Manaar*. The Ministry asked shipowners' organisations to emphasise the importance of warning radio officers when it was time to leave.[77] In February

1940 shipowners and masters were urged to make special arrangements for ensuring that radio officers and engineers were not inadvertently left behind,[78] but confusion could still arise, or the men might put their lives in jeopardy out of a sense of duty towards their shipmates. DEMS gunners might remain closed up at their guns in the hope of either keeping attacking aircraft away while boats were launched or getting a shot at a surfacing submarine. Masters frequently felt that they had to stay behind to make absolutely certain that their ship could not survive the damage it had sustained, and they might involve their chief officer, chief engineer, bosun and carpenter in that assessment. Some masters also felt that they had to make a personal search to make sure no injured or trapped men remained on board. They were also supposed to check that confidential code books had been dumped over the side in a weighted bag or box, and they might think that they ought to try to save the ship's papers, accounts and cash from their safe. In a well-ordered abandonment, arrangements would be made for the master and his final party to be got away in a boat waiting alongside, but it was asking a lot of the men in the boat to hold on patiently right where the next torpedo might strike. Alternatively, a boat could be ordered to lie off but return alongside when signalled that the final party was ready to leave, or a raft might be prepared as their means of escape.

In darkness, bad weather, confusion and haste, arrangements of this kind could not be expected to work smoothly and some of these final parties were lost. The tanker *San Florentino* was torpedoed and sunk on 2 October 1941 after a most gallant defence against a surfaced U-boat. Some of the large final party were waiting alongside on a raft for the master and a few others to climb down when another torpedo struck. The chief officer described the result:

> The torpedo had struck the port side of the ship almost abreast of the raft where all the men were sitting, the chief engineer was thrown to the deck and received terrible injuries and was calling out in agony when a sea washed over the deck, washing him down into the hole amidships and he was not seen again. The captain was also badly injured about the head and face but he asked for a torch and signalled to us in the boats to come and take off the remaining men. Our boat, being so badly damaged could do nothing, and the second officer ... tried to pull over to the ship but the crew could do nothing with the oars in the heavy seas. There were a few more torch flashes from the captain then he was seen to dive overboard followed by the senior [wireless]

operator. Nothing was found of any of the men who had remained on board, with the exception of the third mate and an able seaman.[79]

These two men had an amazing escape. As the ship sank by the stern, they climbed to the fo'c'sle head. Eventually the ship was floating vertically, with the foremast along the surface of the sea and the two men sitting astride the ship's stem a hundred feet up in the air. After thirteen hours without food, water or shelter, they were able to climb hand over hand down the mast's forestay and drop into a boat crewed by volunteers from HMS *Mayflower*.

Final parties who did get away were often compelled to jump and swim for their lives. When the *Aldington Court* was torpedoed on 31 October 1942, 'the captain, second officer, second radio officer and gunner who were left on board jumped into the water as the ship rolled over'.[80] All four men were subsequently picked up by lifeboats. The master of the *Llandaff Castle*, torpedoed a month later, described what happened when his ship broke in two. 'There were still on board the chief, second and third officers, four naval ratings, two Merchant Navy gunners and myself; we all jumped overboard, and climbed on to rafts.'[81] After losing his ship on the same day, the master of the *Trevalgan* reported:

> I saw the chief officer swim to a raft ... and pull the donkeyman on to it. The ship now took such a heavy list that I was able to walk down the ship's side, and the chief officer shouted to me to jump, which I did. I swam to the chief officer's raft and held on to the side ... The backwash [as the ship sank] swept all three of us off the raft, however we managed to scramble back again.[82]

The long history of ordinary shipwrecks in peacetime showed that, when any ship sank, some survivors were likely to find themselves swimming in the sea, yet it was by no means uncommon to find merchant seamen who could not swim a single stroke. Even strong swimmers, who for a short time might find it easier to swim unencumbered, soon felt the need for some personal buoyancy aid. The Board of Trade's most recent pre-war regulations required shipowners to supply enough approved lifejackets for all crew and passengers.[83] To gain approval, a lifejacket had to be capable of supporting 16½ pounds of iron in fresh water for twenty-four hours, and support even an unconscious man with his face clear of the water. The most common type of jacket which gained its buoyancy from cork blocks might weigh 5¼ pounds. A newer type stuffed with kapok fibre could secure the same buoyancy for a weight of 2¼ pounds. The real problem with both types of approved lifejacket was their sheer bulk. It might well be prudent for men to wear their lifejackets all the time in a danger zone, but for working on deck they were cumbersome, while in the engine-room or galley they were too hot as well. In any situation they were likely to catch on projections, hamper movement and obstruct access in confined spaces. In addition, there was a widespread suspicion amongst merchant seamen that anyone wearing a cork lifejacket who dived or jumped into the sea ran the risk of having his neck broken as the force of gravity came into conflict with the buoyant qualities of the cork. In December 1939, press reports of the sinking of the *Navasota* mentioned men losing their lives in precisely that way.[84]

If lives were not to be lost unnecessarily, something needed to be done to provide seamen with a life-preserver which could be worn at all times without interfering too much with routine work. To that end, in December 1939 the Ministry of Shipping began trials of a kapok-filled lifesaving waistcoat. It immediately proved popular with merchant sea-men, although it was recognised that the waistcoat was still unwearable in the engine room. Experience showed that the new waistcoats were effective, and the Ministry began urging shipowners to supply them to their crews, but there was no question that the waistcoat could be a direct replacement for the standard lifejacket, to which it was considered inferior. It was officially regarded as supplementary to the standard type, a decision unwelcome to some shipowners but reflecting sensitivity about the views of the various Merchant Navy unions.

The fifteen (eventually twenty) firms manufacturing the waistcoat found themselves deluged with orders at the start of 1940. In late January, the Ministry began asking shipping organisations and the principal surveyors at the main ports to report on how individual shipping companies were responding to the recommendation about issuing waistcoats. The principal surveyor at Glasgow reported: 'Most of the shipowners in this port have either supplied these to their crews or have given the order for them. They are finding great difficulty in obtaining delivery owing to the great demand with which the factories have been unable to cope.'[85] Elsewhere the position was less satisfactory. Donaldsons were supplying each of their ships with the waistcoats as they arrived in port, but Clan Line, Robertsons and Hogarths still had the matter under consideration. Ellerman's City Line, whose ships were mainly manned by lascar seamen, were supplying kapok waistcoats for all their British officers but the rest of the crew would be provided only with an inflatable rubber ring.[86]

Anxious to avoid giving the Ministry of Shipping an excuse to impose the waistcoats compulsorily, the shipowners' organisations took the lead in pressing their members to comply, and the Executive Council of the National Union of Seamen, meeting on 15 February 1940, noted with satisfaction a decision by the Shipping Federation to supply the waistcoats to all their member companies. Individual seamen who wished to acquire their own personal waistcoat could buy one for ten shillings.[87] In Notice M.182, drawn up in February 1940, the Ministry continued to advise that the standard lifejacket should be used whenever possible, but that all members of crews passing through dangerous areas should be provided with 'a safety appliance which can be worn whilst on duty, preferably in the form of a life-saving waistcoat which provides an extra source of warmth while on deck'.[88] The waistcoats weighed only fifteen ounces.[89]

Private enterprise had its own solutions to offer. Since December 1939, Messrs Gieves of Old Bond Street, the well-known naval outfitters, had been advertising an apparently ordinary cloth waistcoat with a cunningly concealed rubber interlining which could be inflated, through a tube carried in the top pocket, to produce a supporting ring around the chest. Only slightly inflated it could support a fully clothed man while leaving him free to swim. When fully inflated it was claimed to be capable of supporting six men.[90] This rather optimistic claim was reduced to five men in their advertising after March 1940. Priced at three guineas these waistcoats were probably beyond the reach of most merchant seamen. A similar (but cheaper) garment was offered by C. H. Bernard of Harwich in two qualities priced at £2 17s. 6d. and £2 5s. 0d.[91] These waistcoats must have sold reasonably well, as both firms continued to advertise them widely through 1940 and 1941. An interesting product with the same purpose was the Percowear Flotation Jersey.[92] Another firm developed the Vitabuoy overcoat priced at six guineas, advertised as 'waterproof, galeproof, flameproof, and guaranteed to keep wearer afloat for seventy-two hours, conscious or unconscious'.[93] By the middle of 1942 the makers of the Vitabuoy were forced to end production as they could no longer obtain the materials.

By that time it had long been accepted that the safety of merchant seamen ought not to be left to the willingness of particular shipowners to take advice – or the ability of individual seamen to pay out of their own pocket for safety devices from commercial concerns. Prompted by the reports of port surveyors, harassed by the indefatigable Miss Bridget Talbot, and questioned in the House of Commons by such MPs as Eleanor Rathbone and Will Thorne, the Ministry eventually made the

Advertisement, *Daily Telegraph*, 18 December 1939.

kapok waistcoats compulsory, a decision announced publicly by Ronald Cross in a speech at Bootle on 21 July 1940.[94] In deference to representations made through the Chamber of Shipping by the chief superintendent of Ellerman's City Line, their inflatable rubber ring was still acceptable as an alternative to the waistcoat.[95]

In 1942 the Technical Committee of the Chamber of Shipping suggested that the requirement to continue to supply lifejackets in addition to the waistcoats ought to be discontinued 'solely on the score of saving expense'.[96] The Ministry of War Transport refused to take this cheeseparing advice. The lifejacket was still regarded as superior in terms of buoyancy, and each one was inspected and stamped by a Ministry surveyor at the maker's works. The quality of the waistcoats was not so rigorously safeguarded. The potential saving of materials if lifejackets were discontinued was considered minimal and out of all proportion to the potentially adverse effect on the morale of seamen. The attitude of the Merchant Navy unions also had to be taken into account. The Ministry concluded that lifejackets should continue to be supplied as casualty reports showed that crews were always ready to grab their lifejackets if the circumstances allowed.[97] Although two-thirds of the lifejackets on ships in August 1942 were still the old Board of Trade type, improved designs were being developed.

The debate on the relative merits of the lifejacket as compared with the waistcoat was eventually resolved in 1943–44 with the introduction of improved lifejacket designs which used kapok, rather than cork, and could be worn like a waistcoat. For example, the 'Victory' lifejacket could be worn at all times, and was specially designed to allow the wearer to jump overboard without the risk of breaking his neck if he used the correct technique. It was (very optimistically) claimed to keep the head clear of the water; it had a yellow or orange yoke to attract attention and a rope grab handle for use in hauling the wearer from the water. For use in engine rooms, boiler rooms and galleys a type of lifejacket was devised which was normally worn like an apron and, in an emergency, could be raised to the chest and fastened to a back piece to form a serviceable buoyancy aid.[98] But the distribution of new equipment had to be a gradual process in view of the world-wide operations of the Merchant Navy, and the impulse for safety improvements always had to battle with supply difficulties and concerns about the cost.

There was also a constant battle against the insouciance or fatalism of some merchant seamen. The Ministry of War Transport might tell them to keep their lifejackets with them at all times, the shipowners might urge the same precaution, their own unions might plead with them, it might be laid down in masters' standing orders, in 1944 the Crown Film Unit might produce *Lifesaving at Sea* to ram home the message – yet at the crucial moment the lifejacket might not be to hand. Even the senior survivors who were interviewed by the Admiralty sometimes had to admit that they had had to return to their cabin to collect their lifejacket; or that they had been lucky enough to find one lying on the deck; or that they had grabbed a spare one from a locker on the boatdeck; or that they had jumped overboard without a lifejacket. There were also a few merchant seamen who claimed that they did not wish to be kept afloat to face the uncertain fate that might await them once they were clear of the ship. To them a quick end seemed preferable to drowning slowly in a choppy sea, suffering hallucinations and madness brought on by despair, freezing to death, undergoing amputation for frostbite, being incinerated, choking or blinding in fuel oil, being attacked by sharks or barracuda, dying from thirst or sunstroke, being run down or crushed by would-be rescuers, or even being murdered at the hands of the enemy.

6

Face to Face with the Enemy

As British merchant seamen struggled with the multitude of practical problems involved in abandoning a ship on the open sea, they carried at the back of their minds the additional worry that the enemy might attack them while they were helpless. This concern had its origins, perhaps, in the atrocity stories of the First World War and the imaginative works of fiction many seamen would have read when they were boys. The concern had increased with the sinking of the *Athenia*, and the press response built around such emotive words as 'outrage', 'barbarism', 'piracy' and 'inhumanity'. A particularly vivid impression was created by a 1939 *Punch* cartoon showing Hitler as captain of a U-boat crewed by skeletons, and during the winter of 1939–40 there were the regular German announcements of their intention to attack without warning, to treat British merchant vessels as if they were warships, and to operate without restriction in ever-widening areas around Britain's coasts.

Although British newspapers had reported very fairly on the commendable efforts made by German U-boat commanders in the early weeks of the war to treat survivors in strict accordance with international law, merchant seamen and their families continued to be apprehensive about possible action against survivors. There were always a few stories on which worry and rumour could feed. Press reports of the sinking of the *Sneaton* by torpedo and gunfire on 14 October 1939 spoke of the U-boat commander brandishing a pistol, and of a gun being trained on survivors in a lifeboat to compel them to cheer for the benefit of a photographer.[1] In view of his conduct on other occasions, it seems unlikely that Herbert Schultze of *U–48* intended anything more sinister than securing confirmation of his success and a few propaganda pictures, but to British readers the incident looked as if it could very easily have led to a bloodbath.

In reporting the sinking of the *Sea Venture* by gunfire from a U-boat on 20 October 1939, the master commented: 'Whilst pulling away from the ship either the submarine firing was very erratic or else she was firing one gun at the boat.'[2] This may well have been the first hint of deliberate fire being directed at survivors after they had left their ship. Press reports of the bombing of the *Stanburn* ten miles off Flamborough Head on 29 January 1940 stated that survivors were machine-gunned as they attempted to escape in the ship's boats.[3] In the summer of 1940 the accusations became more specific. When the *Abukir* was sunk in the early hours of 28 May by an E-boat (erroneously reported as a U-boat) press reports alleged:

> The Germans swept the waters with the beam of their searchlight and opened fire with a machine-gun at the helpless humanity struggling in the water. A few – a very few – of them succeeded in avoiding the bullets and clinging to a large piece of wreckage. On to it they dragged the chief officer, only to find him dead, killed by a machine-gun bullet through his head. He had been murdered in the water, as a great many others must have been, for the ship had not been subjected to machine-gun attack before she was sunk.[4]

Only three days later, the same newspaper was reporting, under the headline 'U-BOAT COMMANDER'S CALLOUS ACT', the sinking of an unidentified vessel on 27 May. This must have referred to the sinking of the *Sheaf Mead* from which there were only five survivors out of a crew of thirty-six. They told how

> the German commanding officer drove his craft among the men struggling in the water and clinging to a raft, the upturned boats and pieces of wreckage. It was not in order to pick up survivors in accordance with the tradition of the sea, and the dictates of humanity that he came. It was to ask the survivors the name of the ship he had sunk, and to give members of the crew an opportunity to take photographs of his unfortunate victims. And while he did so, the U-boat commander stationed two men with boathooks to fend off and jab at the wretched men who tried to clamber on board, thinking that the U-boat had come to pick them up.[5]

One of the German aircraft which sank five small coasters in the Straits of Dover on 25 July 1940 was accused of having machine-gunned men in the water and in a lifeboat,[6] and the Italian submarine which sank the *St Agnes* on 14 September 1940 was reported to have fired a dozen times at a lifeboat without scoring a single hit.[7] The details of the worst case of all seem to have been considered too horrifying to release to the press. On 23 August, the *Severn Leigh* was torpedoed in mid-Atlantic by a U-boat which subsequently shelled her, first from the port side and then from the starboard side until she sank. The master and twenty-five survivors were lying off the starboard side in a lifeboat, and it is indicative of the apprehension felt by merchant seamen that his report states: 'We in the boat now awaited further developments, fully expecting a burst of shell fire, and was quite resigned to what I then considered inevitable.' The U-boat did them no harm, however, and they rowed over to join the boats from the port side of the ship.

> The first boat, full of water, was occupied by a young deck boy of sixteen years of age, standing up and looking very white and out of his mind, result of pieces of shell in many parts of body and head ... We now proceeded to the second boat, here the sight was ghastly, the boat full of water and riddled, the bosun badly shot in head and body, dead, the chief officer the same, the radio officer his head literally split in two from the crown to the chin, the third officer also injured in head and dead ... The third engineer badly injured in the back, alive, unable to move, and was lifted in the boat, also the cook, badly injured in body. Assistant steward also badly injured, a fireman who was showing shocking injury, his hand blown off, and from elbow to shoulder the muscle torn away showing bone, both legs broken and multiple injuries in body, but alive.[8]

Were incidents of this kind the inevitable outcome of Admiral Doenitz's order No. 154 of late November/early December 1939, which stressed that one must be hard in war, and instructed the U-boats to rescue no one and not to concern themselves with lifeboats? Were they, perhaps, the result of over-zealous officers trying to prove just how hard they could be? Can some be explained as tragic accidents where, in pressing home their attacks, aircraft, E-boats, surface raiders or U-boats failed to notice men who were abandoning ship or were already in the water? Can others be explained as simply cases of distraught survivors assuming that ricochets or poorly aimed shots were being fired at them deliberately? Is it significant that the *Sheaf Mead* and *Severn Leigh* were both sunk by *U–37* commanded by Victor Oehrn, who had been well placed to acquire an insight into Doenitz's thinking during an earlier appointment as a staff officer at U-boat Headquarters? According to an American historian who has had access to an as yet unpublished autobiography by Oehrn, the slaughter of the crew of the *Severn Leigh* was caused by a stray shell. Oehrn was so worried about the likely effect on world opinion that he seriously considered, but in the end rejected, the idea of ensuring that none of the other survivors should live to tell the tale.[9]

Certainly, none of these specific accusations against individual
U-boats was taken up in the war crimes trials held after the war.
Possibly the evidence was regarded as inconclusive, and either the
accused or key prosecution witnesses may no longer have been alive
by the time the war ended. At his own trial, Admiral Doenitz pointed
out that his order No. 154 contained no reference to attacking and
eliminating survivors: it simply directed commanding officers to leave
them to take their chance, rather than risk losing U-boats on the
surface while succouring survivors. In any case, he claimed, the order
was issued only in relation to the particular circumstances in which
operations had to be conducted in the North Sea and other closely
patrolled areas around Britain's shores in the first half of 1940. After
the Norwegian campaign the order fell into abeyance as operations
moved further afield, and it had ceased to apply by November 1940.[10]
One of his most successful U-boat commanders, Otto Kretschmer of
U–99, explained after the war that Doenitz's main objective – bringing
Britain to her knees by a 'tonnage war' – inevitably meant that many
merchant seamen lost their lives; but their deaths were regarded as
a by-product of that strategy, not a goal in itself.[11] Kretschmer's own
attitude to survivors was shown in September 1940 when, although
Doenitz's Order No. 154 had not yet been formally rescinded, he
rescued the sole survivor of the *Baron Blythswood* from a raft, gave
him clothes and cigarettes, and placed him in a lifeboat from the
Invershannon.[12]

The difficulty of applying simple judgements to the behaviour of
combatants in war-time is illustrated by the actions of the Italian submarine *Comandante Cappellini* on 5 January 1941, when sinking the
Shakespear in a three-hour gun action. After two hours the British ship,
down to the last shell, received a direct hit on her gun. The master
then stopped his ship and hoisted a white flag; but, as the crew tried
to abandon ship, the Italians continued to shell her for a further hour.
Thus far the engagement might be listed as a possible war crime but,
once the survivors were off the ship, the Italians allowed eighteen men
from a damaged lifeboat to climb on to the submarine's casing, took
the other lifeboat in tow and headed south at full speed. The third
mate of the British ship was told: 'We are picking you up because we
are not Germans.' He later commented: 'The men on the submarine
treated us very well, they dressed our wounds and gave us brandy and
food, consisting of biscuits and meat, which we greatly appreciated.'
Put back into the lifeboat only four miles from one of the Cape Verde
Islands, the survivors were left to row ashore.[13]

In the great North Atlantic convoy battles of 1941 to 1943, opportunities for U-boats to engage in face to face contact with survivors were limited. They were generally too busy trying to manoeuvre into position for a further attack, and too concerned about possible counter measures by escorting ships and aircraft, to waste time on rescue, interrogation or more sinister activities. But in more distant waters or in attacks on ships sailing alone, U-boat commanders were often anxious to surface and contact the survivors who, since they were not privy to the innermost thoughts of Admiral Doenitz and his U-boat officers, continued to be apprehensive when they saw the enemy approaching. Exaggerated dockside rumours, press reports, accusations by leader writers that the enemy often machine-gunned lifeboats,[14] and an alliterative reference by the Prime Minister himself to 'merciless murdering and marauding',[15] all contributed to their fears.

In fact the main purpose of these contacts was intelligence gathering. Identification of the class of ship and its tonnage was an integral part of the attack procedure, and if the name of the ship could be obtained that would be a useful confirmation of the success and a check on the accuracy of the visual identification. The information would be useful in many ways. German naval intelligence could maintain an accurate 'profit and loss' account of Britain's merchant tonnage; German propaganda could use the names to boost the credibility of its claims about the U-boats' effectiveness; disguised surface raiders could avoid adopting the cover-name of a vessel which no longer existed; and, at a personal level, the entitlement of U-boat commanders to coveted decorations could be established. Knowledge of the cargo could be useful in such matters as gauging the value of each sinking, indicating where Britain was obtaining essential supplies or where military stores were being built up, and providing clues about the level of US aid to Britain, especially prior to 1942. Information about the route which had been laid down for the ship might reveal where it would be profitable to concentrate future U-boat, surface raider or mining operations. It could also show the extent to which Britain's merchant tonnage was being used at less than optimum efficiency through being forced to adopt evasive routeing.

British naval intelligence also found the face to face encounters useful. Senior survivors were later questioned about such matters as the type of submarine, the condition of her hull, her armament, the appearance of the officers, the dress of the crew, their morale and their nationality. On this last point survivors' evidence was often misleading: small, swarthy men who did not correspond to the Nordic stereotype were often mistakenly assumed to be Italians. Although U-boat identification numbers were not displayed, British intelligence could sometimes, as their data bank built up, identify a particular U-boat from unofficial insignia on uniform caps, private badges painted on conning towers and other apparently insignificant items.

Although eager to obtain information, U-boat commanders exercised considerable caution in approaching lifeboats and rafts. Look-outs would be posted to scan each sector of the horizon, and survivors would be covered by men armed with submachine-guns or other small arms – and possibly by light anti-aircraft weapons. To men who had only narrowly escaped with their lives from their sinking ship, this display of force could seem like the prelude to a massacre, and in subsequent press reports it could easily be made to look like a shameful example of bullying and browbeating of helpless men. In reality, the posting of armed men was merely a prudent precaution which a commanding officer of any nationality might have ordered in similar circumstances. Survivors had to be discouraged from clambering onto the U-boat's casing as a place of refuge, since this might interfere with the operational efficiency of the boat if she needed to dive in an emergency, or they might try to overpower members of the crew. Apocryphal stories of unarmed survivors trying to storm on board went the rounds of U-boat crews – and it could not always be assumed that the survivors were unarmed.

In July 1940 there were press reports of survivors from an unidentified ship who had taken three rifles on their raft. They tried without success to attract rescuers by firing tracer bullets into the air at night, lost two rifles when their raft overturned, and 'ostentatiously threw overboard the one remaining rifle' when a surfaced U-boat approached and trained a machine-gun on them six days after their vessel sank.[16] Survivors occasionally mention shooting at sharks from lifeboats, although one suspects that those who took pistols with them when abandoning ship were probably motivated more by their possible value in keeping order in the boat than by any intention to launch an assault on a U-boat. The DEMS gunners of the *Athelqueen* actually took a Lewis gun and ammunition into the lifeboat when she was torpedoed and shelled on 15 March 1942 by the Italian submarine *Enrico Tazzoli*;[17] and the master of the *Llandaff Castle*, recalling his encounter with *U–177* which torpedoed his ship on 30 November 1942, commented: 'I was sorry that I did not have a rifle with a high explosive shell in it, as I feel that I could have damaged or sunk this submarine.'[18] That he was not the only person thinking along these lines is shown by the fact that, at a meeting in January 1943, the Admiralty's Merchant Ships Technical Committee was told that 'many suggestions' had been received about how survivors might attack U-boats which approached them, but the Admiralty had 'consistently set its face against any such policy, which it is considered would undoubtedly lead to reprisals against the crews of sunken merchant ships'.[19] One can hardly blame U-boat commanders for putting on a show of force to discourage any possibility of surprise attack by desperate survivors.

In reality, most survivors would have been in no state to offer any resistance. They usually answered willingly enough the few simple questions put to them. If it was thought that more information might be revealed by a man who was isolated from the prying eyes and support of his shipmates, a survivor would sometimes be called on board the U-boat to be interrogated below deck. The more common practice in these encounters, however, was for the questions to be just shouted down to men in a boat or on a raft and, even if the senior surviving officers kept quiet to hide both their status and knowledge, someone would usually supply the answers, either because they were too shocked to act differently, too unintelligent to dissemble, or too eager to placate a threatening foe. Indeed, many merchant seamen were inclined to look upon giving such details as ship's name, cargo and where bound as no different to the name, rank and number which people in the armed forces were required to give. A few truculent individuals could be less co-operative. From his raft on 23 November 1940, the radio officer of the *Tymeric* simply told the U-boat commander to go to hell.[20] Survivors from other ships gave misleading answers, and on 17 February 1943 the chief officer of the *Llanashe*, having decided to answer truthfully, spoke with such a pronounced Welsh accent that, after ascertaining the vessel's name with great difficulty, the commander of *U–182* gave up and steamed away without further questioning.[21]

Incidental to this intelligence gathering, some German commanders appeared glad of an opportunity to offer help to survivors. This may have been on the assumption that they would reveal more information while the help was being given, but may equally have been out of genuine humanitarian concern. Men in boats were often given the distance and course to steer for the nearest landfall. Considerate acts of this kind were by no means rare in 1942. The commander of *U–103* told survivors from the *Stanbank* 'that the war would soon be over and [gave] the men in the boat twenty-five cigarettes and a box of matches'.[22] The master of the *Athelknight* identified the second-in-command of *U–172* as the man giving directions to survivors. '[He] told me to come alongside when he would give us some bread. We did so, and he handed us several five-pound loaves. This bread was very hard, and only two of the loaves were any good, the others being mouldy. [He said,] "I am very sorry for you fellows", and our men in the boat shouted back "We are sorry, too".' [23] After sinking the *Anglo Canadian*, the commander of *U–153*

> wanted to know whether there were any members of the crew still in the water. The third officer could not say whether there were any survivors in the water or not, so the commander turned on a spotlight and searched the surrounding wreckage ... The engineer lieutenant gave us the contents of a water breaker and fifteen American cigarettes but no food ... We asked him for a bottle of whisky, but none was forthcoming.[24]

U–155 torpedoed and sank the *Empire Arnold* to the east of Trinidad on 4 August 1942. The chief officer later gave an account of what happened when the U-boat approached the ship's lifeboats:

> [He] asked if I had any wounded, and I pointed out one man, who was badly burnt about the eyes and hands. We put him on board the submarine, where he was given medical attention, and was subsequently put in the other boat. [When a survivor was sighted clinging to flotsam,] the submarine went over to the packing case; the commander told the boy to jump into the sea, and one of the crew from the submarine ... dived in and brought the boy safely to the submarine. The commander treated him very kindly [before putting him in a lifeboat].[25]

Along with all the evidence of U-boats showing this kind of consideration for survivors, there were still some reports which hinted at a more brutal approach. The master of the *Inversuir*, sunk by Herbert Schultze of *U–48* on 2 June 1941, thought that the submarine 'appeared to be machine-gunning the boats'.[26]

Some survivors from the *British Resource*, sunk by *U–124* on 14 March 1942, tried to swim to the U-boat to avoid the burning oil on the sea. 'As they got within reach, they were brutally waved away and the submarine went full ahead and steamed through them.' [27] On 25 June 1942 an almost naked apprentice from the *Putney Hill* managed to scramble on to *U–203*. He was given a cigarette, but no clothes and nothing to drink, and he was eventually ordered to jump into the sea twenty yards from an overcrowded raft even though he had told the Germans that he could not swim. An officer from the raft swam to tow him to safety.[28]

The fundamental problem facing any U-boat commander was, of course, that he could not accommodate any significant number of survivors without impairing the ability of his boat to dive and conduct further operations. Captains of surface raiders, whether major warships or auxiliary cruisers, having more space on board, could approach survivors without any major worries on that score. Beginning with the pocket battleships *Admiral Graf Spee* and *Deutschland* in 1939, the surface raiders' most successful period was in 1940 and 1941, years in which they sank forty-eight and forty-six British vessels respectively as well as many belonging to Britain's allies.

When a major warship attacked a convoy, as for example, the *Admiral Scheer*'s attack on Convoy HX84 on 5 November 1940 or the *Admiral Hipper*'s attack on Convoy SLS65 on 12 February 1941, the merchant ships were legitimate targets under international law and the raider was under no obligation to make any provision for the crews of vessels which were sunk. That responsibility, if they could discharge it, lay with those who had organised and commanded the convoy. Survivors had to take their chance on the open sea, as in many of the sinkings by U-boats, while the raider performed her primary task of attacking as many ships as possible before dispersal, darkness or bad visibility enabled them to make good their escape. The general orders for the *Bismarck*'s foray into the Atlantic in May 1941 emphasised that, in any attack on a convoy, attempts to rescue survivors must neither endanger German vessels nor stand in the way of sinking further merchant ships, although a small one might be spared to engage in rescue work.[29] Possibly the orders may have been drafted to remind the man in command of the *Bismarck* operation, Admiral Günther Lütjens, that he was not to waste time rescuing survivors as he had done two months earlier when, in command of the *Scharnhorst* and *Gneisenau*, he had sunk sixteen ships, twelve of them British, from dispersed convoys off Halifax.

All of the successes of the *Admiral Graf Spee*, the *Deutschland* and the disguised auxiliary cruisers, however, were achieved in attacks on unescorted merchant ships. So, also, were some of the sinkings by the *Admiral Scheer*, *Scharnhorst*, *Gneisenau* and *Admiral Hipper*. Then, with one or two possible exceptions, the German captains seem to have tried to ensure the safety of the survivors as required by international law and the custom of the sea. In this they were not being merely altruistic: it was in their own interest to ensure, as far as possible, that survivors should become prisoners-of-war – unable to report their attacker's name, area of operations or the disguise adopted by an auxiliary cruiser, and unable to serve on any other ship. Occasionally a German captain might be content to leave survivors in their boats, if he wanted to direct attention to an area which he was intending to leave very shortly; and in darkness a few lifeboats or rafts, loaded with survivors who would sooner face the perils of the sea than captivity, managed to evade the search mounted by the Germans.

Once it was established that a merchant ship was no longer offering resistance, using her radio or attempting to flee, a boarding party would be sent across to scuttle the ship or take her in prize. If it had been necessary to shell her into submission, the boarding party usually included a doctor and sick-berth attendants who could give immediate attention to any wounded members of the crew and administer morphine if required. Dr Wenzel and the boarding officer from the German auxiliary cruiser *Pinguin* rescued the gravely wounded and unconscious British second officer from the burning bridge of the *Benavon* on 12 September 1940, incurring burns themselves in doing so.[30]

If survivors had already abandoned ship, they would be ordered to come alongside the raider, and men in the water or on rafts would be rescued by the raider's own boats. If the crew had remained on board their ship, and there was no great need to hurry, they would be allowed to collect a few essential items such as warm clothing, blankets, toiletries and valuables before climbing down into the boats to row over to the raider. In this way their future privations might be eased and they would not deplete the raider's own stocks. Captain Ernst-Felix Krüder of the *Pinguin* actually had a printed list prepared advising survivors what kind of things they would find useful. Captain Theodor Detmers of the auxiliary cruiser *Kormoran* even ordered his boarding party to bring back clothing for two women passengers of the *Afric Star* who were wearing only bathing costumes, having been sunbathing at the time of the attack.[31] Some of the other raiders took care to transfer stocks of food acceptable to lascar prisoners.

Once on board the raider, survivors would be searched and listed, before being shown to their accommodation. This necessarily varied according to the ship's size and construction, but the Germans almost always seem to have been able to provide Europeans with separate accommodation from the lascars and Chinese, to keep officers separate from ratings, and to make special arrangements to keep any women segregated from the rest. The relative spaciousness of the accommodation varied according to the number of vessels the raider had sunk. What would have appeared positively generous space early in a voyage could look very crowded indeed later. By 8 October 1940, for example, the auxiliary cruiser *Thor* had 368 survivors on board, a total which had been accumulated in the course of three months' operations in the Central and South Atlantic. In December 1940 the *Pinguin* had over 400 prisoners. The quality of food depended on how recently and generously the raider had been able to take on supplies, either from one of her own supply ships or from a well-provisioned prize. European prisoners generally received the same food as the German crew, but food for the lascars and Chinese was prepared by their own cooks under German supervision. In some raiders the lascars and Chinese were given the opportunity to engage in some work alongside the German sailors. There were inevitably complaints from the prisoners about the amount of time they were kept shut up below decks, but the Germans tried to be as generous as possible in allowing men to exercise on the open deck. The privilege was necessarily limited by weather conditions, by operational considerations when attacking other targets or meeting supply vessels, and by the relationship between prisoner numbers, area of deck space and the number of guards available.[32]

The work of German medical officers in caring for the sick and wounded among the survivors was in the highest tradition of the medical profession. Under the difficult conditions presented by a rolling and pitching ship, they carried out complex emergency operations such as amputations and removing shell splinters. Afterwards they attended conscientiously to the general medical needs of the prisoners, although sometimes irritated by a tendency to hypochondria among the lascars. When a prisoner died on board one of the raiders, the Germans were meticulous in observing all the formalities of burial at sea: the raider stopped, its ensign at half-mast, a proper canvas shroud for the body covered by the appropriate national flag (even if it had to be made specially), a guard to present arms, bosun's pipes, sometimes even the ship's band to provide music.

After the war, some of the captains of German raiders took pains to emphasise the humane way in which survivors had been treated. Kurt Weyher wrote: 'Whenever the last shot had been fired, the concepts *friend* and *foe* ceased for us of the *Orion*. Those in the water then became exclusively survivors of shipwreck, to be treated as such.'[33] Detmers, in describing how two of his seamen from the *Kormoran* had jumped into the sea to rescue an unconscious survivor from the *British Union*, commented: 'It was typical of my men: they were ruthless in action, but afterwards there was nothing they wouldn't do to help their victims.'[34] Admiral Bernhard Rogge, formerly captain of the raider *Atlantis*, quoted from her log:

I have tried to make war in accordance with the old raider tradition of 'fairness', by which I mean that where possible I never fired for longer than was absolutely necessary to break down the enemy's resistance and destroy his wireless ... We have treated our prisoners and survivors as we would wish to be treated ourselves in similar circumstances; we have tried to make their lot as easy as possible.[35]

British survivors of ships sunk by surface raiders generally showed appreciation of the way they were treated. In a foreword to Rogge's book, Captain J. Armstrong White of the *City of Bagdad*, sunk by the *Atlantis* on 11 July 1940, described him as 'correct and humane in every detail', and added 'the greater majority of his prisoners first began to respect, and then to like him'.[36] Captain Patrick Dove of the *Africa Shell*, sunk on 15 November 1939 by the *Admiral Graf Spee*, thought that Captain Hans Langsdorff was 'a gentleman, and much too humane for the job he was doing'.[37] Conditions on the *Pinguin* were acknowledged by the fourth officer of the *Port Wellington* to be as good as prisoners could expect, with fairly plentiful food and an hour's exercise on deck three times a day,[38] while the master of the *Demeterton* reported that they were well treated on the *Scharnhorst*, even being able to get a haircut or shave and have beer from the enemy ship's canteen.[39]

This all sounds rather cosy and civilised, and it is well to remember that the evidence comes mainly from officers whose conditions were probably more comfortable than those enjoyed by British ratings and lascars. Survivors taken prisoner by major warships operating in the North Atlantic would only spend, at most, a few weeks aboard a raider before being landed at one of the French Biscay ports such as Brest or La Rochelle. Those taken in the South Atlantic or Indian Ocean would have to spend far longer on the raider. As their numbers built up they would place such a strain on the accommodation and victualling as to become something of an unwelcome burden to their captors. It is understandable, therefore, that captains of raiders welcomed an opportunity to offload their prisoners by placing them under guard on board another ship. This might be one of the supply ships which the Kriegsmarine ran very efficiently to rendezvous with raiders in lonely parts of the world's oceans, or one of the German merchant ships directed to try to reach German-occupied territory by breaking through the Allied blockade, or a prize captured intact by the raider and also directed to run the blockade. Transfers of this kind at least relieved the prisoners of the worry that the raider might be brought to action and sunk by British forces while they were still on board her; but, if their new prison was less likely to become involved in a fight to the death, living conditions were almost certain to be far worse. Accommodation for the prisoners had to be improvised, food supplies and storage were very limited, sanitary arrangements were probably quite primitive and, with only a handful of guards, the prisoners had to be kept battened below decks for most of the time.

When the *Admiral Graf Spee* was driven to take refuge in Montevideo, on 13 December 1939, she was obliged to release to the neutral Uruguayan authorities the captains and other senior officers whom she had taken from the British ships she had sunk, but it was discovered that most of the survivors from those ships had already been transferred to her supply ship, the *Altmark*. The master of the *Ashlea*, having spent some weeks as a prisoner on the supply ship before being returned to the pocket battleship, was able to give an account of the conditions:

> Things were pretty rotten. The treatment we received whilst on board was definitely not humane. They seemed to want to humiliate us as much as possible. Our convenience consisted of a ten gallon drum which we had to take on deck and empty ourselves before our crew and amidst the laughs and jeers of the Germans ... There were only about twenty pans in which to wash and these we all had to share including the lascars most of whom had skin disease. Food was very scarce and only once a week did we have meat. We had mostly black bread and sausage ... The prison officer and the captain were definitely unfriendly. [The prison officer was] a fat and offensive man.[40]

The British press was quick to condemn these conditions. The *Manchester Guardian* labelled the *Altmark*'s captain 'a hard-bitten Nazi' and described his command as a 'slave-ship' and a 'floating concentration camp' where the mattresses were 'covered in lice and vermin'.[41] On 16 February 1940 the *Altmark*, trying to reach a German port, was intercepted by British destroyers in Norwegian territorial waters and driven into Jösing Fiord where, the Norwegians having declined to act, the German ship was boarded by men from HMS *Cossack* and 299 British merchant seamen were rescued. Their accounts of their ordeal provided plenty of ammunition for British propaganda about German inhumanity.

Once they had the use of the French Biscay ports, the Germans might have expected to find it easier to evade the blockade and land their prisoners safely, but the approach to a German occupied port, with the risk of interception by the Royal Navy, was always a time of great tension for the German crew and for the survivors from merchant vessels who

were their prisoners. Two of the early attempts ended in disaster for
the Germans. On 3 September 1940 the British submarine HMS *Truant*
intercepted the cargo ship *Tropic Sea* in the Bay of Biscay. Taken as a
prize by the auxiliary cruiser *Orion* in the South Pacific, and with a
German prize crew, this Norwegian vessel was carrying the master and
twenty-three other survivors from the British cargo ship *Haxby* as well
as her own Norwegian crew. The Germans ordered everyone into the
lifeboats and scuttled the *Tropic Sea* with demolition charges. The
captain of the *Truant* managed to cram all the British survivors plus
the Norwegian captain and his wife into the submarine and take them
to Gibraltar; a British flying boat later picked up more Norwegians
from a lifeboat, while the Germans landed in Spain. It had been a
turbulent half-year for the men of the *Haxby*. On passage from Glasgow
to Texas, their ship had been shelled into submission by the *Orion* on
24 April in mid-Atlantic and sixteen of their shipmates had been killed.
As prisoners on the raider they had been carried round Cape Horn
into the Pacific Ocean, and they had been aboard her while she laid
mines in the approaches to Auckland, New Zealand. Then they had
been put on board the *Tropic Sea* on 30 June and brought back halfway
round the world, to finish their voyage in September on board a British
submarine.[42]

Later in the same month another German prize, the Norwegian
Tirranna, was torpedoed and sunk by HMS *Tuna* off the mouth of the
Gironde estuary while she was waiting for minesweepers to make sure
the channel was clear. She was carrying over 270 survivors, including
some women and children, from two Norwegian ships and the British
vessels *Scientist*, *City of Bagdad* and *Kemmendine*, all victims of the auxiliary
cruiser *Atlantis*. Most of the prisoners on the *Tirranna* were saved, but
over sixty, mostly Indians, lost their lives.[43]

After that, the Germans became more successful in passing their
blockade runners through the Bay of Biscay to Bordeaux. For example,
the *Nordvard*, another Norwegian prize carrying over 170 prisoners,
reached Bordeaux in November 1940, followed by the *Rio Grande* with
over 300 prisoners in December 1940, the *Storstad* with well over 500
in February 1941, the *Portland* with over 300 in March (after the failure
of an attempt by prisoners to seize the ship), the *Tannenfels* with over
one hundred and the *Ermland* with yet more prisoners in April, and
the *Dresden* in May. Few of the British survivors who were transported
as prisoners on these ships had a good word to say for the conditions
in which they had to live. Rats, vermin, primitive sanitation, inadequate
ventilation, nauseating stench, overcrowding, unappetising food and

lack of exercise seem to have been the norm on these voyages, especially while passing through the tropics. The fourth officer of the *Port Wellington* described conditions on the *Storstad* as 'absolutely foul ... entirely unsuitable for carrying prisoners',[44] an opinion endorsed by the fifth engineer of the *Nowshera*.[45]

The worst conditions of all, however, were probably those found on board the Yugoslav ship *Durmitor*. Captured in the Indian Ocean by the *Atlantis* in October 1940, she was given a small German prize crew and ordered to carry 260 survivors from other ships to Italian Somaliland. Captain Rogge of the *Atlantis* admitted that the Yugoslav ship was

> ill-equipped to carry extra people. The conditions in which the prisoners would have to live were frankly bad, for they would have to be accommodated in the holds on top of the cargo of salt, without mattresses. Only those over fifty years of age were allowed mattresses ... We could only give the *Durmitor* a week's supply of bread, while drinking water was available in only small quantities and there was no water at all for washing ... Her top speed was only seven knots. She was crawling with cockroaches, bugs and rats.[46]

When she ran out of coal, the Germans rigged sails and burned hatch-covers, doors, furniture and anything else which could be burned in the boilers until, on 23 November, their drinking water totally exhausted, they reached Kismayu where their suffering prisoners were handed over to the Italian authorities.

Towards the end of 1940, the inconvenience of carrying too many survivors from ships which they had captured or sunk was particularly acute for the German auxiliary cruisers *Komet* and *Orion* which, together with their accompanying supply ship *Kulmerland*, were operating in the Pacific Ocean. As a result of sinking the passenger liner *Rangitane* and a very successful operation against British phosphate ships off Nauru, the number of prisoners exceeded 600. In desperation, the senior German officer, Captain Eyssen of the *Komet*, took his ships to Emirau Island, northeast of New Guinea, and put ashore 343 Europeans and 171 Chinese and Kanakas on 21 December. He left them with tents and food, but they did not have to wait long before they were rescued by a British ship on the 29th.[47]

During the summer and autumn of 1941, the German raiders continued to ship survivors whom they had taken prisoner to French Biscay ports when opportunity offered, although on June 23 British warships succeeded in intercepting the supply ship *Alstertor* west of Gibraltar and releasing 220 prisoners of various nationalities, including seventy-eight from the British ships *Rabaul* and *Trafalgar*;[48] both of which had fallen victim to the *Atlantis* in the previous month. The eagerness of the captains of the German raiders to pass on the survivors they accumulated, and the efficiency of the German navy in arranging for suitable vessels to collect them all over the world, had one great benefit for British merchant seamen: very few of them were on board those raiders which were eventually tracked down and sunk by British forces. The greatest loss of British lives in such an encounter was in the sinking of the German auxiliary cruiser *Pinguin* by HMS *Cornwall* on 8 May 1941. The *Pinguin* still had on board about 240 survivors, including men from the *Clan Buchanan*, *Empire Light* and *British Emperor*, when a shell from the *Cornwall* set off the raider's mines in a tremendous explosion. Only sixty Germans and twenty-seven of their prisoners lived to be rescued by the British cruiser's boats.[49]

After Japan entered the war, in December 1941, German raiders usually preferred to send their prisoners to Japan or Japanese-held ports, such as Singapore or Tanjong Priok, rather than attempting to pass them through the surface and air patrols of the Bay of Biscay. In any case, by 1942 the German surface offensive on British merchant shipping had shot its bolt and losses from that source had diminished to a trickle. The really serious danger in the 'tonnage war' was from the submarines of the three Axis powers. On 3 January 1942 Hitler discussed the war at sea with the Japanese ambassador in Berlin, Baron Oshima. They were concerned about the capacity of the United States to build new ships in considerable numbers, but Hitler claimed that there would still be problems in finding enough trained seamen to man them, especially if submarines struck without warning in order to increase casualties among merchant seamen. He even suggested that, when countries were fighting for their very existence, they could not afford humanitarian principles and he would have to order U-boats to surface and fire on survivors in lifeboats.[50] Oshima replied that Japan would have to adopt the same policy.

It may be that, preoccupied with the land campaign in Russia, Hitler never formally issued an order to attack survivors; or Raeder and Doenitz may have convinced him that it would damage the morale of German submariners who were likely to be on the receiving end if the British and Americans chose to take reprisals. In May Doenitz was arguing that one result of the development of a new proximity pistol for torpedoes would inevitably be an increase in the casualties among merchant seamen 'who would not be able to save themselves due to the rapid sinking of the ship'.[51] Another approach to depriving Britain and America of skilled manpower for their shipping was an order, issued in June, which urged U-boats to take prisoner whenever possible the captains and chief engineers of the ships they sank.[52] These measures did not, however, fully satisfy Hitler. He was so incensed by the RAF's bombing raids on German cities and by reports that British destroyers had fired on survivors from the German minelayer *Ulm* that, chatting over dinner on 6 September, he said that the British would have to be dealt with on the basis of 'an eye for an eye and a tooth for a tooth'. He suggested an immediate announcement that U-boats would 'shell the survivors of torpedoed ships regardless of whether they are soldiers or civilians, women or children'. He even speculated that, if an exchange of reprisals escalated, 'we will retort by hanging the captains of all ships sunk! The Merchant Navy would then begin to act very differently. The Japanese do this, while we entertain them with coffee and cognac.'[53] These remarks sound like an example of Hitler's thinking aloud, a mere exploration of possibilities rather than framing a firm operational order.

After the war Doenitz claimed that he had neither received nor issued any order of that kind, and there is no evidence from the way U-boats operated that any such policy was generally adopted in 1942 or 1943. The official US naval historian, Samuel Eliot Morison, acknowledged that, in their operations off the east coast of the United States, U-boats 'refrained from machine-gunning survivors in lifeboats,' although he does cite three untypical incidents during the first quarter of 1942: two of firing while boats were being lowered and one of survivors being fired on in the water.[54] The first two cases involved *U–126* commanded by Ernst Bauer; the other allegation concerned *U–156* commanded by Werner Hartenstein.

If Hartenstein deliberately fired on men in this way, his conduct towards survivors seems to have been puzzlingly inconsistent. On 17 May 1942, after sinking the British ship *Barrdale*, he picked up a seaman clinging to wreckage and transferred him to a lifeboat.[55] After *U–156* used her guns to sink the *Willimantic* on 24 June the ship's second officer, in charge of a lifeboat, reported: 'I heard another cry for help nearer the ship and started searching in that direction. The submarine fired his machine gun at us, but I still continued searching, until a few well-directed bursts convinced me that he wanted us to keep away from the ship, which was now blazing furiously.'[56] Yet Hartenstein, joking that it was a present for Mr Churchill, also provided the survivors with a chart. He also took his U-boat in a search of the area to reassure the men in the boats that none of their shipmates needed picking up from the water.

On 12 September 1942, having torpedoed and sunk the British passenger liner *Laconia* in the South Atlantic, Hartenstein was horrified to find that, in addition to a large crew, Polish guards, and British servicemen and their families, the liner was carrying about 1800 Italian prisoners-of-war. Seeing the potential scale of the tragedy, and its implications for Italo-German relations, Hartenstein began rounding up boats and rafts and taking people from the water, irrespective of nationality, on to *U–156*. At one stage he had as many as 193 extra people on board. When he radioed U-boat Headquarters for instructions, Doenitz ordered *U–506*, *U–507* and the Italian *Comandante Cappellini* to join in the rescue work. He also asked the Vichy French government to send warships from Dakar to pick up survivors.

In the early hours of 13 September, Hartenstein broadcast a plain language message promising that he would not attack any vessel which was prepared to help with the rescue. Many Italians had already gone down with the ship, but over the next three days Hartenstein helped to organise the survivors, treated the injured, and took strings of lifeboats in tow. *U–506* and *U–507* joined in the work on the 15th, and the Italian submarine arrived the following day. On the 16th, however, despite having lifeboats alongside and a Red Cross flag clearly displayed, *U–156* was attacked and damaged by an American Liberator bomber operating from Ascension Island. One of the bombs destroyed a lifeboat full of Italians. The next day *U–507* was bombed while she had more than one hundred survivors on board, but she was able to pass them over to the Vichy French sloop *Annamite*, and that vessel, together with the cruiser *Gloire*, then took over responsibility for the rescue work. In all, between 1100 and 1200 people were rescued. Precise figures are hard to establish, but it is clear that about three-quarters of the Italian prisoners-of-war did not survive.

Doenitz lost no time in drawing his conclusions from this humanitarian episode: 'I realised that in no circumstances must I ever again risk the loss of a boat and its crew in an enterprise of a similar nature.' [57] While the rescue had been in progress, the Kriegsmarine report on the alleged firing by British destroyers on the survivors from the *Ulm* had been completed. It had drawn attention to accusations of other attacks on German survivors during the second Battle of Narvik and during the invasion of Crete. Doenitz concluded that humanitarian considerations would have to give way to a ruthless realism. On 17 September he drew up what came to be known as the '*Laconia* Order':

Face to Face with the Enemy 121

1. No attempt of any kind must be made to rescue members of ships sunk, and this includes picking up persons in the water and putting them in lifeboats, righting capsized lifeboats, and handing over food and water. Rescue runs counter to the most elementary demands of warfare for the destruction of enemy ships and crews.

2. Orders for bringing back captains and chief engineers still apply.

3. Rescue the shipwrecked only if their statements will be of value to your boat.

4. Be harsh. Bear in mind that the enemy takes no regard of women and children in his bombing attacks on German cities.[58]

At a conference with Raeder, Doenitz and other admirals held at the Reich Chancellery on 28 September, Hitler endorsed this harsher attitude with the comment: 'It is very much to our disadvantage if a large percentage of the crews of sunken ships is able to go to sea again in new ships.'[59]

The '*Laconia* Order' lacked clarity. Doenitz always maintained that, in view of the increasing threat from radar-equipped aircraft, its purpose was to forbid his U-boats from endangering themselves while succouring survivors, and he insisted that it contained nothing whatsoever about taking active measures to massacre them instead. His critics have alleged that, at the very least, the order was capable of being interpreted as encouraging direct action against survivors, especially in its reference to the destruction of ships *and crews*, and by its appeal to the emotions in its final injunction. Much would depend on the way the order was supplemented by oral advice at captains' training courses and at the routine briefing and debriefing sessions for each patrol. Korvetten-kapitän Moehle, who commanded the Fifth U-boat Flotilla at Kiel from the middle of 1941 to the end of the war, thought that the order meant that crews should be regarded as legitimate objects of attack, but that it might have been made deliberately ambiguous because it was contrary to international law and would create a conflict of conscience for many U-boat captains. Although he had to pass on the order, he felt it to be wrong in his own innermost conscience.[60]

In fairness to Doenitz it has to be said that, when the German Foreign Office wrote to draw his attention to a (certainly over-optimistic) British claim that 87 per cent of the crews were being rescued after their merchant ships had been sunk, he replied on 4 April 1943: 'A directive to take action against lifeboats of sunken vessels and crew members drifting in the sea would, for psychological reasons, hardly be acceptable to U-boat crews, since it would be contrary to the innermost feelings of all sailors.'[61] But, of course, the real impact of the '*Laconia* Order' can only be understood by reference to what happened when survivors and U-boat men came face to face. In view of their apprehension about air patrols, these face to face contacts were mainly in the more distant theatres of operations such as West African waters, the South Atlantic and the Indian Ocean.

Whenever possible, U-boat commanders appear to have been eager to obey the order to seize the captains and chief engineers of merchant ships. To thwart this intention, senior survivors generally resorted to hiding their uniforms and hoping that their crew would say that they had gone down with the ship. In the view of the master of the *Empire Guidon*, 'life on a raft is far from pleasant, but anything is better than life in an enemy submarine'.[62] Some U-boats were so keen to carry off a prisoner that, if they could not identify the senior officers, they just took any officer, or even an apprentice or able seaman. While some masters were content to let this happen, others felt obliged to own up rather than allow one of their subordinates to be carried off in their stead. Of course, a survivor who was taken prisoner by a U-boat was exposed to the same risks as the U-boat's own crew if she were lost before the end of the patrol. One such tragedy was the loss of Captain Moss, of the *St Usk*, when *U–161* was bombed and sunk in September 1943.[63]

Other aspects of the '*Laconia* Order' made very little difference to the way survivors were treated. They were not routinely massacred by the Germans. Some U-boat commanders still apologised for having to sink their ships, and offered them advice about such matters as the position of the sinking, the distance from land and the best course to steer. Within a few weeks of the order's being broadcast, some survivors were even receiving the kind of help expressly forbidden by Doenitz. A lifeboat from the *Glendene* was given eight gallons of water by *U–125* on 8 October 1942.[64] Survivors from the *Ross* received eight packets of cigarettes from *U–159* on 29 October.[65] On 2 November, nineteen men from a leaking lifeboat belonging to the *Llandilo* were invited to take refuge on the casing of *U–172* while the Germans checked the boat and helped to bail it out.[66] *U–161* supplied a boat from the *Ripley* with fourteen pounds of bread, some pemmican and two gallons of water on 12 December. The Germans also gave clothes to two naked survivors.[67] Bandages for an injured man from the *East Wales* were provided by *U–159* on 16 December.[68]

Other U-boats were less helpful. While this might take the form of simply ignoring survivors altogether, or turning a deaf ear to their request for a position fix and course to steer, others could be altogether more threatening. The report of the master of the *Hopetarn*, sunk in the Indian Ocean on 29 May 1943 by *U–198*, contains such comments as:

> For the moment it seemed as if he was going to ram our lifeboat ... He again ordered us alongside, stating that unless we did so immediately he would fire on the boat ... He [said] 'It is war, *your war*, you are fighting for Churchill, for Roosevelt, for the rich man and the Jew, and now for the Bolshevik. If you reach land safely, don't go back to sea.' ... One of the German sailors on the deck began punching me in the ribs ... The submarine then steamed away, and as she did so her stern swung round, caught the side of the [small] lifeboat, and nearly capsized it ... The submarine, without any warning, steamed off at full speed, dragging the [larger] lifeboat with it, and to save the boat from being swamped we had to cut the line.[69]

As soon as *U–172* surfaced to approach the boats of the *Fort Chilcotin*, after torpedoing her on 24 July 1943, the survivors were alarmed to hear the rattle of machine-gun fire and they feared the worst. Kapitän-leutnant Carl Emmermann later explained, while questioning the *Fort Chilcotin*'s bosun, that he did not do 'that sort of thing', and that he had only been clearing his guns,[70] but it is easy to see how an entirely innocent procedure of this kind might lead frightened men to conclude that they were being attacked. Even Emmermann's disclaimer might be seen as implying that other U-boat commanders would 'do that sort of thing', and merchant seamen were convinced that they did. At the conference of the International Transport Federation held in London on 30–31 January 1943, a resolution was passed unanimously 'condemning the criminal methods of the seamen of Axis countries ... in torpedoing merchant ships on sight without warning, without giving crews and civilian passengers time to take to the lifeboats, and with shelling and machine-gunning lifeboats'.[71] Similar accusations and demands for retribution featured prominently in the speeches of Charles Jarman, the acting General Secretary of the National Union of Seamen.[72]

If the actions of some German U-boat commanders in regard to survivors can be difficult to interpret because of the fog of propaganda, ambiguity, uncertainty, misunderstanding and suspicion in which they are enveloped, the guilt of certain Japanese submarine commanders is more clearly established. Because they regarded the Pacific Ocean as their main theatre, their operations in the Indian Ocean tended to be limited and sporadic, but these included several well-documented examples of deliberate attacks on survivors after they had abandoned ship. The first of these occurred on 4 January 1942 when, after torpedoing the small British ship *Kwangtung* south of Java, the Japanese submarine *I–156* surfaced and deliberately rammed the lifeboats, smashing them to pieces and leaving a few of their occupants clinging to the wreckage. Just twelve survivors out of a crew of ninety-eight were picked up by another vessel two days later.[73]

Lieutenant-Commander Kazuro Ebato, of the Japanese submarine *RO–110*, adopted the same inhuman tactic after sinking the *Daisy Moller* in the Bay of Bengal on 14 December 1943.[74] All seventy-one members of her crew had managed to get away safely from the sinking ship, and with the Indian coast only a few miles away their survival should have been assured; but, after destroying the lifeboats by ramming, the Japanese machine-gunned the men struggling in the water and on rafts. On damaged rafts, thirteen survivors managed to reach the shore, and another three were picked up by fishermen: the rest had been callously slaughtered.

Commander Nakagawa's behaviour towards survivors was even more savage. In May 1942, when in command of *I–177* he had already earned his place in the register of infamy by torpedoing the fully lit hospital ship *Centaur* forty-three miles east of Brisbane. She sank in three minutes, and only sixty-four of the 363 people on board survived.[75] On that occasion Nakagawa had refrained from attacking the survivors, but he showed no such restraint in February 1944 when, in command of *I–37*, he sank three British ships in the course of a single week. His first victim, the tanker *British Chivalry*, was torpedoed on the 22nd, southwest of the Maldive Islands in 0°50'S 68°00'E. Most of the crew managed to get away from the ship in two lifeboats and on rafts, and the submarine ordered the lifeboats to come alongside. After the master had been taken on board the submarine, and courteously saluted by the Japanese, the submarine moved away; then it returned. In the words of the *British Chivalry*'s chief officer:

> The submarine steamed backwards and forwards, machine-gunning the boats each time she passed at very short range. I and my crew immediately jumped into the water for safety, but the men in the other boat crouched down in the bottom, consequently each time the submarine passed, he was able to fire down into the boat, killing or wounding most of the crew.

At one time the submarine steamed through the men in the water, and as he did so he put his helm over and swung his stern amongst them ... Both lifeboats were holed and filled rapidly; several men attempted to bail out the starboard boat, but as they stood up, so they were shot down by the submarine ... Captain Hill (our master) was made to stand on the deck of the submarine to witness the machine-gunning of the boats and the men in the water.[76]

When the submarine finally went away, the surprisingly high number of thirty-nine survivors, from a crew of fifty-nine, were still alive to climb aboard one riddled lifeboat and a raft. Some of them were seriously injured, and they still had to face thirty-seven days adrift before they were rescued.

Four days later, having moved to 9°00'S 70°00'E, Nakagawa torpedoed the British cargo ship *Sutlej*, which sank in four minutes. He then spent an hour steaming through survivors in the water and machine-gunning them. He also rammed the rafts to which other survivors were clinging, a tactic which proved to be rather ineffective, as the submarine's bow wave pushed the rafts aside just before impact, but of the seventy-three crew only twenty-five remained alive, and they had to wait forty-seven days before they were picked up.[77]

Three days after sinking the *Sutlej*, Nakagawa scored another success by sinking the *Ascot* in approximately 5°00'S 63°00'E. All but seven of her crew of fifty-four managed to get away from the sinking ship, in two lifeboats and a raft, all of which were summoned alongside the submarine. Captain Travers was ordered on board; then the Japanese slashed his hands and threw him into the sea while they set about ramming his lifeboat. 'The submarine then began machine-gunning all the men in the water from the captain's boat, the water-logged chief officer's boat and the raft; all the men who remained on the raft were killed outright or died later from their wounds.'[78] The machine-gunning went on for two hours. When the submarine turned her attention to finishing off the *Ascot*, some of the survivors who were still alive climbed on board a lifeboat, which then attempted to tow away a raft carrying a few of their shipmates, but they were pursued by the submarine and subjected to further machine-gun fire. As a final act of vindictiveness, Commander Nakagawa rounded off his week's villainy by towing away the lifeboat, containing one wounded man feigning death, and setting it adrift two miles away so that any survivors still in the water would be unable to reach it. Next day seven men on a damaged raft, commanded by a young cadet, managed to pick up the wounded man from the waterlogged boat, and they were fortunate enough to be rescued by a Dutch ship two days after the sinking.

More Japanese submarine atrocities occurred in the following month. On 18 March, thirty-two of the sixty-five crew from the *Nancy Moller* died when she was torpedoed south of Ceylon by the *I-165*. Lieutenant Shimezu took one British gunner prisoner. He had two Chinese seamen shot on the submarine's foredeck, then cruised around ramming the rafts and machine-gunning men in the water. The survivors were rescued from four rafts by a British ship on the 22nd.[79]

A total of ninety-eight passengers and crew from the Dutch ship *Tjisalak* perished after she was torpedoed and shelled by the *I-8* on the 26th. Many of those who survived the sinking, including the British gunners, were ordered from their lifeboats on to the submarine's casing, where Lieutenant-Commander Tatsunoseke Ariizumi ordered them to remove their lifejackets and then had them systematically butchered, some by shooting, some by sword strokes, some by being hit with a sledgehammer, and the rest by being tied together in groups and thrown into the sea. The only five survivors, three of them wounded, who were rescued by an American ship two days later, had all miraculously survived both the sinking of their own ship and a visit to the deck of *I-8*.[80]

It is hardly credible that these despicable attacks made on survivors in the four-month period December 1943 to March 1944 could have been the work of a few individual psychopaths working entirely on their own initiative. The incidents look more like a planned campaign, especially when one considers the chillingly clear wording of an order issued by the Commander-in-Chief of the Japanese First Submarine Force on 19 February: 'Do not stop with the sinking of enemy ships and cargoes; at the same time that you carry out the complete destruction of the crews of the enemy ships, if possible, seize part of the crew and endeavour to secure information about the enemy.'[81]

In this same period occurred an atrocity by Japanese surface forces. When the Japanese cruiser *Tone* sank the British motor vessel *Behar* about 800 miles south-southwest of Cocos Island on 9 March, only three of the British ship's crew were killed in the attack; 108 survivors were taken on board the cruiser. Captain Symonds of the *Behar* had ordered his DEMS gunners not to return fire for fear of provoking Japanese reprisals, but many of the survivors were beaten, tied up, poorly fed and generally maltreated, and one of the two women passengers was punched in the face. In taking so many survivors on board his ship, Captain Mayazumi was in breach of operational orders issued in February by Admiral Takasu, Commander-in-Chief of the Southwest Area Fleet, that only people who might be worth interrogating were to be taken prisoner and the rest killed.

While returning to Java, and also after reaching Tanjong Priok, Mayazumi was censured by his immediate superior, Admiral Sakonju, who would at first only accept sixteen prisoners from among the more important crew members and passengers. When Mayazumi asked what he was to do with the remaining survivors he was ordered to dispose of them. The admiral rejected all the pleas of the *Tone*'s Christian captain to be allowed to hand them over to a prisoner-of-war camp, where they could be employed on airfield construction or other work. The *Tone*'s second-in-command, Commander Mii, met with a better response. Meeting Sakonju socially, he managed to extract permission to land a few Indian seamen, and courageously put twenty ashore before an order arrived authorising only ten. Faced with a direct order to dispose of all the remaining survivors from the *Behar*, Captain Mayazumi sailed for Singapore and, although Commander Mii refused to take part, a group of junior officers carried out the slaughter of twenty-seven Europeans and about forty-five Indians during the night, while the captain stayed well out of the way on the ship's bridge. After the war Mayazumi explained to war crimes investigators that, as instructed by one of Sakonju's staff officers, the executions had been

> carried out with the least possible pain and suffering ... the prisoners being taken out one by one as if for further interrogation, then knocked unconscious and killed while still in that state. The execution [was to] be carried out by a well educated graduate of the Naval College so as to avoid cruelty ... Courteous treatment of the bodies was ordered ... Later I heard a sword had been used to cut the jugular vein and a thrust was made into the heart to ensure against failure.[82]

Commander Mii heard that they had been beheaded after being kicked in the testicles. Whatever the intended ritual, nothing can disguise the fact that a combination of superior orders, Samurai tradition, the spirit of Japanese naval education and probably some unskilled attempts at surgical precision produced what can only be described as a disgraceful and wanton atrocity on helpless prisoners as the *Tone* approached the entrance to Bangka Straits around midnight of 18/19 March 1944.

In the same period as this cluster of Japanese atrocities was taking place, there occurred the only fully proven instance of survivors being deliberately massacred by the crew of a German U-boat. On 13 March 1944, in the Atlantic 300 miles from the African coast and just south of the Equator, Kapitänleutnant Heinz Eck, commanding *U–852*, sank the British-chartered Greek steamer *Peleus*, whose crew included eight British seamen. He then spent five hours cruising around in the darkness machine-gunning and throwing grenades at the rafts and wreckage. He attempted to justify this action with the explanation that he was intent on destroying all evidence of the sinking so that reconnaissance aircraft would not be able to detect that a U-boat was operating in the area. His prime responsibility for ensuring the safety of his boat and crew had to take precedence over the fate of any survivors who happened to be clinging to the rafts and wreckage which he had to destroy. In other words, the survivors were not the targets; they just happened to be holding on to the targets. That looks like mere sophistry. He could not hope to remove the surface evidence of a sinking and, if he was really so concerned about aircraft, one would have expected him to use the rest of the night to get as far away from the scene as possible. His real purpose can only have been to annihilate the survivors, and he very nearly succeeded. Just three men, one of them British, lived to be rescued after a further twenty-five days adrift.[83]

In response to some misgivings among his own crew, Eck sought to justify his action. Instead of showing what he considered to be misplaced sympathy for the enemy, he urged them to think of the wives and children in Germany, who became victims of enemy air raids.[84] That was an interesting echo of the injunction in Doenitz's 'Laconia Order', issued eighteen months earlier. At the end of the war, British investigators searched among the German records to see whether some of the crews of ships which had been lost with all hands might also have been deliberately killed by German U-boat commanders who thought like Heinz Eck, but they were unable to find any comparable examples.[85]

There can be no doubt that if the Germans, Italians and Japanese had consistently treated survivors as legitimate targets casualty rates among merchant seamen would have been very much higher, and the manning of ships would have been a bigger problem for the British government throughout the war. Luckily, such incidents involved only a tiny fraction of the total number of vessels which were sunk. Of course, the vast majority of merchant seamen who survived the sinking of their ships, especially those involved in the North Atlantic convoy battles, never had any face to face encounter with the enemy. For them, once they had left their ships, the sea itself offered more than enough daunting challenge, suffering and danger without human intervention.

7

Vessel Abandoned!

When merchant ships had to be abandoned, the first and most pressing problem for the survivors was to get well clear of the sinking vessel. What had recently represented established order and familiar routines – their home, their place of work, their social centre – could quickly become an unpredictable threat to their lives. The people in greatest danger were those who, for whatever reason, found themselves forced to swim, but even those on board rafts or lifeboats were by no means immune from the suction and turbulence created by a sinking ship. Survivors' reports frequently mention this problem:

> As the ship went down, the suction was so great that I was unable to hold on to the raft and was taken down some fifty or sixty feet.[1]

> As the ship rolled over on the boat and sank, the falls became entangled round my feet and I was dragged down with the ship; somehow I got clear and shot to the surface, but was at once drawn down by the suction of the ship. I came up for the second time, but as I rose to the surface, I hit my head on a piece of wreckage which partially stunned me.[2]

> The senior wireless operator told me that he was taken down to a considerable depth ... and had heard two dull explosions apparently from the boilers, which blew him to the surface.[3]

> The suction drew the lifeboat over the top of the wreck. Everybody aboard clung to the gunwhale, expecting it to be drawn under, but there was a sudden rush of air from the ship which lifted the lifeboat up, as the vessel slipped quietly under.[4]

Those who were not in danger of being carried down by the sinking ship might find that they faced new dangers as buoyant deck cargo, rafts and damaged lifeboats came hurtling to the surface with tremendous force after breaking free at considerable depth; sometimes oil from a tanker's cargo or from a motorship's bunkers choked, burned and blinded the unfortunate survivors who found themselves compelled to swim in it and made it much harder for would-be rescuers to haul them into a boat or onto a raft.

When petroleum products caught fire on the surface of the sea the results could be unspeakably horrific, a truly terrifying way for men to die. The effect was vividly described by the third officer of the tanker *Caspia* after she had been torpedoed ten miles south of Beirut on 16 April 1942:

> The benzine from the tanks poured on to the water and caught fire ... I lay flat in the bottom of the boat as the flames swept round and saw that the crew in my boat jumped overboard into the flames ... Seeing that there was a small clear channel through the flames, I dived overboard and swam toward this channel. Some of the crew did not wait long enough to see which way the blazing oil was running and consequently swam blindly into the worst part of the blazing sea. Ten of the crew besides myself saw this small clear channel through the flames and made for it. We had to swim 400 yards through the flames and every one of us received severe burns. The ship's carpenter had his eyes badly burned and became hysterical and started swimming madly round towards the flames, but Able Seaman Shearer went to his rescue, towed him clear of the flames and kept him afloat for one and a half hours.[5]

For those survivors who managed to get well clear of the ship, swimming in the open sea hundreds, possibly thousands, of miles from land was a dauntingly stressful and exhausting experience. Their eyes being only a few inches above the surface of the water, they could see only a very limited distance, even in calm weather, and they might be totally unaware that boats or rafts were close at hand. In a choppy sea they would occasionally catch a tantalising glimpse of a possible refuge, but repeatedly lose sight of it as wave crests or large swells intervened. The fortunate ones would gratefully hang on to any piece of buoyant wreckage which seemed to offer support, but a promising piece could remain frustratingly outside their reach as the wind blew it to leeward faster than they could swim after it, or it might slip through their grasp if it were coated with oil or ice. If they tried to climb on to it, the change in the centre of gravity could cause it to roll over infuriatingly. All these difficulties were made worse when ships were sunk during the hours of darkness. Very powerful swimmers soon found that their strength began to ebb away; non-swimmers struggled against their panic, bewilderment and hopelessness.

A non-swimmer from the *Putney Hill*, sunk on the night of 25/26 June

1942 east of the Bahamas, found himself in the sea after his lifeboat filled with water and capsized:

> Most of the crew swam to one of the two rafts, while several clung to the upturned boat. I could not swim and drifted around for a few minutes, then sighting an oar I managed to struggle towards it and grab hold of it. A few minutes later [another survivor] joined me on the oar, but he could not swim either, and together we drifted for about half a mile away from the rafts and boats. [He] suddenly became panicky and went for me, having completely lost his head, and as neither of us could swim I had no alternative but to push him off the oar.[6]

There is no way of knowing how many merchant seamen were drawn down by their sinking ship, how many swimmers were burned to death by their own inflammable cargo, how many drowned because they had gone over the side without their lifejackets, or how many were attacked by sharks and barracuda. Swimmers were often afraid of being torn to pieces by predatory fish, although attacks of this kind are mentioned in only a small number of survivors' reports. A post-war Medical Research Council study concluded that their 'dramatic nature ... far exceeded their numerical importance'.[7] Nevertheless, for survivors the fear itself could have a debilitating effect, and those who actually experienced an attack were unlikely to have found reassurance in the evidence of its rarity, even if they had known of it.

Captain Caird of the *Eurylochus*, a victim of the raider *Kormoran* on 29 January 1941, described how, while he and other survivors were on rafts, 'sharks were our greatest danger, however by splashing we succeeded in keeping them at bay ... The Chinese bosun had one arm blown away and a shark took a foot ... When one raft overturned I understand that the No. 2 carpenter was got by a shark.' He commended Cadet Hay who swam to rescue the radio officer. 'Sharks could be plainly seen, however he succeeded in his task. A shark finally tore one leg from his trousers but he was unscathed.' Caird considered the sharks 'were even a greater menace than thirst'.[8]

Some survivors reported their experiences in a surprisingly objective way. The surgeon of the *Eurylochus* described kicking his legs and splashing the water to keep sharks away, and expressed the belief that 'sharks are shy, and cannot see well at night'.[9] The master of the *Empress of Canada*, torpedoed north of Ascension Island on 13 March 1943, also offered an interesting analysis:

> A lot of people were bitten by sharks; I was not bitten myself during

the two hours I spent swimming around, but I was smothered with fuel oil which probably kept them away, as they don't like the taste of it. Several people were suffering from barracuda bites; I think the sharks are worse, but the barracuda are more annoying as they bite slowly.[10]

It is a strange paradox, that the oil which was such a menace to many survivors may have saved the lives of others by discouraging the sharks. A modern book on survival recommends swimmers to stay among the oil if sharks are present, but advises that they should stay as still as possible rather than swimming or splashing.[11]

Many seamen died from the effects of their actual immersion in the sea itself. Some of these deaths arose from swimmers choking on vomit brought on by the motion of the waves or by swallowing seawater and oil; other deaths came from heart attacks caused by the shock of immersion or by hyperventilation; many were cases of drowning as men could no longer breathe when exhaustion, unconsciousness, a badly adjusted lifejacket or rough sea conditions caused their faces to become submerged; some simply lost hope and gave up the struggle, a condition which a number of reports claim to have been common among lascars. Very cold sea temperatures could exert a powerful, even decisive, influence on how long swimmers could remain alive. Recent studies at the Institute of Naval Medicine have concluded that immersion in very cold water probably most often kills very quickly through hastening the onset of the conditions outlined above.[12] It is less common for it to cause actual hypothermia by reducing the core temperature of the body below about 77° Fahrenheit (25° Centigrade) when the vital organs of the body can no longer function.

The ability to withstand very cold temperatures varied from one survivor to another, according to such factors as age and fitness, determination, the insulation provided by body fat and clothing, how long they remained in the water, and what conditions they had to face when removed from the water. Men taken on to rafts or open lifeboats might die as their core temperature continued to fall, while men rescued by a ship where warmth and skilled medical attention were available would have a better chance of staying alive, even though they might lose hands or feet through frostbite. Because of these variables, post-war studies differ from one another in their calculations of how long swimmers can survive at any given sea temperature.

While both Robin and Lee agree that above 77° F the water temperature is unlikely to be a dangerous factor, in warmer conditions sunburn, heatstroke and thirst begin to take their toll.

Degrees F	Molnar[13]	Robin[14]	Lee[15]
40/41	minutes only	½–3 hours	1 hour
59/60	under 5 hours	2–24 hours	7 hours
68+		< 40 hours	< 16 hours
77+		no limit	no limit

Even without detailed statistical analysis, survivors in war-time were perfectly well aware that cold kills, the sea kills, sharks kill, the shock of an underwater explosion kills. They were eager to find some refuge out of the water as quickly as possible. Although there were examples of survivors in overcrowded boats or on rafts refusing to allow swimmers to join them for fear of adding to their own immediate danger, those who had been fortunate enough to reach a place of relative safety generally appreciated the importance of picking up anyone still in the water, and that task was usually given high priority. It was work sometimes fraught with difficulties and disappointments:

We heard others calling out in the water but they had no lights and we were helpless on the raft as we had no means of manoeuvring it to the men.[16] (*Cingalese Prince*)

Just after we had got into the boat there was a shout from the water 'Help, help, I cannot swim'. Without a moment's hesitation, the bosun who had only just been picked up from the water, dived overboard and swam off to the man calling ... It was a very dark night ... but after about five minutes the bosun, G. Christie, came back to the boat bringing with him one of the military gunners.[17] (*Benmohr*)

The lifeboats sailed through the wreckage, hoping to pick up survivors, but it was a vain search. All that was seen was the captain's hat and a mutilated body.[18] (*Calchas*)

They rescued [the chief engineer] with the aid of a boathook. He was almost finished and said afterwards he couldn't have held on much longer. He was also a very heavy man and they had great difficulty in getting him aboard.[19] (*Dagomba*)

I tried to pick up the other men, but this was not easy, as there was a big hole in the lifeboat, the rudder was gone, and the wind and current were strong, causing the boat to drift. Owing to eight of the men being injured, there were only young boys left to row.[20] (*Baron Dechmont*)

A particularly graphic illustration of the effect of extreme cold on this type of rescue work is provided by the report of the master of the *Chulmleigh*, which grounded on a reef in snowy weather south of Spitzbergen at 2330 on 5 November 1942 when independently routed for North Russia:

I heard a cry for help from the port side, so I ran down the deck with my torch and saw two men in the water. I called to the crew in No. 2 port lifeboat to pick them up, but the men appeared to be dazed and took no notice. The boat was still alongside so I went down into it and managed to get hold of one man, with the assistance of the bosun and one of the apprentices. We had a terrible job getting this man into the boat, as the others would not help us, but eventually we succeeded and after having a drink of brandy he was all right. I then tried to pick up the second man, a Royal Marine gunner, but when we reached him he was floating with his head fallen forward into the water and appeared lifeless ... I felt the man's pulse, but could feel nothing, presumably he was dead as the water was very cold; eventually we had to give up the attempt and let him go. I could not understand the attitude of the rest of the crew at all, they were quite useless.[21]

Even when swimmers had been picked up, or succeeded in reaching a lifeboat or raft by their own efforts, they often found that at first they were only marginally better off. Survivors on rafts or clinging to the keel of a capsized lifeboat might continue to be soaked to the skin, repeatedly drenched by flying spray or breaking waves; lifeboats which had been damaged by enemy action or while being launched could quickly become flooded to the point where the sea would spill over the gunwales as fast as frantic men could bail it out; and ostensibly sound wooden lifeboats could also fill with water because prolonged hot, dry weather or rough treatment had caused the seams to open up. This last condition would generally cure itself after a time as the planks would swell in the water and the boat could be bailed out. In traditionally constructed wooden boats survivors would always have to contend with a certain amount of seawater swilling around in the bottom.

From the earliest days of the war, it had been obvious that more might be done to improve merchant seamen's survival chances in the immediate aftermath of a sinking. Provision of rafts, self-igniting lights for rafts and lifebuoys, and improvements in lifejackets were important innovations, and many more ideas emerged from the hard-won direct experience of survivors.

As soon as the Germans adopted the policy of sinking vessels without warning at night, reports began to come in of ships' lifeboats or other rescue craft being able to hear, but unable to locate, lifejacketed survivors who drifted away in the darkness. For anyone who had come to value the small hand-held, battery-operated flashlight during the winter blackout of 1939–40, the solution was obvious and cheap. Miss Bridget Talbot demanded that merchant seamen should be supplied with a sea-proof electric torch so that they could indicate their position, and she eventually turned her hand to inventing a suitable light. Eleanor Rathbone put the idea to the Minister of Shipping, in an oral question on 5 March 1940, and was told by Sir John Gilmour that, although the Ministry was considering the idea, there were doubts about whether it might lead to even more deaths if other swimmers should mistake a man's individual light for a light on a raft.[22] When Will Adamson, a Labour MP, raised the issue again a month later, he was assured by the new Minister of Shipping, R. S. Hudson, that individual lights were being discussed with manufacturers. Eleanor Rathbone seized her opportunity, in a supplementary question, to suggest that the objection advanced by Hudson's predecessor could be overcome by making lifejacket lights a different colour from those mounted on rafts.

Despite the reservations still felt in the Ministry, advertisements began to appear in the shipping press for such products as the 'Wefco' watertight torch, the 'Winckler' lifejacket light, the 'Easco' light and the 'GEC' light.[23] The 'Winckler' light was a one-piece device nine inches long, weighing one pound, powered by batteries lasting forty-eight hours, automatically lighting up on immersion, and visible for half a mile. The 'Easco' was a two-piece device, with the battery carried in a pocket of the lifejacket and with a short flex connecting it to a light clipped to the shoulder. It lit up when a small captive jack-plug was inserted into the top of the battery holder. It had two great advantages: at nine ounces it weighed only just over half as much as its rival, and it cost only seven shillings and sixpence, complete with battery. It was initially claimed to have the same duration and visibility as the 'Winckler', but by 1943, with a U2 battery, a duration of only twelve hours was claimed.[24] The General Electric Company offered an even cheaper light for only five shillings.

When representatives of the shipowners were consulted by the Ministry of Shipping in May 1940 they expressed opposition to the lights on the grounds that they would lead inevitably to violations of the blackout on ships,[25] although there was some suspicion among the Ministry's officials that they were really concerned about the cost. Mr Plumb of the Ministry approached the matter in a different way. After examining the available

Advertisement for the Easco Life-Jacket Light. *Merchant Navy Journal* (1942).

casualty reports, he calculated that of the 1342 lives lost through enemy action up to 22 May only 10 per cent had occurred at night, and that the number who might have been saved by lifejacket lights was exceptionally small.[26] He concluded that the available evidence would not even justify the production of a sizable number of lights for trial purposes. Plumb's scepticism was not, however, shared by others in the Ministry, and by July it had been decided to follow the usual practice with innovations by introducing the lights on a trial basis on board ships owned or managed by the Ministry of Shipping,[27] while some shipping companies had already begun to issue them voluntarily.

The lights, by now red in colour, were an immediate success and came to be very highly regarded by merchant seamen. Pressure soon built up to have them made a compulsory requirement on all British ships, a view urged by Bridget Talbot in a letter to *The Times* in September,[28] and by Eleanor Rathbone in a parliamentary question in October.[29] They were eventually made compulsory in March 1941 under the Merchant Shipping (Additional Lifesaving Appliances), No. 3 Rules.[30] In March 1942 an unfortunate wrangle about patent rights between Easco and another manufacturer, Oldham and Son, demonstrated that commercial concerns and seamen swimming for their lives could view the lights from very different perspectives.[31]

There were the usual wartime difficulties in producing and distributing the lights. Survivors from some ships, such as the *Benmohr* and *Hertford*, sunk in 1942 complained that they had by then not received them;[32] and when the *Empress of Canada* was sunk in 1943 there were no red lights for the passengers' lifejackets, although the crew had them.[33] After lights had been issued, there were occasional problems with dead batteries, blown bulbs or damaged flex, and some shipping companies complained that the lights were being used so irresponsibly by seamen reading in bunks that bulbs and batteries had to be frequently replaced.[34] Generally, however, they worked well:

> Everyone was wearing a lifejacket, fitted with a red light. These red lights are wonderful but on this occasion several failed to work ... Whilst I was in the water I had had to hold the red light from my lifejacket in my hand with my arm out of the water, as otherwise it could not have been seen.[35] (*Ciscar*, 1941)

> I could see several red lights around me in the water ... We had frequent lifeboat drills, during which all the lights on the belts were tested ... So far as I know all the crew who were wearing lifebelts with red lights were picked up.[36] (*Sheaf Mount*, 1942)

We all had lights and whistles on our lifejackets, which were instrumental in most of us being picked up.[37] (*Kingswood*, 1943)

I was wearing my lifejacket, but the red light was not working ... The boats searched amongst the wreckage for survivors [and] at a conservative estimate thirty-five lives were saved by the red lights and whistles attached to the lifejackets.[38] (*Phemius*, 1943)

The lifejacket lights are a good example of a relatively simple and cost-effective innovation which fully justified the Ministry of War Transport's claim that by 1944 they had saved 'countless lives'.[39]

Alongside the campaign for the lights, another group of interested individuals had been conducting their own campaign to force the government to insist on each merchant ship having a motor lifeboat. Under the pre-war Board of Trade regulations, ships were not required by law to have a motor lifeboat unless they carried more than thirteen lifeboats. In other words, a motor lifeboat was only required on large passenger ships, although owners of cargo ships might voluntarily provide one as a means of communicating with the shore when a vessel was anchored in an open roadstead. In November 1939 John I. Thornycroft and Company, manufacturers of boat engines, placed an advertisement drawing attention to the fact that survivors from many ships had to depend on rowing boats. It urged that 'every merchantman should carry at least one power-propelled boat to shepherd the others and take them in tow'.[40] A. P. Chalkley, the editor of *Motor Boat and Yachting*, weighed in with his support, arguing that the provision of motor boats need not be expensive. In his view 500 boats would cost about £150,000, which could be financed by the Red Cross or by public subscription.[41] Not content with putting his idea in print, the editor pursued it through correspondence, only to find that the British Red Cross Society considered it outside the scope of its activities and that the Ministry of Shipping were undecided. In January 1940, therefore, he modified his approach slightly by suggesting that the Ministry should, at the very least, see that the new ships it was having built were each equipped with a motor boat, which would only add £300 or one-sixth of one per cent to the cost.[42]

By February, Chalkley had failed to persuade three London daily newspapers to take up the matter, but there was support from other shipping publications which were critical of the Ministry for being unable to make up its mind.[43] Ellen Wilkinson, the left-wing Labour MP for Jarrow, carried the campaign into the House of Commons and, in response to a question from her, Sir Arthur Salter announced on 14 February that all new ocean-going ships being built on government account would be equipped with a motor lifeboat, and that shipping companies building ships on their own account were being recommended to follow the government's example.[44] If the Ministry of Shipping had thought that this would satisfy the campaigners they were instantly shown how wrong they were. Wilkinson followed up immediately with a supplementary question arguing that smaller vessels also needed a motor boat, and Chalkley rushed into print with an article claiming victory for his magazine's campaign and putting forward a new demand that, logically, the government 'should not hesitate a day' before ordering all existing ships to be provided with a motor lifeboat. He insisted that, at a cost of £100 to £200 each, one lifeboat for each ship could have a motor installed during a couple of days in port, and it would be better for the government and owners to get on with it 'rather than that they should be forced to it by the seamen and public opinion'.[45]

Pressure on the Ministry of Shipping was maintained throughout 1940. Chalkley was critical of the inadequate power of the engines and the large number of different lifeboat designs being provided for ships under construction, and he printed articles showing how motors might be easily fitted to existing oared lifeboats.[46] Thornycroft's advertisements stressed the valuable role played by the *Athenia*'s motor boat, whose engine had run continuously for six hours,[47] and C. J. Hellberg, marine superintendent of the Austin Motor Company, began to look into the question of supplying engines. Having been a merchant seaman himself for fourteen years, he was keenly interested in maritime safety questions. In Parliament, Ellen Wilkinson secured the backing of Ben Smith, David Adams and Emmanuel Shinwell but, after accepting office as a Junior Minister in the coalition government formed by Churchill in May 1940, she had to withdraw from campaigning publicly. It was Smith who put down a question asking when it would be made compulsory for existing ships to carry a motor lifeboat. The then Minister of Shipping, Ronald Cross, told him that so many boats would need to be converted, and such extensive alterations would be required to the lowering gear, that the idea was not practical.[48] Chalkley would not accept that. In August he accused the Ministry of wishing to avoid the subject and claimed that their inaction would lead to deaths;[49] in October he lambasted the shipowners because, as revealed the previous month,[50] only a third of the ships being built at their expense were being fitted with a motor boat. He charged them with either not believing 'that the motor lifeboats would be helpful in saving the lives of their crews or [being unwilling] to incur the very small expenditure involved'.[51]

The Ministry of Shipping was still examining the matter, and its representatives discussed it with the Admiralty's merchant shipping and repairs division on 14 October. Shortage of skilled labour to undertake the conversion work, and a shortage of suitable engines, were identified as the main obstacles, and an idea was put forward for using the engine manufacturers themselves to carry out the conversion work.[52] In the same month a lead to the shipowners was given by the Clan Line, which placed an order for fifty engines to be used for converting boats on their existing ships. Enquiries made by the Ministry with engine manufacturers revealed that supply problems would not prove insuperable. In the November issue of *Motor Boat and Yachting*, Chalkley announced with justifiable satisfaction, and with generous acknowledgement of Hellberg's contribution, that the Ministry of Shipping was sending a strong recommendation to shipowners that one lifeboat should be converted on every existing ship over 2000 gross tons.[53]

Chalkley estimated that the number of boats requiring conversion would be about 2000 so that, with the production of engines running at only thirty to forty a week and the availability of ships in United Kingdom ports being unpredictable in wartime, it would still take some time before every ship had a motor lifeboat. The Ministry ordered 500 engines from the Morris Motor Company.[54] A Morris Vedette nine horsepower engine installed with two ten-gallon petrol tanks in a twenty-seven-foot lifeboat belonging to the Prince Line reduced the carrying capacity from forty-eight men to forty-five, but was claimed to be capable of powering the boat for twenty-nine hours at five knots.[55] A large order was also given to the Austin Motor Company. By March 1942 they had supplied 600 engines of ten horsepower giving a range in excess of 200 miles at five or six knots, and the Ministry awarded them a contract for a further 1000 at fifty per week. By that time, there was even a suggestion that the larger ships ought to have two motor lifeboats instead of one.[56]

When Chalkley and his allies first launched their campaign for motor lifeboats in the winter of 1939–40 they had seen the main value of such boats as allowing crews of vessels sunk in the North Sea, the mouth of the English Channel or within, say, 150 miles of the Irish or Scottish coasts to reach land within about twenty-four hours – instead of having to suffer the privations of several days adrift in those latitudes during winter. As the battle moved out into the wider oceans, many sinkings

Our men depend on

Austins The Austin Motor Company is proud that Austin equipment has been singled out for its dependability to help the men of the Merchant Service at sea. The new motor lifeboats being put into service by the Ministry of War Transport are powered with 10 h.p. Austin Engines with special reduction gear for greater power when getting away from a ship's side in heavy seas. Another notable feature of these boats is the Austin Manual Fire and Bilge Pump — designed to require the minimum effort in operation. Wherever and whenever our men stand, in need of help they can depend on Austin equipment never to let them down.

Austin Lifeboat Engine

Austin Manual Fire and Bilge Pump.

AUSTIN

SHIPS' LIFEBOAT

ENGINES

THE AUSTIN MOTOR CO. LIMITED, BIRMINGHAM

Our thanks to the Merchant Navy wherever they plough the seas for the magnificent part they are playing today with such complete disregard for danger . . .

An appreciation by JAMES STOTT LTD, makers of Cotton Sailcloths and Awning Canvases, OLDHAM, LANCS

Advertisement from *Merchant Navy Journal* (1942).

occurred so far from land that motor boats lacked the range to fill that role, but they could still save many lives by towing boats and rafts away from the sinking ship, searching for men in the water, gathering liferafts together and redistributing survivors between them, recovering supplies from surplus rafts, intercepting a possible rescue vessel sighted some way off, and assisting other boats and rafts to get alongside any vessel coming to their rescue. When their fuel had been exhausted they could still function as ordinary lifeboats, since they were required to carry oars, mast and sails, although the drag of the propeller would not have improved their handling under sail.

The results of supplying motor lifeboats were probably a good deal less impressive than their advocates might have hoped. Motor boats were as vulnerable as other lifeboats to damage from enemy action and from accidents while they were being lowered into the water. Indeed, one might have expected them to be slightly more vulnerable on account of the fire hazard of the fuel carried and the extra weight of the engine during launching. If the sample of 209 ships analysed in the Medical Research Council's post-war study was typical of casualties as a whole,[57] their finding that, on average, sinking ships managed to launch only 52.8 per cent of their lifeboats successfully would imply that survivors from about half of the cargo ships equipped with four lifeboats were likely to have to manage without a motor boat.

Some survivors' reports showed that, even when a motor boat was launched, there was no guarantee that the engine would work under the harsh conditions in which it was required to function:

The Morris motor in the lifeboat was out of order, as the magneto was wet and too near the bottom of the boat, where the water was a foot deep. There was only one-eighth of an inch between the propellor [sic] and the stern post, and the propellor became badly jammed against it.[58] (*Thursobank*, 1942)

The magneto was saturated and although the engineers worked on it every day they could not get it to spark. I consider something should be done to make the magnetos in lifeboats watertight.[59] (*Ross*, 1942)

The motor only functioned for a short time, and then broke down as the carburettor and jets became fouled with salt.[60] (*Hartington*, 1942)

The experience of survivors from other ships was much more positive. The master of the *Fort Chilcotin* was able to use his motor boat to collect men from rafts and to tow another lifeboat until they could get organised. He reported that 'the motor functioned splendidly', and he suggested that ships 'should be provided with two motor boats, one carried on each side, so that there would be a better chance of one getting away from the ship'.[61] The motor boat of the *Kingswood* worked well for over two hours picking up swimmers spread over a wide area through abandoning the vessel while she still had way on her. Only when all had been recovered did the engine eventually break down.[62] After the *John Holt* had been sunk, on 5 March 1944, the chief officer was able to use the motor boat to tow three other lifeboats through the night covering twenty-three miles in under eleven hours until the ninety-five survivors were picked up.[63] This is a good illustration of the capabilities of the nine or ten horsepower engines provided for lifeboats. Not a single man was lost apart from the master and a passenger taken prisoner by *U–66*. Chalkley, Hellberg and their associates would have considered the lives of merchant seamen saved when lifeboat engines functioned efficiently were ample reward for all their efforts during 1940.

Another lifeboat problem demanding attention was what happened when a lifeboat capsized. Traditional wooden lifeboats may have been constructed with techniques which would have been familiar to Drake and Raleigh but, fitted with buoyancy tanks, they were undoubtedly resilient. They might be blown into the sea by explosions, peppered with bullets and shrapnel, partially burnt, dropped from a great height during launching, float to the surface after being carried down by a sinking ship, or be swamped by heavy seas – but they almost always floated after a fashion. Even when they floated in a capsized position, lives could be saved if exhausted and waterlogged swimmers could contrive to climb onto the upturned hull. That would always be a difficult task. Darkness, cold, oil or injuries would make it more difficult, and it often had to be done several times as men could easily slide off or be washed off. All lifeboats were fitted with a line looped around the outside for swimmers to grasp. Although that would be under water when the boat had capsized, it might provide a foothold. If the detachable skates, fitted to allow a lifeboat to slide down the side of a listing ship, had not been removed, they might offer a means of reaching the keel. But it was soon realised that something more was required.

Various ingenious pragmatic solutions were evolved by individual mates and carpenters. By 1942 the Ministry of War Transport was also insisting on all lifeboats having bilge rails (sometimes called bilge keels) fitted where the vertical side of the boat curves round to become the flat bottom.[64] These bilge rails provided an intermediate handhold for a man trying to haul himself out of the water, and a place for men holding on to the keel itself to brace their feet. In addition, grab lines were secured round the bottom of all lifeboats. Containers holding at least two gallons of water were tied to these lines so that they could be reached, even though the rest of a capsized boat's provisions were inaccessible.[65] To meet the needs of survivors adrift with no access to provisions, suggestions were made from time to time that seamen should be provided with an iron ration to be carried on their persons, but the Ministry of War Transport rejected the idea as having too many practical difficulties.[66] Some seamen did, however, carry a small bar of, say, chocolate or a small bottle of spirits in their lifejackets.

Survivors clinging to capsized lifeboats would normally have no alternative but to drift and hope to be picked up within a day or two at the most, but in favourable sea conditions it was sometimes possible for desperate men to right the boat by their own efforts. The chief officer of the *Richmond Castle* described his technique:

> We righted the boat by means of keel grab rails. We got as many men as possible on to the bottom of the upturned boat and by putting our feet against the keel and putting our full weight on the keel grab lines we eventually righted the boat. When the boat was righted it was found that some of the equipment was lost ... The second officer made an attempt to right No. 4 boat which was floating keel up among the wreckage, but he was unsuccessful.[67]

The master of the *Putney Hill* climbed on to the bottom of his capsized boat with a group of volunteers. They turned the boat broadside to the swell and began rocking it until it turned over 'after about twenty minutes of real hard work'.[68] It was obviously a task requiring strength, co-ordination and luck. Survivors from the *Lulworth Hill*, in her carpenter's words, found it 'difficult and dangerous, as several large sharks could be seen nearby. Eventually we made many attempts, but all were unsuccessful and our strength was soon exhausted.'[69]

A serious problem with which almost all survivors had to contend was the danger of death from exposure. Most of them would be wet through from swimming, from breaking waves and driven spray, from rain, or from sitting in leaky or flooded boats. When that was combined with cold winds and low air temperatures, especially at night, energy drained away, morale was destroyed, the ability to carry out necessary duties was impaired and men began to die. Open lifeboats offered very little shelter, so in early 1940 the Ministry of Shipping brought in modified rules which, among other things, required that lifeboats should be provided with a canvas hood which could be rigged to provide shelter in the forward end of the boat. Boats were also required to carry a number of blankets,[70] standardised in 1942 as six good woollen blankets in a waterproof cover. The hood, which also served to keep out spray, could be made by any competent sailmaker but received mixed reports from survivors. In October 1941, for example, the chief officer of the *Empire Wave* 'found it very good indeed', and the master of the *Hazelside* considered it 'of great value in keeping the men warm and out of the weather'.[71] Other reports claimed that hoods got in the way of bailing, rowing, streaming the sea anchor or tending the sails; and if too many men huddled forward a lifeboat became difficult to steer.

If boats could be kept drier, survivors would be more comfortable, but even constant bailing was seldom enough to get rid of all the water slopping around in the bottom of a boat. Using the traditional bailer, buckets, tin helmets, shoes and bare hands was back-breaking work, so in 1941 the Ministry of War Transport was persuaded to consider installing a semi-rotary hand pump as well as the bailers. The pump was another project of C. J. Hellberg, in collaboration with L. P. Lord. Both men were employed by the Austin Motor Company, and they had used the resources of the firm at Longbridge to develop a robust and efficient pump. They had even taken medical opinion and carried out experiments to discover the ideal length for the pump handle. It was claimed that a man could operate the pump continuously for up to two and a half hours, clearing ten gallons a minute, and projecting a spray for thirty feet if required to suppress oil burning on the surface of the sea. Hellberg used his formidable powers of advocacy to plead that these pumps should be made compulsory: in July the Ministry placed a contract for 15,000, of which Austin had delivered 12,000 by the end of March 1942.[72] Hand bailing was still needed if a boat filled with water, and the pump could become blocked with bits of rubbish in the bottom of the boat, but used at suitable intervals pumps could often keep the water level down to an irreducible minimum.

During 1941 experts at the Ministry of War Transport were busily engaged in designing a special garment which would protect survivors from exposure. The idea was not original; exposure suits had been produced in Sweden, Norway and the USA, but they were considered to be too bulky, too complicated or too costly. The Ministry experts were looking for something light and simple which could be donned quickly. They came up with a two-piece garment in yellow waterproof material. The bottom half consisted of trousers with integral covering for the feet and incorporating crepe rubber soles: the upper half consisted of a jacket with elasticated wrists on the sleeves and a hood to protect the head and neck.[73] The whole thing weighed no more than two and three-quarter pounds, and it came ingeniously folded to fit inside the hood making a flat package about the size of an A4 envelope. It was intended to be carried and put on only when the survivor was safely installed in a boat or on a raft. All these 'exposure suits' were the same size. Since they were intended to be worn over normal clothing they were so large that they looked as if they might comfortably house two small thin men. Once the design had been settled, the Ministry ordered 100,000 of the suits in the late summer of 1941 and distributed them to ships as quickly as possible.

The driving force behind the design of the 'exposure suit' was T. E. Metcalfe, who had been a civil servant in various Ministries since 1900. Before the war he had been in the safety division of the Board of Trade's Mercantile Marine Department. On the outbreak of war he had been put in charge of the lifesaving section, where he continued under the Ministry of Shipping and then the Ministry of War Transport. His involvement in all the lifesaving innovations relating to survivors from merchant ships earned him the respect of politicians, shipowners and the various maritime unions. For his work on the 'exposure suit', the Royal Society of Arts awarded him the 1941 Thomas Gray Memorial Prize 'for an invention advancing the science and practice of navigation'. By the time he retired in May 1944 over 300,000 of the suits had been produced, and in recognition of his important contribution to safety at sea Charles Jarman, acting General Secretary of the National Union of Seamen, presented him with the first Honorary Life Membership card of that union.[74]

In service the suits were all too often missing when they were most needed. It was expecting too much that seamen would carry lifejackets and 'exposure suits' everywhere as they went about their normal duties, and since they were separate from the lifejacket the suits were easily lost or mislaid in the frantic business of abandoning ship, or swimming, or scrambling on to rafts. On some ships they were stowed in the lifeboats, but they would not then be available to survivors who found themselves on an upturned boat, raft or piece of flotsam. What was really needed was a pocket specially designed for carrying the suit in the lifejacket cover. That was not provided, but some seamen improvised their own.

Survivors' reports from 1942 show that the suits provided worthwhile protection for a time, although they also had their drawbacks and they were too flimsy for prolonged wear. All the survivors from the *Earlston*, sunk on 5 July 1942 en route to North Russia with convoy PQ17, had suits, but some men refused to wear them in the lifeboat because, even in the Arctic, they caused so much perspiration that clothes became wet.[75] The master of the *Bolton Castle*, sunk in the same convoy, claimed that water in the bottom of the boat made his men uncomfortable despite their wearing the suits, and he had to remove the bottom part of his own suit because he found it too cumbersome while he was moving about tending the sails.[76] The master of the *Medon* described the suits as 'very troublesome and filled with water', a complaint endorsed by the chief engineer of the *Hartington*,[77] but the third officer of the *Sylvia de Larrinaga* thought that, despite getting damp inside, they were useful at night, while the chief officer of the *Teesbank* described them as 'most useful'.[78] Outside their primary purpose, the yellow colour of the 'exposure suits' improved the chances of survivors being seen by potential rescuers, and with their waterproof fabric they could be used as improvised rainwater catchers.

At the same time as they were developing the 'exposure suits', the Ministry of War Transport had been discussing with the oil tanker companies whether anything might be done to improve the survival chances of seamen who faced a terrifying death when petroleum cargoes caught fire after tankers had been attacked. Stories circulated of men running along the deck with their clothes ablaze, men leaping overboard into a burning sea, lifeboats engulfed in a sea of flames, burned men dying in agony, and blackened corpses disintegrating as rescuers tried to haul them into a boat. Compassion demanded that some effort should be made to protect them, and so did the national interest in sustaining the morale of the tanker crews. Two different approaches to the problem were explored: providing protection for the individual seaman and collective protection for the lifeboat and its occupants.

To protect individuals while they were launching or rowing a boat, a one-piece garment of light, fire-proofed fabric was devised. It consisted of a hood with a mica eyepiece, a very full, thigh-length cloak or smock, and gauntlets to cover the hands. It was intended that this garment should be carried around with the lifejacket, and presumably the 'exposure suit', and it was claimed that it could be slipped on in an instant over the top of the lifejacket. The intention was praiseworthy but was hardly likely to be practical in a sudden emergency. Regulations concerning the suits were issued in August 1941.[79] They were to be supplied at government expense, as were manual pumps to spray water over the lifeboat and an 8ft x 6ft asbestos blanket to shield the occupants. Tanker owners were required, at their own expense, to arrange for lifeboats to be painted with fireproof paint, and for their canvas covers, masts, sails and oars to be fireproofed.

Protection for the boat was probably a more promising approach than trying to provide protection for individuals. Tankers were given priority in the issuing of the semi-rotary hand pumps, and in having their lifeboats modified to take an engine. A powered boat was likely to get away from a burning ship and through patches of oil burning on the sea much more quickly than one driven by men at the oars who, by the nature of their task, could not shelter under a canvas cover or an asbestos blanket. It was thought that steel lifeboats would provide greater protection than the traditional clinker-built wooden boats. In July 1942 about half of the British oil-tanker fleet was equipped with steel boats and, at that stage, the Ministry of War Transport decided to make them mandatory for both new and existing tankers.[80]

By the beginning of 1943 a special technical panel of the Tanker Tonnage Committee, under the chairmanship of Mr John Lamb, technical manager of the Anglo-Saxon Petroleum Company, had produced a design for the safest possible steel boat.[81] It included quick-release lifting hooks, covered cabins forward and aft (the latter housing an engine and the helmsman), and a centre section covered by a quick-closing asbestos canopy in three sections, all cooled by water sprayed from the hand pump. From within this centre section the boat could be driven forward, if the engine failed, by Fleming gear. This system of propulsion, first developed in the 1920s, allowed the propeller to be driven by several men pumping handles and it could give a speed of about three knots for a limited period. As compared with rowing, it had the advantage of requiring less skill and the men would be less exposed, but the boat still carried oars for use as a last resort. The time taken up in testing prototypes, checking the implications of its weight of over seven tons for the various types of davit, and finding supplies of suitable sheet steel caused unavoidable delays. The Ministry was unable to place the first bulk order for 500 of these boats until the autumn of 1943.[82] By the time they were being installed in any numbers the worst period for shipping losses was over. The delay was fiercely criticised in a letter to *The Times* from Bridget Talbot, combative as ever in the merchant seamen's cause.[83]

Appreciating the production difficulties, Lamb's technical panel had also produced a design for adapting and fireproofing existing wooden boats carried by tankers. This incorporated many of the features of the steel boat, such as the cabins, canopy and Fleming gear, together with some metal sheathing and external blisters to provide both buoyancy and insulation. It was claimed that the conversion could be completed in four or five days and only added just over a third of a ton to the four-ton weight of a typical lifeboat. The capacity of a twenty-four-foot boat was reduced from thirty-two to twenty-seven men. In June 1943 an unmanned converted boat was tested on Merseyside to see how well it could stand up to oil burning on the surface of seawater.[84] It was found that, after four minutes, the cabin temperatures had been in the 70s and 80s Fahrenheit, while under the canopy it had reached 114° F.

> For a subsequent test, however, ten officials of the Anglo-Saxon Company (led by Mr Lamb) and of the Grayson, Rollo & Clover Docks Ltd, were in the boat, and themselves operated the pumps. Thus, actual conditions were much more nearly simulated; and, perhaps equally important, the party were able to gauge at any rate approximately, the psychological reactions to the experience. [After three minutes in the burning oil,] it was found that Mr Lamb's party, though rather wet, were otherwise but slightly discomforted. Smoke and steam were present inside the boat under the hood, but the concentration could not be regarded as dangerous. Indeed, those of the party who kept their heads low had no complaint to make on this score.[85]

By the autumn the Ministry of War Transport had set up a programme for converting the wooden boats still remaining on tankers,[86] but Lamb's conversion design had come too late to have much effect on casualties among the tanker crews. Nevertheless, one has to admire the willingness shown by him and his associates to put their own safety at risk before expecting merchant seamen to rely on their proposed design.

The shore staffs of the tanker companies were very active in looking for other ways of improving the safety of the men at sea. They tried unsuccessfully to develop a viable oil repellent which could be thrown into the sea or poured over individual seamen to clear thick oil from the vicinity of swimmers; the Shell group developed special soaps and solvents to allow oil-covered men in lifeboats to clean oil off the skin, especially on the face; and, in association with Siebe Gorman, the Eagle Oil Company developed a rubber helmet and mask so that survivors could breathe and see while swimming in oil. In 1944 this 'Eagle Protective Mask' was adopted by the Ministry of War Transport for issue to all tanker crews, and the Royal Society of Arts awarded it the Thomas Gray Prize.[87]

Another example of the lively interest in safety matters taken by shore-side employees of shipping companies was an improved lifeboat designed by Francis H. Lowe, an accountant who had risen to be Joint Managing Director of the Lamport and Holt Line. After eighteen months of research he was able to stage a demonstration in May 1943, when the new boat so impressed officials of the Ministry of War Transport that they were reported to have congratulated the designer on producing the world's safest ship's lifeboat.[88] Taking the standard double-ended lifeboat as a starting point, Lowe added a raised and decked-in section at bow and stern which, supplemented by canvas screens and covers, provided better shelter in heavy weather. The raised sections could also house buoyancy tanks at a greater height above the water line, and buoyancy was further enhanced by the addition of a large fender filled with cork or kapok along the outside of the gunwale for three-quarters of its length. Even when lowered almost vertically into the (admittedly sheltered) water of Liverpool's Alexandra Dock, or when rolled over through 100 degrees, the boat quickly righted itself and floated satisfactorily. The boat was fitted with additional water tanks and an improved rudder mounted on a continuous pintle and controlled by a yoke and lines rather than a tiller.[89]

Press reports describing the Lowe lifeboat as 'unsinkable' were probably over-optimistic, but it certainly seems to have incorporated impressive buoyancy characteristics. Some of these boats were provided for ships, mainly those belonging to Lamport and Holt, and one was reported to have carried eighty-four survivors to safety, even though it was only certified for fifty-five. Very generously, Lowe refused to make personal profit, and he declined to take out patents on the design. Moved by the plight of survivors, he insisted: 'When something is produced which will save life at sea, I think it should be available to all men.'[90] The Lowe lifeboat could not be introduced in large numbers before hostilities came to an end.

The Medical Research Council's post-war study analysed the sinking of 448 ships (almost all merchant vessels) carrying a total of 27,000 people. There was insufficient information to make separate calculations of the number of deaths which occurred on board the ships, while they were being abandoned, or while people were swimming; but the study concluded that 26 per cent of the people who had been on the ships must have lost their lives in the period between the attack itself and the time when survivors were on board lifeboats, rafts or other rescue craft safely away from the sinking ship. Unsurprisingly, it was found that the death rate for ships abandoned in darkness was about double that for ships abandoned in daylight; and for ships abandoned when the wind was at Force 5 or above on the Beaufort scale it was almost double the rate compared with abandonments when the wind was below Force 5.[91] A further 6 per cent died later, either in the lifecraft or shortly after rescue, and 68 per cent of the 27,000 people involved in the sinkings analysed in the study survived.

For survivors on rafts or in boats immediately after a sinking, the first few hours were a particularly anxious time. Could their craft survive in the existing weather conditions? Did it need repairing? Could they survive the excruciating discomfort? What could be done for the injured? Could they find shipmates still in the water? How many more survivors could their craft hold? What was the enemy going to do? Would showing lights bring swimmers, other lifecraft and rescuers to them, or attract the enemy? Ought they to row, hoist sail, drift or stream a sea anchor? Was rowing worthwhile as a means of keeping warm or did it simply waste energy? Might it be possible to reboard their ship next morning? What were their chances of being picked up? As they grappled with these problems, a great deal could depend on the qualities of leadership shown by those who assumed command because of their former rank on board the ship or those who simply took the lead, irrespective of former status, because they had the necessary personal qualities brought out by the crisis. How decisions were made on rafts depended on what collection of survivors had been brought together by pure chance, and how many were still physically and mentally capable of giving a lead. In lifeboats there would generally be an officer or certificated lifeboatman designated to take charge, but if that person were missing, for some reason, the responsibility might devolve on someone ill-equipped to discharge it.

For example, when the *Calchas* was torpedoed on 21 April 1941, the second officer was not available to take charge of his lifeboat as he was still at his action station by the gun. The third engineer was ordered to take the boat away, but eventually had to hand the tiller to someone else so that he could lead the bailing of the flooded boat. In his subsequent report to the owners, he explained that in the end he put an able seaman in charge, 'evidently a practical sailing boat man, my own experience of sail being nil'.[92] In fact, the master, all four deck officers and six of the engineers were lost in the *Calchas*, and her other boats were got away under the command of the bosun, carpenter, chief steward, an able seaman and a leading seaman. In the case of the *California Star*, sunk on 4 March 1943, the purser, who had never sailed a boat before, found himself in charge when the U-boat took away the second officer as a prisoner. Luckily, the purser was able to gather up the master from a raft next morning, but only after a difficult and inept struggle to bring the boat alongside the raft.[93] There were a number of instances where trainee officers in their teens – variously called

apprentices, cadets or midshipmen – took charge of lifeboats, and
sometimes the task fell to officers from the armed forces who happened
to have been travelling as passengers.

In fact, few merchant seamen were really familiar with handling open
boats, whether under oars or sail. The third engineer of the *Calchas*
provided a thoughtful analysis of the difficulty of rowing:

> With the present type [of oars] as used by *inexperienced* oarsmen there
> is nothing to locate the oar in the rowlock, it is either too far out over
> the side or the reverse. While rowing in a heavy sea the oar is revolving,
> the pull of the hands tending to turn the blade of the oar horizontal
> instead of vertical as it should be when pulling. Feathering of oars looks
> very nice in a dock or harbour but it is not practicable in the open sea.
> This could be rectified by shipping the oar in something the same way
> as in pleasure boats on lakes etc., the oar being located in a pin rowlock
> which locates the oar, and keeps its blade vertical at all times, thus
> ensuring the maximum efficiency from the pull.[94]

In a post-war memoir, the fourth officer of the *Macon* wrote that in the
ships of the Blue Funnel Line most able seamen and deck hands could
handle oars, 'but engine room and catering staff had little experience
of this task and were often very awkward, and unfamiliarity with boat
work was the cause of much loss of life which might have been avoided'.[95]

It was fortunate that a great many survivors spent only a brief time
in their lifeboats or rafts. The Medical Research Council analysis of
622 war-time lifeboat voyages and 137 raft voyages found that almost
30 per cent of the boats had been picked up during the first day adrift,
14 per cent during the second day, and a further 7 per cent during
the third day. Almost 50 per cent of the rafts were found on the first
day, 13 per cent on the second day and 3 per cent on the third day.
Half of the boats and two-thirds of the rafts carrying survivors had,
therefore, been found inside three days.[96]

Some of these very speedy rescues came about through ships being
sunk so near the coast that their lifeboats were able to reach the shore
unaided or were soon found by local fishing boats or shore-based rescue
craft. This was a common experience when vessels were sunk by mines
(and sometimes by aircraft), and also when they were sunk off neutral
coasts such as those of Spain, Portugal or their colonies. The master
and six other survivors, paddling a raft with bits of driftwood after the
Baron Newlands had been sunk in thirty seconds off the coast of Liberia
at 2045 on 16 March 1942, reported: '[At 1500 next day] we contacted
three native canoes, which took aboard the seven survivors, including

myself, from the raft. Two of these canoes landed four men at Grand Cester and the other canoe landed two men and myself at Piccaninni Cove, which was nine miles further up the coast.' [97]

Other speedy rescues came about because the ship had been able to transmit a distress message giving an accurate position, and that message had been promptly acted upon by a shore station. An excellent example is provided by the rescue of all seventy-nine crew, nine gunners and twelve passengers from the *Glenshiel*. Torpedoed at 0230 on 3 April 1942 in 1°00'S 78°11'E, her first attempt to transmit a distress message was unsuccessful because of damage caused by the explosion, but she stayed afloat long enough for the set to be repaired. Before she was finally abandoned at 0351 a distress message had been transmitted, and acknowledged by Colombo, 500 miles away. In the master's own words:

> I gave a talk to the survivors in order to keep up their morale, informing them we had received a reply to our SOS and that we were sure of being picked up. I particularly stress[ed] the importance of keeping the boats together so as to present a more conspicuous object for ships on the lookout for us ... At 1700 I sighted a ship on the horizon which turned out to be HMS *Fortune*, a destroyer, sent out to look for us. The *Fortune* had received a wireless signal ordering her to search for us at 0900 in the morning while she was 260 miles away.[98]

In some cases survivors owed their mercifully brief time adrift to the pure chance of their ships having been sunk in a busy shipping lane, especially one frequented by neutral vessels. Many British merchant seamen owed their lives to the fact that Spanish and Portuguese vessels continued to run to their African possessions and to Latin American ports. In the later years of the war, more and more survivors were picked up after being first sighted by reconnaissance aircraft.

The best chance of all for a speedy rescue came, however, when ships were sunk in convoy, or when warships were in the immediate vicinity. The plight of survivors would then be known on board other vessels, and both escorting warships and other merchant vessels were prepared to take considerable risks in order pluck them to safety. At the time, survivors were often impatient, even furious, at being made to wait while escorts went U-boat hunting or merchant vessels swept by rather than risk collisions with following vessels, but the general picture is one of rescues carried out with both speed and great bravery:

> HMS *Javelin* returned amongst us as we were struggling in the water and dropped over two 'Carley's' floats. She then proceeded with her

companion HMS *Jackal* in an endeavour to locate the submarine. After about an hour and a quarter the *Javelin* returned and picked us out of the water ... They picked the men up by nets which they threw over the side. Some of the men, however, were not fit enough even to climb up these nets, so the *Javelin* put her own men over the side to loosen the wreckage and rescue them.[99] (*Cedarbank*, 1940)

The destroyer, which was HMS *Harvester*, came up and gave us two ropes and we made the boat fast. We waited our chance and then scrambled on to the destroyer ... Later that morning we found a raft with eight men on it, but one Chinaman was killed whilst trying to board the destroyer. He was crushed between the raft and the ship's side. There was one Chinaman who had gone mad left on the raft and the ship's doctor jumped over the side to try to save him. The doctor got into difficulties ... and a lieutenant dived over the side, reached the Chinaman, knocked him on the head, and then fastened a rope round him and brought him back to the ship.[100] (*Silverpine*, 1940)

Soon after the ship went we hailed the SS *Stork* as she passed and she replied that the next ship astern would pick us up. This was the *Sedantes* whom we also hailed, but she passed on; we were eventually picked up by the rescue ship from our column, the SS *Petrel*. She lowered two boats and was stopped for over two hours picking up survivors.[101] (*Ciscar*, 1941)

We burned several red flares from the boats, and after two hours HMS *Campanula* picked us up ... There were quite a lot of survivors on board the *Campanula*. I was told by some of the survivors that this corvette went to the rescue of the *Aguila*. The corvette saw the red lights on the men's jackets but she could not stop in time and overran these men. She threw heaving lines to the men in the water, but they could not hang on to them.[102] (*Aldergrove*, 1941)

Experience of this kind of rescue work in the early part of the war quickly showed that the arrangements were far from ideal. Nominating the last merchant ship in each column to act as rescue ship inevitably added to the number of vessels straggling astern of the convoy, and the temptation to shield them while they were carrying out the rescue work or trying to catch up with the convoy tended to distract escorts from their main protective role. In any case, the merchant vessels concerned often had such a high freeboard that survivors had difficulty in climbing on board and, even when they could get on board, their rescuer would almost certainly have neither a doctor nor enough suitable accommodation. An escort vessel engaged on rescue work would have the advantage of lower freeboard, greater speed and manoeuvrability, and might well have a doctor or sick berth attendants; but the rest of the convoy would be deprived of possibly a quarter or a third of its protection until the escort regained her proper station.

The outstanding demonstration of the folly of organising the rescue of survivors in this way came on 17–18 October 1940, when the slow convoy SC7 from Canada was in the northwest approaches to the British Isles. The escort, which eventually amounted to three sloops and two corvettes, was no match for a group of U-boats commanded by aces such as Bleichrodt, Endrass, Frauenheim, Kretschmer, Moehle and Schepke. One sloop spent so long hunting a U-boat that she never regained touch with the convoy, and a corvette was detached to escort a damaged merchant ship. A total of twenty merchant ships were sent to the bottom and the surviving ships became dispersed, while the three remaining escorts chased around searching unsuccessfully for the enemy and stopping to pick up survivors from the ships which had gone down. The Dutch merchant vessel *Boekelo* was sunk when she stopped to rescue survivors from the British *Beatus*. More than half the merchant ships were lost, and afterwards HMS *Fowey* landed over 150 British, Allied and neutral survivors, HMS *Bluebell* almost 250 and HMS *Leith* over one hundred. Later more survivors were picked up by the salvage tug *Salvonia*, sent out to tow in a damaged ship which had remained afloat.[103]

One must admire the humanitarian principles of the captains of the escort vessels, but it is hard to quarrel with Dan van der Vat's judgement that they 'were completely ineffective, spending their time rescuing survivors, and thus abandoning their stations, which made it all the easier for the Germans to pick off the most profitable targets'.[104] Two nights later, 19/20 October, the U-boats which still had torpedoes joined with Prien and Liebe in savaging the following convoy HX79, which lost twelve ships in spite of having a much stronger escort. One of the torpedoed merchant ships was the 5452-ton *Loch Lomond*, sunk while attempting to carry out her designated duty as rescue ship; and the convoy escort which rescued her survivors was the minesweeper HMS *Jason*, whose captain claimed to have picked up 720 survivors from sunken merchantmen in the space of six weeks.[105]

A month before these disasters, the Commander-in-Chief, Western Approaches, Admiral Sir Martin Dunbar-Nasmith, had written to the Admiralty suggesting that if special ships were attached to convoys for rescue duties the escorts could concentrate on their defensive role and it would be good for the morale of merchant seamen.[106] In the light of the rescue problems of SC7 and HX79, the case was irrefutable; and during January 1941 the first three of the specialised rescue ships came into service. Nine more were added during 1941, four during 1942, seven in 1943 and one in 1944. They were small ships with a low freeboard and straight sides to make it easy to haul survivors on board. They averaged about 1500 tons, but the *Walmer Castle* was only 906 tons and the *Perth* was the largest at 2258 tons. The ships needed to be faster than the average convoy, so that they could catch up after effecting a rescue. They also had to have space to accommodate survivors and a hospital for treating the injured. These criteria were found in certain passenger/cargo vessels from the coasting or Mediterranean trades. In the last few months of the war, five corvettes were also converted for this role.

The rescue ships were based on the Clyde where the responsibility for meeting their shore requirements was shared between their commercial owners and a young naval officer, Lieutenant L. F. Martyn. The rescue ships were commanded and manned by merchant seamen (usually their normal crews familiar with how they were best manoeuvred), but they also carried Royal Navy specialists such as a doctor, sick-berth staff and communications staff in addition to the usual DEMS gunners to man their array of weapons. They did not claim the immunity of hospital ships, because that would have meant being illuminated at night and betraying a convoy's position.

The men of the rescue ships developed their own specialised techniques: for hauling on board injured men in special baskets or Neil Robertson stretchers; for rigging scrambling nets, not only against the ship's side but also on twelve-foot long booms projecting at right angles from the side; for using motor boats to pick up swimmers; for fishing men out of the water with hooks attached to twenty-foot long bamboo poles; and for cleaning up oil-caked survivors. They also volunteered to go down the scrambling nets to help up survivors who were too exhausted or waterlogged to help themselves. Even off-duty engine-room staff joined in this work.

Rescues were generally a race against time. Survivors from the *Aymeric* found themselves in the sea within five minutes of her being torpedoed near the southern tip of Greenland at 2240 on 16 May 1943. Her master commented bitterly:

A frigate steamed close to me, so close indeed that I could easily have swum to it. I shouted out to the frigate, asking her to pick us up, as the water was bitterly cold, and I knew the men would not be able to last very long in it. The frigate did not stop, but simply signalled to the Rescue Ship *Copeland*, which was four miles astern. About forty minutes later the *Copeland* arrived on the scene, but by this time many of the men had frozen to death.[107]

The *Copeland* managed to pick up twenty-four men, and HM Trawler *Northern Wave* another fourteen. The master of the *Copeland* reported with satisfaction:

> All my crew worked magnificently to save them by jumping on rafts, bending lines on them, and getting them on board in the quickest possible time. Other willing hands attended to their needs on board and also carried out artificial respiration for those who required same. [At times, Boatswain William Moffat] went down the life nets, waist deep in icy cold water, to bend a line on some helpless seaman.[108]

Six rescued lascars died subsequently on board the *Copeland* and seven on the *Northern Wave*.

The challenge for the naval doctors who served in rescue ships was discussed in a paper by Surgeon Rear-Admiral J. W. McNee in 1945. He pointed out that some of the rescued men would be suffering from low morale and hysteria.

> Medical officers have in such circumstances never hesitated to use morphine freely at once, followed later, if necessary, by heavy doses of luminal or bromides ... I hold the personal opinion that it is undesirable to appoint very young medical officers with only three or six months of hospital experience to Rescue Ships, where all kinds of emergency work including major surgery may be required at any time. Nor should men who prove to be 'bad sailors' be retained in this service – these small ships were never meant for Atlantic rollers and they are to say the least, 'lively' ... The medical officer in this service has rather a roughish job.[109]

Two of the rescue ships were withdrawn when it was found that they were unsuitable for the type of work involved. Others had a tragically brief career. The tiny *Walmer Castle* lasted only nine days before she was bombed and sunk with the loss of eleven crew and twenty of the eighty-one survivors she had rescued on her first convoy; the *St Sunniva* simply disappeared with all hands on her first convoy, probably capsized by the weight of ice on her upperworks. The *Pinto* made eight trips without being called on to effect a single rescue, and was then torpedoed by *U–482* on 8 September 1944 as she stopped to pick up survivors from the whale-oil tanker *Empire Heritage*. Others had long and distinguished careers: the *Zamalek* picked up 617 survivors from sixty-four convoys, the *Rathlin* 634 from sixty convoys, the *Perth* 455 from sixty, the *Copeland* 433 from seventy-two, and the *Stockport* 413 from only fifteen convoys. This last named rescue ship was torpedoed by *U–604* on 24 February 1943 with the loss of sixty-four crew and ninety-one people she had rescued.

The Admiralty and the Ministry of War Transport were never able to find enough vessels suitable for conversion into specialised rescue ships (hence the eventual introduction of converted corvettes). The need for convoy escorts or ordinary merchantmen to engage in rescue work themselves persisted, therefore, throughout the war.[110] Nevertheless, by the time the war ended, the converted rescue ships had escorted about 800 convoys, mostly across the Atlantic, but also to Russia and Gibraltar. They had rescued 4194 survivors, mainly merchant seamen but including some from sunken escorts and four from a U-boat. 2296 of the survivors were from Britain and the Commonwealth, 951 from the USA, four from Germany, and the rest from Allied and neutral ships.[111] The operations of these rescue ships ensured that many merchant seamen had to spend only a relatively short period waiting for rescue after their ships had been sunk; but for those whose ships were sunk while sailing independently in distant waters, or while straggling from a convoy, or survivors simply left astern after being overlooked in the turmoil of a convoy night action, the only hope of reaching safety might lie in their own ability to face the formidable challenge of a lengthy boat or raft voyage.

8

Lifeboat and Raft Voyages

In the early months of the war, when most of the U-boat sinkings were in the northwest or southwest approaches to the British Isles, survivors who had to depend on their own efforts to reach safety did not necessarily have to embark on a lengthy lifeboat voyage. But even a short open boat voyage in the North Atlantic was enough to reveal some of the discomforts and problems inescapable on such voyages. Most of the crew of the *Arlington Court* were picked up by a neutral vessel soon after their ship was torpedoed in the southwestern approaches on 16 November 1939, but seven men found themselves adrift in a small boat. Malcolm Morrison, an eighteen-year-old deckhand from the Isle of Lewis, was the only one who knew how to set a sail. Under his leadership they sailed their boat through gale conditions until they were picked up by a neutral tanker in the mouth of the English Channel. In reporting that Morrison was to receive the official congratulations of the Admiralty, British newspapers emphasised the hardship of living on biscuits, condensed milk and corned beef, with hardly any fresh water to drink. They also wrote of the constant bailing and the cold, and the severe frostbite from which the men were suffering when they were rescued.[1]

The *Langleeford* was torpedoed by *U–26* in 50°54′N 11°20′W on Wednesday 14 February 1940. Two lifeboats got away, with eighteen men in one, commanded by the master, and fourteen in the other, commanded by the chief officer. The Germans gave them some rum, cigarettes, bandages and biscuits to supplement the water, biscuits and condensed milk carried in the boats, and they were advised that the southwest coast of Ireland lay seventy or eighty miles away on a course of 060. The boats kept together until 1800, when the master suggested tying them together so that they would not lose touch during the night, but the chief officer preferred to take advantage of the fine weather by rowing until midnight before giving his men a chance to sleep.

By 0400 the next day the wind had picked up, and they were able to sail, the two boats being two miles apart with the master's boat falling further behind. Land, thought to be fifteen miles distant, was sighted at 1000. The chief officer described the difficulty of actually getting ashore:

> We sailed until 5.45 p.m., when we were a quarter of a mile off Curry Head [almost certainly Kerry Head, the southern shore of the mouth of the River Shannon] so we got the oars out and tried to row. We could not make it, however, so we decided to make for Loop Head [the Shannon's north bank]. We sailed until 10 o'clock, and although it was a matter of only nine miles, we made only five ... It rained all during the night ... we were all wet from the rain and our feet were in water which the boat was making in the bottom. About seven men suffered from what the doctor ashore told us was a form of trench feet, and one man, much older than the rest, who had been in the water before getting into the boat and was therefore wet to start with, died of exposure.[2]

On Friday morning they found themselves out of sight of land once more, and it took them ten hours of effort before they were able to land at Ross, near Loop Head at 1725. The master's boat was still missing, and Irish air reconnaissance on Saturday afternoon failed to spot it, but by the end of the afternoon it was reported to have landed safely at Ballyheige, near Kerry Head. The experience of the survivors from the *Langleeford* illustrates that, even with a reasonably fresh crew where debilitation from food and water shortage had not yet set in, lifeboats were difficult to row and sail. On a relatively short voyage they landed some sixty miles further north than intended, presumably because of compass error or leeway in the ESE wind. For much of the time they must have made good a course between 020 and 030 instead of the 060 advised by the Germans. Their experience also illustrates how difficult it was for boats to remain in company, and how quickly the feet of survivors deteriorated when they were constantly immersed in cold water.

  Six months later, as more ships were being sunk further out in the Atlantic, the full horror of protracted lifeboat voyages, even in summer, began to be revealed. When the *Severn Leigh* was sunk in 54°31'N 25°41'W, about 550 miles west of Ireland, on 23 August 1940, thirty-four of her crew of forty-two were left adrift in one lifeboat and two rafts. The master had the two rafts tied together and on them he placed five men seriously wounded by the U-boat's shelling with eight fit men to look after them. Hoping that his radio distress call would bring rescuers to the scene, he gave orders for the lifeboat to tow the rafts, but the tow rope kept parting and their speed was only about half a knot. Two of the injured men died during the first night, and on the afternoon of the following day they suffered the disappointment of seeing a ship pass by five miles away despite their efforts to attract attention with flares and white cloths tied to oars held aloft.

Through the night of 24/25 August the master wrestled with an appalling decision. He thought they would never reach land trying to tow the rafts, but if all crowded into the boat there would be no room to lay out the injured men.

> It was a case of sacrificing twenty-nine men for the three injured men, or sacrificing the three injured men for the twenty-nine able men. I therefore consulted my second officer, chief engineer, and the sound and able men, pointing out the bare hope that it was possible without the rafts to reach land in ten days, but the longer action was delayed, the lesser would the hope be, and so it was decided to abandon the rafts with the three injured men left on. Although it was to me a terrible action, yet, my duty lay in the fact of my endeavour [sic] to save as many as possible.[3]

Leaving the injured men with some water and biscuits, the lifeboat with the remaining twenty-nine survivors was able to make four or five knots. The boat was well supplied with several bottles of whisky, biscuits, tinned milk and tinned meat, but only carried twenty gallons of fresh water. The master had managed to take his sextant and chronometer, but the absence of the necessary mathematical tables prevented accurate navigation, and the boat was forced too far northwards to reach Ireland, which must have been their intended destination. His report sets out some of the difficulties of the voyage:

27 August Men beginning to clamour for water.

28 August An endeavour was made to catch rain from the sail, but was tainted with salt ... Compass lamp continually going out.

30 August [Lying to sea anchors during gale] To avoid disaster, the oars were used to keep boat's head to seas. No one wanted any food, but a ration of water was issued. By 2 pm the seas were so large and dangerous and the men in a weakened state they were unable to pull the oars, boat laying under bare pole ... I decided to take a chance and ran before the gale ... We managed very well, however, and but for occasional swamping weathered the storm.

31 August One keg of water ended and the second was opened up and it was discovered that during the night ... some of the water had been pillaged.

1 September [Four men had now died.] At 7 a.m. a passenger boat passed us about three ship's lengths away but no notice of us was taken.

2 September Our water was becoming very low, and I realised that unless succour came soon we would all perish ... I think now many of my men lost hope, for they one after the other died.

3 September [Rain to drink] Food we did not require, only water. Our mouths were like blotting paper and all were in a very weakened state.

4 September Land was sighted, and although we endeavoured to reach it, we were gradually blown away. It transpired after that this was the Flannan Isles ... During the night two men died, making a total of nineteen.[4]

On 5 September, at the end of a voyage of 850 miles, the ten survivors landed at Northton, on the Isle of Lewis, and after being cared for by local people they were transferred to hospital in Stornoway, one further man dying on the way. Miraculously, on the day their boat reached land, one of the injured men who had been abandoned on the raft was landed at Halifax, Nova Scotia, by a British warship which had come across the raft by chance in mid-Atlantic.

Twelve days later, during a gale, the Ellerman liner *City of Benares* was sunk by *U–48* five hundred miles out in the Atlantic. She was carrying about 400 passengers, ninety of whom were children being evacuated to North America under a government scheme. Some life-boats managed to get away from the ship, but over 300 passengers died either on the ship or while waiting for rescue in the boats. Only thirteen of the children on the evacuation scheme were saved. Most of the boats were picked up on the day after the sinking, but one boat carrying, among others, six children and two of their adult escorts was adrift for eight days before it was spotted by a Sunderland flying boat which directed a destroyer to the rescue.[5] Dan van der Vat has claimed that this sinking made an even bigger impression on British public opinion than the loss of the *Athenia* a year earlier.[6] Certainly newspaper accounts of children bravely singing in the lifeboats, of two little girls clinging through the night to the keel of a capsized boat, of the sufferings of those who had to survive for eight days, and the appalling death toll all served to focus public attention once more on the question of survival at sea.

A retired captain of the Royal Navy felt moved to offer the readers of *The Times* the rather impractical suggestion that ships' lifeboats ought to incorporate the self-righting, self-baling and anti-swamping devices which were a feature of the boats maintained by the Royal National Life-Boat Institution.[7] In Parliament, Robert Gibson, the Labour MP for Greenock, raised the general question whether lifeboat drills were adequate and claimed that there was evidence that merchant ships' crews were unable to lower boats in an emergency.[8] He also questioned the wisdom of using a ship like the *City of Benares* with a crew consisting largely of lascars who were 'obviously not suited to the cold North Atlantic winds'.[9] The scheme for shipping children overseas had to be abandoned.

During the second year of the war, the number of very long lifeboat voyages increased, and particularly tragic examples received press attention even at a time of strict censorship. The sympathy of newspaper readers was aroused by accounts of a seventy-day voyage by a lifeboat from the *Anglo Saxon* during which five men died and only two lived to land in the Bahamas;[10] a lifeboat from the *Carlton* from which four men were rescued after eighteen days during which twelve of their shipmates had died;[11] and a voyage of 1500 miles to Brazil in twenty-three days by a lifeboat from the *Britannia* during which forty-four people died from wounds and exposure, leaving thirty-eight survivors.[12]

As evidence about lifeboat voyages was systematically gathered from survivors, experts in the Admiralty, Ministry of Shipping, shipping companies and Merchant Navy unions were busily engaged in evaluating ideas for tackling the problems. The first half of 1941 was a particularly fertile period for innovations, a number of which have already been discussed, and the Ministry of War Transport, created on 1 May 1941, was soon able to establish a good reputation on the strength of ideas inherited from its predecessor. Much was expected from the development of a portable radio transmitter and receiver for use in lifeboats. This idea had been around since 1914, when some lifeboats of the Cunard liner *Aquitania* had been equipped with radio, and pre-war regulations had stipulated that every motorboat should be equipped with radio but, since only the largest passenger liners were required to carry motorboats at that time, the vast majority of Britain's merchant fleet entered the war without a suitable set. If all ocean-going ships were to carry a lifeboat radio, they would be able to transmit a distress message, even if a ship's main set had been destroyed in an attack. Lengthy lifeboat voyages would be unnecessary, as help could be summoned from the shore or from any ships in the vicinity, and the ability to receive time signals would make an important contribution to the more accurate navigation of lifeboats. As well as helping to ensure the safety of survivors, lifeboat radios would also provide an operational bonus in allowing the Admiralty to build up a quicker and fuller picture of enemy activity.

In 1941 the International Marine Radio Company, in consultation with the Ministry of War Transport, managed to produce a transmitter and receiver which were thought to satisfy the Ministry's essential criteria – watertight, light, portable, simple to operate and robust. The transmitter was packed in a small suitcase secured with straps. It was powered by a newly invented dry acid battery and, although it contained only a single valve, it was claimed to have a range of 200 miles. As well as having a morse key, it could also transmit an SOS signal automatically. Publicity material promised that it was light enough to be carried down a ladder into a lifeboat; but being watertight and buoyant it could, if necessary, withstand being thrown into the sea for a boat to recover. The receiver was a separate item, carried by a strap over the shoulder and only about a quarter the size of the transmitter.[13]

After promising trials, the set was put into full production, and in June foreign-going ships were required to carry one under the Merchant Shipping (Additional Lifesaving Appliances) (No. 4) Rules, 1941.[14] The radio required a special topmast, which could be hoisted above the lifeboat's mast to give adequate height to the aerial. One boat each side was required to carry such a topmast, as it was hoped that at least one of them would be able to get safely away from the ship, with the radio being embarked at the last moment. The Radio Officers' Union welcomed the new equipment, and reported enthusiastically to their members:

> Signals from a lifeboat containing seventeen men were heard by a destroyer at a distance of ninety miles, and the men were picked up within seven hours; another boat, 230 miles from land, was located by direction-finding apparatus at coast stations, and ships were able to rescue the men.[15]

Sadly, survivors often found that the sets did not live up to the publicity which accompanied their introduction. The master of the *Macon*, torpedoed near the Azores on 24 July, found that the set 'went for twenty seconds and then petered out, due to the battery being run down';[16] the master of the *Tunisia*, sunk by a German aircraft west of Ireland on 4 August, condemned the radio sets as 'too delicate for use in boats';[17] and the master of the *Thistleglen*, torpedoed on 10 September east of Cape Farewell, Greenland, confessed that 'the set had become wet and therefore unusable'.[18] The master of the *Hazelside*, torpedoed in the South Atlantic on 28 October, reported: 'We later managed to send out about ten SOS transmissions from the boat's W/T set but I have not heard that any of these messages were picked up.'[19] He had no better luck in trying to gain radio contact with ships which were clearly in sight, until he resorted to the older technology of lamp signals.

During 1942, the Admiralty interviewers heard these sorry tales repeated and embellished over and over again: radio sets were forgotten in the scramble to abandon ship; the smaller receiving set was left behind; the set fell out of the boat as it was being launched or when it capsized; the set could not be carried to the boat because of the vessel's heavy list; it was washed overboard; no one in the lifeboat knew how to operate the radio; the set was dead or soaked; the range was inadequate; there was too much atmospheric interference; regular transmissions went apparently unheard either by other ships or by shore stations. Captain Shaw of the *Peisander*, torpedoed in the North Atlantic on 17 May 1942, seems to have been particularly embittered by the failure of the radio as his boats tried to reach the US coast in the area of Nantucket. He complained to the owners that his radio officer had not understood the set: 'I don't understand much about wireless but to me a good shake to the set with a slap at its side seemed rough treatment for a delicate instrument. I was beginning to wonder how he would like the same treatment.'[20] At his Admiralty interview he commented tartly, 'I was of the opinion by this time that I could have shouted ashore with a megaphone more successfully'.[21]

Just occasionally there were more favourable reports. Even the master of the *Peisander* had to admit that his boat's receiver had picked up useful time signals. East of Durban, survivors in a lifeboat from the *Empire Guidon* picked up a faint reply to their radio signal on 1 November 1942, and an aircraft found them within an hour, followed by a ship shortly afterwards.[22] A month later, a distress call from a lifeboat of the *Llandaff Castle*, northeast of Durban, was also instrumental in bringing an aircraft and ships to the rescue.[23] Probably the most remarkable result was obtained by a lifeboat from the *George H. Jones* which, five days after the ship had been sunk north of the Azores, managed to make contact at a range of over one hundred miles with a British escort vessel on 16 June 1942. In this case the lifeboat radio set was not the standard British issue. It was an American design, manufactured by the Barke Electrical Company of Erie, Pennsylvania, and it did not rely on batteries.[24] Power for its radio telephone was generated by manually cranking a handle on the completely waterproof set, a feature that came to be incorporated in British sets later in the war.

The Ministry of War Transport was far from complacent about the difficulties survivors were having with the lifeboat radios. In December 1941 it issued a notice emphasising the importance of adhering strictly to the makers' instructions about servicing the battery. It was acknowledged that the set was not completely waterproof and that it would benefit from a waterproof cover. Users were advised against leaving the set in the bottom of the lifeboat, where it would often have to lie in water, or trying to drop it directly into a boat, as both boat and set might be damaged.[25] By the time a revised version was issued in May 1943 the latest lifeboat radios were said to be watertight, and further advice was given on protecting the older sets against water. Very detailed instructions emphasised the importance of carrying a spare battery and rotating it systematically with the one in the set. Survivors were also shown how they could use the receiver to obtain an approximate fix on any shore station which could be heard.[26] Improved types of lifeboat radio set were invented right up to the end of the war, and the whole issue was kept under examination by a technical committee established by the Ministry. The Radio Officers' Union was generous in its recognition that the Ministry and the shipowners were genuinely trying to provide the best possible sets and that 'no question of expense [was] being allowed to interfere with this ideal'.[27]

Reports for 1943 and 1944 indicated, nevertheless, that survivors continued to find that attempts to use the lifeboat radio were more likely to prove frustrating than successful, even though great ingenuity was sometimes shown in improvising additional power by adapting batteries from signalling lamps, torches, or the red lifejacket lights. Occasionally, however, the sets proved their worth. Two lifeboats from the *Hopetarn* were rescued two days after she had been torpedoed in May 1943. Their radio signal had been received by a passing vessel. The *Hopetarn*'s master, in commending an apprentice and a radio officer who had risked their lives to save the set just before the ship sank, stated: 'Had it not been for the distress messages we transmitted with this set, I do not think we could possibly have been rescued so quickly.'[28] Another very satisfied user was the master of the *Fort La Maune*, torpedoed east of Socotra on 25 January 1944. Radio signals from his boat were picked up by a ship a hundred miles away, and he was also able to exchange messages with aircraft.[29]

By 1943 American and British reconnaissance aircraft were sometimes

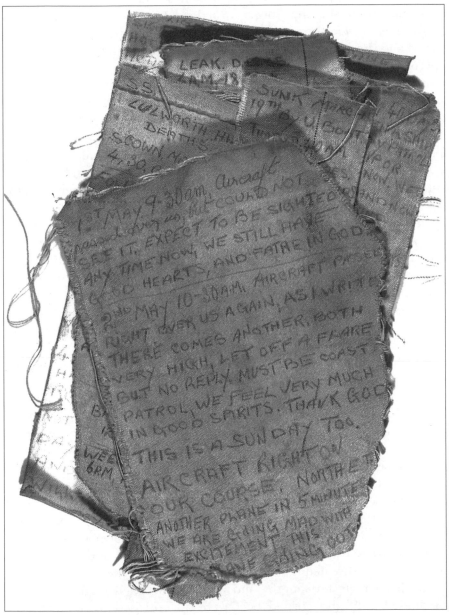

Pages from the log, written on pieces of sailcloth by Carpenter Kenneth Cooke, to record a fifty-day raft voyage after the *Lulworth Hill* had been torpedoed in the South Atlantic on 19 March 1943. (*Imperial War Museum*)

able to parachute radio sets and supplies to survivors from merchant ships. Two men from the *Lulworth Hill* were supplied with a set in this way on 2 May 1943. They had been drifting on a raft for forty-four days since their ship had been torpedoed by the Italian submarine *Leonardo da Vinci* in the South Atlantic about midway between Ascension Island and the African coast. After two days puzzling over the book of instructions, almost indecipherable after a soaking in seawater, they sent up the aerial on the kite provided, and one cranked the handle while the other tapped out SOS messages. This enabled aircraft to visit them and drop further supplies on two more days. One of these aircraft dropped a note to say that their signal was being heard in West Africa and Ascension Island although by then they were 400 miles from the West African coast. The radio handle became too stiff to turn by 7 May, but on that day a British destroyer rescued them. It was their fiftieth day on the raft.[30]

Another of the many initiatives taken in the first half of 1941 by the Ministry of Shipping and implemented by its successor, the Ministry of War Transport, was an investigation into the adequacy of the food and water supplies carried in lifeboats and rafts. The longer men had to spend in lifecraft, the more crucially important victualling became, but it could not be solved by simply increasing the quantity of supplies. Engines, canvas canopies, radios, aerial masts, blankets, extra food would all take up space which might be needed by survivors, especially when something like half of the lifeboats failed to get away from the sinking ships and the presence of DEMS gunners and additional radio officers increased the size of the crews.

Every ship's lifeboat was certified to carry a number of people which varied with the cubic capacity of the boat. A fairly typical Class 1 lifeboat twenty-four feet long would be approved for thirty-six persons, and it would be required to carry two pints of water, two pounds of biscuits and a one pound tin of condensed milk for each person. After the outbreak of war, boats usually carried tins of corned beef or other meat also. During the first half of 1941, examination of survivors' reports and discussions, involving the Ministry, Chamber of Shipping, Merchant Navy Unions, nutrition and medical experts and other interested parties, revealed a general consensus that the supplies were totally inadequate for lengthy and arduous lifeboat voyages. Biscuits, condensed milk and corned beef were all criticised by survivors as causing thirst. The Admiralty Merchant Ships' Technical Committee probably spoke for most of those involved in the discussions when they urged the abolition of the standard ship's biscuit which can rarely be eaten by survivors in boats after the first twenty-four hours and which is very bulky. The solution appears to lie in suitable concentrates and ... any additional stowage space so released should be devoted to additional water supplies. Concentrates should be suitably packed (not in bulk) and sealed to prevent deterioration.[31]

A passenger who survived a 630-mile lifeboat voyage to the Cape Verde Islands in sixteen days after the *Calchas* was torpedoed on 21 April 1941 wrote to Lawrence Holt, managing partner of the Blue Funnel Line, setting out his views on the lifeboat rations:

Is it not possible to find something better in the way of biscuits? ... There is something definitely wrong here, The food value of those which were supplied in our boat is very low, and again they are so extremely hard as to be quite impossible for many to eat, especially in a hot climate with such extremely limited supply of liquid. Ordinary Spratt's Puppy Biscuits would be better ...

It is amazing to me that modern science has not devised a more appropriate food for lifeboats. I am quite sure that it could be done if scope were given: the trouble is that old and antiquated ideas and customs are still being adhered to and practical experience not listened to.[32]

The criticism was a little harsh: the search for more suitable food was well advanced.

Food manufacturers co-operated willingly with the Ministry. As early as September 1940, Horlicks were manufacturing a vacuum-sealed pack of malted milk tablets,[33] and, although some experts in the Ministry of Shipping initially preferred to retain the condensed milk ration, the Senior Medical Inspector, Dr Tinker, calculated that if a case of forty-eight tins of milk were replaced by the equivalent food value of concentrated milk tablets, storage space would be released for an extra three and a half gallons of water.[34] Other well-known firms such as Fry and Rowntree developed a formula to make chocolate with greatly reduced thirst-provoking qualities; food manufacturers such as Bovril concocted a concentrated tinned meat product called 'pemmican'; and bakers collaborated in finding a recipe for a thinner and softer biscuit with a rather higher fat content which would still keep for a long time without deterioration.

By July 1941 the Ministry of War Transport was able to issue a new schedule of lifeboat rations, and with a real sense of urgency required them to have been implemented by 30 September. Lifeboats were to carry chocolate, milk tablets, pemmican and biscuits on a scale of fourteen ounces for each man for whom the boat was certified. They were all to be packed in sealed and rustproof metal containers of small size, and the foods were to be easily subdivided so that they could be rationed fairly. Since the new rations were markedly less bulky than those previously supplied, the extra stowage space was to be used to increase the allowance of fresh water almost threefold, to 112 ounces per man.[35] This extra fresh water was a very significant contribution towards enabling men to survive longer lifeboat voyages. Every raft was to carry six gallons of water and five pounds of each of the four foods. In an attempt to combat frostbite and 'trench foot' (sometimes called 'immersion foot') the new regulations also required each boat and raft to carry a one gallon can of oil with which survivors could massage their feet and legs daily.

In welcoming the new scales, the Merchant Navy Navigators' and Engineer Officers' Union explained to its members that pemmican was 'a highly nutritious – and, incidentally, expensive – concentrated food', the particular importance of the extra water was stressed, and the officials of the Ministry of War Transport were congratulated 'upon the very thorough and scientific manner in which they have dealt with their very humane task of introducing long overdue improvements'.[36] The Technical Committee of the Chamber of Shipping backed up the new approach to nutrition with a leaflet outlining what were then thought to be the most effective practical approaches to the whole question of survival in lifeboats and rafts,[37] and in October 1941, at the request of the Royal Navy's Medical Department, the Medical Research Council set up a high-powered Committee on the Care of Shipwrecked Personnel.[38]

The introduction of new lifeboat rations and the discussions of the Committee on the Care of Shipwrecked Personnel were taking place at a particularly difficult time. The average monthly loss of British shipping through enemy action was to rise from just over 235,000 tons in 1941 to just over 289,000 tons in 1942,[39] while the average monthly number killed among the crews, including DEMS gunners, was to rise from 653 in 1941 to 811 in 1942.[40]

Public sympathy for the sufferings of merchant seamen was constantly reinforced by advertisements and appeals from various maritime charities, the Merchant Navy Comforts Fund, National Savings, and the government's own campaigns with slogans like 'Let your SHOPPING help our SHIPPING'. One Ministry of Food advertisement featured a sinking ship with the blunt exhortation 'Your bread costs ships. Eat home-grown potatoes instead!'[41] The *Daily Mirror* published two very effective cartoons: one, showing a ship about to strike a mine representing luxury imports, appeared on 26 February 1942,[42] and was followed on 6 March by a particularly dramatic cartoon by Zec featuring an exhausted survivor clinging to a raft in rough seas. The caption referred to a recent decision to allow the price of petrol to go up by a penny a gallon.[43] This infuriated the government, who threatened to use the Defence Regulations to close down the paper for creating despair and defeatism. The Home Secretary, Herbert Morrison, explained to the House of Commons:

> The implication [of the cartoon] was that the brave men of the Mercantile Marine, whom I would not put in the same street as some of the people who write these things ... were sacrificing their lives merely in order that the petrol combine should make another penny a gallon.[44]

That reaction seems excessive; the cartoon could just as easily be interpreted as a reminder to petrol users that the seamen who brought it to Britain sometimes had to pay a far higher price than an extra penny. Other newspapers made the same point in a different way. The *Daily Express* printed an official photograph of a blazing tanker above reports of the successful prosecution of two men from Coventry for obtaining additional petrol to which they were not entitled.[45] But long after the details of ministerial indignation and newspaper stories had been forgotten, the image drawn by Zec lived on in people's minds whenever they saw the words 'merchant seaman'.

It would be a mistake to suppose that after 30 September 1941 lifeboats on all British merchant ships carried identical supplies. The Ministry succeeded in arranging for the new rations to be manufactured in sufficient quantities, but distribution to ports abroad was uneven, and as late as the middle of 1942 survivors from ships such as the *Cape of Good Hope* and *Willimantic* could still find themselves adrift in boats which lacked the concentrated foods. Other ships which had received the new foods simply put them in the boats alongside the old rations, so they were quite generously victualled until the old stocks deteriorated.

Shipowners or individual ship's officers might add their own supplementary rations with things like boiled sweets or chewing gum; and Lawrence Holt set an example which deserved to be more widely followed when he took the advice of the second steward of the *Calchas* and the second officer of the *Macon* and began placing prunes, raisins and peanuts in the lifeboats of his companies' ships.[46] These additional items received glowing endorsements from survivors. When a ship took some time to sink, stewards might be able to put extra food into the boats, and after a sinking some boats were able to boost their food and water supplies by salvaging stocks from surplus rafts and damaged boats.

Occasionally food might also be recovered from among the floating debris, and some survivors were lucky enough to catch seabirds and fish, or gather edible creatures from floating seaweed. Given that an assortment of fish hooks and some line involved trifling expense and took up little space, it is surprising that many lifeboats did not carry them as standard equipment. This was often commented on adversely in survivors' reports, which sometimes gave details of ingenious improvisations of hooks or harpoons. In October 1942 the Chamber of Shipping made an arrangement with its members for placing fishing tackle in boats and rafts,[47] but even in 1944 survivors from ships such as the *Fort La Maune* and *British Chivalry* were still complaining about the absence of hooks and lines.[48] Of course, that does not necessarily mean that they had never been supplied: they could have been mislaid or lain hidden in some corner of the boat, or they might have been stolen.

The new lifeboat rations received very mixed reports from the men who had to depend on them for their lives. From some they received an unqualified endorsement; the third officer of the *Thursobank* spoke of the 'excellence of the new concentrated food, which sustained us very well during the time we were in the boat',[49] while the chief officer of the *Empire Arnold* reported that 'no one complained about the food, and everybody felt well fed'.[50] Others were far from complimentary. The master of the *Peisander* was as blistering in his comments on the provisions as he had been about the lifeboat radio:

> The biscuits were as hard as bell metal and after three or four days of trying to chew them with my false teeth, my gums became so tender, that I finally had to pound them into powder before I could masticate them at all ... When I eventually arrived home I gave one of them to my Scottie dog, who promptly took it away and buried it! The pemmican tasted somewhat like Stockholm tar and sawdust and I found that my throat contracted and simply refused to swallow it.[51]

The master of the *Stanbank* described pemmican spread on biscuits as 'very unpalatable',[52] yet the third officer of the *Sylvia de Larrinaga* thought it 'very palatable'.[53]

Pemmican was the most common target for criticism, mainly for provoking thirst and having an unpleasant taste, but it also received a few positive reports:

The pemmican made several men sick when first issued and they refused to eat any more of it.[54] (*Earlston*)

The pemmican has a very unpleasant taste but I see no reason why anyone who is hungry could not eat it. The coolies ate it, but no one asked for more.[55] (*Weirbank*)

The men enjoyed the pemmican.[56] (*Empire Arnold*)

The coloured men liked the pemmican a great deal more than the Europeans did.[57] (*Glendene*)

The pemmican was not liked by anyone, but after telling them that it was good for them they all ate it.[58] (*Ross*)

We also had some tins of sausages in the boats which the lascars would not touch – they even refused to eat the pemmican, fearing it might contain pork.[59] (*Teesbank*)

In some cases, when survivors had been supplied with American pemmican or given German pemmican by U-boats, the foreign versions were preferred to the standard British issue. American pemmican, with a considerable fruit and nut content, was said to taste better and be easier to swallow. Some survivors claimed that the British version was improved by mixing with a little seawater.

The range of these comments shows what a difficult task the Ministry of War Transport faced in deciding how lifeboats should be victualled and how to respond to survivors' experiences. Subjective judgements were influenced not only by the qualities of the food itself but by such factors as individual tastes, cultural and religious background, temperature, seasickness, size of water ration, length of voyage, morale and leadership. In any case, many reports spoke of a loss of appetite after a few days, which meant that survivors usually stopped feeling hungry. Milk tablets and chocolate generally received more favourable reports than pemmican, but they also had their critics for being thirst-inducing or sticking in the throat or making men feel sick.

The great majority of reports offer no qualitative judgement on the food provided. Most senior survivors were realistic enough to accept that they could not expect to eat well in a lifeboat, while after being rescued they were probably so grateful for having survived at all that an analytical appraisal of food quality would have been far from their minds. Possibly interviews with fo'c'sle hands would have obtained a more forthright appraisal: some of them had honed their critical skills in the hard-lying tramp steamers of the inter-war years when many shipping companies were widely known by nicknames incorporating words like 'hungry' and 'starvation'.

The Medical Research Council's post-war study, based on a small sample of comments, found sixteen claiming to have liked chocolate and four to have disliked it. Condensed milk also had a favourable rating of four to one. With milk tablets the picture was more ambivalent, six liking and eight disliking them. Only five liked pemmican, while nineteen reported unfavourably, and biscuits received only one favourable mention to seven against. All the figures are simply raw scores of the number of times each food received a comment which could be classified in this way; they are not percentages. It is, perhaps, indicative of variations in comment-provoking potential that of eighty-nine mentions of biscuits only eight offered an opinion, while sixty-eight mentions of pemmican produced twenty-four opinions.[60] The same study calculated that, excluding cases where survivors had no food whatsoever, 'men adrift in boats and rafts were able to obtain, on the average, only about 300 to 500 calories a day. Nevertheless many men survived for long periods on this amount of food, even at relatively low temperatures.'[61]

The authorities ashore and the men at sea were all agreed that a supply of fresh water was the overriding requirement for survival. Survivors' reports contained graphic descriptions of swollen tongues, cracked lips, inability to swallow food and other symptoms of dehydration which soon began to sap the energy and the will of men cast adrift for longer than a day or two. After a time thirst could threaten both discipline and sanity itself, with the added torment of being surrounded by seawater which all expert opinion advised should not be drunk.

After the *Athelknight* had been sunk by *U–172* on 27 May 1942 in mid-Atlantic, the second officer confronted this problem among the men in his lifeboat. 'Several men had been drinking salt water during the nights, when I was asleep, but they never attempted to do so during the day, and when I taxed them with doing so they said they were only gargling and rinsing out their mouths; I think the men who drank the sea water suffered most, and were definitely the most seriously sick men when they reached hospital.' The chief officer, in command of a different lifeboat, noticed a puzzling phenomenon. 'The carpenter, a Russian, often used to drink salt water and said it had no effect on him, as he drank salt water regularly when on board ship, and was used to it, but I was afraid his example might have a bad effect on the other men and tried to stop him.'[62]

The master of the *California Star*, sunk by *U–515* on 4 March 1943, reported: 'There were four men who refused to do anything. They would not bail or look-out, and even stole the fresh water from the forward tank. I threatened to stop their rations, and they then began drinking salt water. One of the crew died [after] drinking considerable quantities of salt water.' [63]

Of his experiences during a fifty-day raft voyage in 1943, the carpenter of the *Lulworth Hill* commented:

> Our greatest problem was water, all of us suffered from intense thirst, and after a while I noticed some of the survivors drinking salt water … As they drank more and more, they rapidly became delirious, imagining they could see rivers of water and snow. One man became very troublesome, and had to be forcibly held down until he became too exhausted to struggle any more … Some died from drinking salt water, others from exhaustion, and I think in many cases the men gave up hope, and lost the urge to struggle on for their lives.[64]

Statistics on matters of this kind have to be treated with considerable caution, since few lifeboats or rafts contained survivors with medical qualifications. There is no reliable way of distinguishing between deaths caused by thirst and deaths from other causes, and there is no way of quantifying the amount of liquid some survivors were able to obtain from rainfall or raw fish. An examination of lifeboat and raft voyages during 1940–44 where there was clear information about duration, water ration, number of survivors at risk and number of deaths from all causes indicates that a ration of four ounces per man per day may have been a critical level:[65]

Voyage	Daily ration under 4 oz. water			Daily ration over 4 oz. water		
(Days)	At risk	Died	%	At risk	Died	%
3–6	507	142	28	497	7	1
6 15	431	80	19	867	73	8
15–32	167	53	32	305	22	7
32+	78	70	90	118	2	2

In January 1942, the Royal Navy's Director-General of Medical Services, Surgeon Rear-Admiral Sheldon Dudley, produced a paper outlining some very preliminary thoughts of the Medical Research Council's Committee on the Care of Shipwrecked Personnel, of which he was chairman. The committee consisted of eminent RN, RAF and civilian doctors. Dudley asserted that water was the only ration that really mattered on physiological grounds, although some food might be needed for psychological reasons. For physiological efficiency men needed two pints of water each day in temperate climates, and even more in the tropics. He warned: 'Progressive deterioration is inevitable below the physiological minimum.' He speculated that it might eventually become necessary to carry more water, even if it meant reducing the number of survivors a boat or raft could accommodate. Meanwhile, his committee was examining the possibilities of reducing water loss through the lungs and skin, and producing drinkable water from seawater by means of stills or chemicals.[66]

In practice, the actual food and water rations doled out to survivors in boats and rafts depended on a number of unpredictable variables. Obviously, the supplies provided had to be calculated on the number of occupants for whom the lifecraft was certified, but their adequacy would be determined by whether, as sometimes happened, the craft was overcrowded by 50 per cent or occupied to a mere fraction of its capacity. Another important factor was whether supplies had been boosted from redundant and damaged lifecraft, or lost during launching when traditional water-storage breakers (small wooden casks) were prone to being lost overboard or having their bungs knocked out. A third variable was the estimated length of time survivors were likely to have to spend in their lifecraft. It might well be that, when survivors reached safety, only 23 per cent of the boats and 10 per cent of the rafts had needed to spend longer than a week adrift,[67] but the prudent policy was to base rations on the worst-case assumption that the lifecraft would have to reach land unaided.

A calculation of that kind had to begin with the position of the sinking. That would usually be known with reasonable accuracy by the master and his deck officers, and possibly by apprentices or cadets if they had been keeping bridge watches. Sometimes it was provided, or at least confirmed, by surfaced German or Italian U-boats. Ministry of War Transport advice was to keep all members of the crew informed by posting regularly updated notices or placing the information in lifeboats. A destination then had to be selected, but that could not be simply a matter of choosing the nearest point of land: the direction of prevailing winds and ocean currents (often with significant seasonal variations), the location of the most frequented shipping routes, the desirability of avoiding dangerous or enemy-occupied coastlines, and the chances of missing a tiny island such as Bermuda or Ascension all had to be taken into account. Given all the uncertainties, and the differences in how fully informed people were on these issues, it is easy to see why they could lead to sharp disagreements between officers in charge of different boats or men in the same boat. Calculations had to be made about the distance to be covered, how fast the boat could be expected to sail and what safety margin to allow, before the food and water rations could be determined.

A suitable chart setting out the key items of information was obviously essential to enable the navigational problems to be considered, and yet for more than two and a half years of war the practice in many ships was to rely on transferring charts from the chartroom into the boats just before abandoning ship, even at the risk of either not having enough time or losing them in the confusion of getting the boats away. In the absence of a chart, a page torn from a school atlas or a map in a diary might suffice, or, as in the case of the *Lapwing*, torpedoed southwest of Ireland on 26 September 1941, a chart might have to be constructed from whatever could be remembered of the longitude and latitude of a few key landmarks like Ushant, the Smalls and Cape Clear.[68]

It seems extraordinary that a chart drawn in that way enabled the boat from the *Lapwing* to be navigated to Ireland in a voyage lasting fifteen days, and even more extraordinary that suitable charts had not been made universally available in lifeboats at a much earlier date. They could have been produced quite cheaply and would have taken up very little space.

Some British and Allied merchant ships managed to acquire from the Hydrographic Office of the US Navy very detailed weather charts of the oceans. Before the war, these charts had been provided free of charge to vessels which supplied meteorological information but, even if they had to be bought, the purchase price of ten cents each meant that the expense of placing them in lifeboats and rafts was minimal. Despite the admonition, printed in red, 'This chart should not be used for navigational purposes', they were perfectly adequate for emergency use, and they continued to be carried in the lifeboats of some merchant ships to the end of the war.

In the interests of its members, the Navigators' and Engineer Officers' Union collaborated with two nautical instrument makers and chart agents – Kelvin, Bottomley and Bird, and Henry Hughes – to produce a modified version of the American chart of the North Atlantic. This showed not only the coasts, lines of longitude and latitude, and ocean currents, but also details of wind strength, direction and frequency for each five degree section. The chart was printed in waterproof ink on waterproof linen, and in March 1942 it was offered free to members of the union. Charts of the South Atlantic and Indian Ocean were announced the following month.[69] The South Atlantic chart was 'found very useful indeed', in navigating a lifeboat from the *Trevilley* some 415 miles in seven and a half days after she had been torpedoed on 12 September 1942.[70]

At the end of October 1942 a special packet of Admiralty charts was published, complete with protractor and squared paper, for use in navigating lifeboats, and after seeing a set the London correspondent of the *Manchester Guardian* felt so impressed (and optimistic) that he hastened to assure his readers that 'the full instructions on the back for using them make it possible for any intelligent non-skilled passenger to undertake navigation of the boat'.[71]

In addition to a chart, reasonably accurate navigation required a number of other items. Each boat was provided with a magnetic compass, but it was assumed that other equipment, such as chronometer, sextants and copies of the nautical almanac and nautical tables, would be transferred into lifeboats when the time came to abandon ship, since they were too valuable to be stowed permanently in the boats. Even if these things were safely got away from the sinking ship, they would remain inaccessible to many survivors if, as happened more often than not, boats became separated from one another. Comments by survivors from ships sunk in 1941 and 1942 show some of the difficulties.

A rough sextant had been fashioned, and was tested using Polaris ... It was realised, however, that this was very approximate, being sixty miles either way, and really very unsatisfactory.[72] (*Memnon*)

We checked the compass morning and night by the rising and setting of the sun.[73] (*Calchas*)

The [compass] error was not constant, so I decided to take little notice of it, and steer by the sun and stars.[74] (*Mattawin*)

My compass had been badly knocked about, so I steered mainly by the pole star. I made a measure out of two pieces of wood in the form of a pair of dividers, and morning and evening I measured the angle of the pole star. This worked so well that I was only three miles out of my reckoning when picked up [after seven days adrift].[75] (*Empire Arnold*)

After one month of sailing, beating, drifting in gales and calms, etc., without instruments save watch and compass, my reckoning may be far from accurate.[76] [When picked up, at the end of forty-one days, he found he was 830 miles from the position he had calculated.] (*Medon*)

In 1943, as a further service to its members, the Navigators' and Engineer Officers' Union prepared tables of the sun's declination and the right ascension and declination of the principal stars up to the end of 1945. They were printed as a four-page waterproof booklet and issued free to members of the unions which had combined to form the Merchant Navy Officers' Federation. They also provided a diagram for converting the altitude of the Pole Star into an approximate latitude. Knowing the problems of boat navigation without a sextant, the Federation endorsed a miniature sextant, only one inch deep by four and a half inches in diameter and accurate to within five minutes of arc, which they urged the Ministry of War Transport to supply to ships, but this idea was never adopted.[77]

Success on long boat voyages did not depend solely on skilful navigation: the skills of boat handling were also of crucial importance. Half a century later, when lone yachtsmen sail around the world using satellite navigation, self-steering gear and self-reefing nylon sails, it may be difficult to appreciate just how difficult it was to sail a wartime lifeboat. The canvas lugsail was heavy to hoist or reef; it took a strong wind from well abaft the beam to achieve a speed of five or six knots (two or three being more usual), a motorboat's propeller became a useless drag after the fuel was used up, and a side-wind might cause the boat to make more leeway than headway. A direct course towards a chosen destination would often prove impossible. Then those in command had to settle for whatever course, reasonably close to the one required, the boat would lie, and hope to adjust the course in the opposite direction later.

The trickiest decision of all for those in command was recognising when wind and sea conditions in which the boat was bowling along at an exhilarating speed were approaching the point where the boat might be driven under, broach to or have her sails and mast carry away. Then the sails would have to be lowered, the boat turned across the weather to face into the wind and sea, and a canvas drogue called a sea anchor streamed on the end of a rope to steady the boat. The oars would be needed to ensure that the boat met each succeeding sea bow-on. A crew's ability to carry out that kind of manoeuvre, or to lay the boat on the opposite tack, might be expected to improve slightly in the first two or three days of a voyage, as they became more familiar with boat work, but thereafter the effects of hunger, thirst, exposure, ailments, injuries, exhaustion and depression would tend to produce a marked and dangerous deterioration in performance.

The shortage of really experienced and competent boat handlers featured regularly in reports made by survivors, and it is clear that

those few who did know what was required had to shoulder a very
onerous work load during long and arduous boat voyages.

> For the first three days ... I was doing all the sailing, after which time
> I trained some of the others to assist me.[78] (*Empire Wave*)

> It was some time before we could get the mast secured and the jib-sail
> set as none of the men, except myself, knew how to handle a boat, [and]
> the only two able seamen had but three months sea experience.[79] (*Induna*)

> Able Seaman Blake Bremer ... is a trawler man and a very handy man
> in small boats, and it was due to his help and valuable assistance and
> devotion to duty that everything went so well in the boats during the
> nine and a half days.[80] (*Stanbank*)

> I steered at the tiller for the first forty-eight hours at one stretch, but
> found the strain on my eyes too much so one or two of the men took
> a turn occasionally.[81] (*Empire Arnold*)

The many reports of this kind revealed a very serious skill deficit
which amply justified a complaint from Vice-Admiral E. A. Taylor MP:
'The ignorance of the men is appalling, and that applies to some of
the officers too',[82] but war-time training could not make this good
because the real art of boat-handling came from hands-on experience
rather than text-books or instruction. It was fortunate for their shipmates if pure chance placed them in a boat with someone like the
Earlston's Newfoundland fisherman, the *Peterton*'s chief engineer keen
on yachting, the *Aldington Court*'s Latvian bosun who was an expert
boatman, the *Ripley*'s West Indian able seaman who had spent most of
his life in small boats, or the *Larchbank*'s Bengali greaser who was
familiar with river craft.

All lifeboat voyages involved suffering and tested the endurance of
survivors, but the nature of that suffering and endurance varied considerably with the latitude and time of year. For survivors adrift in the
North Atlantic, and even more markedly in the Arctic Ocean, the great
enemy was the cold. It is impossible to read the survivors' reports of
lifeboat voyages in those seas without marvelling at their courage and
determination. The second officer of the *Induna*, a straggler from
convoy PQ13 to North Russia, described how, after she was sunk on
30 March 1942, seven of his men died during their first night in the
boat, and others followed on subsequent days.

> It was bitterly cold, everyone suffered from frost bite in their hands and
> feet, but not in their faces ... The seas were continually breaking over

the sides of the boat. My feet were wet all the time ... The food was quite good, but the water was frozen into a solid block. We sucked the ice to moisten our mouths, having to burst the breakers to get at the ice ... We rowed in spells to keep ourselves warm, but our hands were so numb that it was all we could do to hang on to the oars.[83]

An apprentice who took charge of a lifeboat containing thirty-three survivors after the *Shillong* had been torpedoed in the North Atlantic on 4 April 1943 gave a touching account of the conditions:

We were all suffering agonies from the bitter cold, our feet and hands soon became numbed and lifeless, and everybody suffered with cramp in the stomach. At times our outer garments were frozen stiff, and there was a film of ice over everything ... We massaged our faces, hands and feet with the massage oil, but this did not seem very beneficial ... A number of the men died each day from exposure; all the natives except three died during the first three days.[84]

After eight days adrift, only seven men survived to be picked up by the rescue ship *Zamalek*, and six of the seven survivors had to undergo amputations after they reached hospital in Halifax, Nova Scotia.

Experiences such as these may be contrasted with the problems of survivors whose ships were sunk in the tropics. After a seven-day, 480-mile lifeboat voyage when the *Empire Arnold* was torpedoed, her chief officer reported:

Until 9 August, the weather was hot, and we felt the sun rather badly, as we were very crowded in the boat and were all badly burned. I used the tannic acid from the first aid case for the bad burns, but this did not help very much. The men took turns holding each others' ankles so that they could take dips in the sea to keep cool, but the salt water combined with the sun only made it worse.[85]

Of her twenty-seven-day voyage during September and October 1942 in one of the lifeboats from the *Laconia*, Doris Hawkins wrote:

We became thinner daily, and we were hollow-eyed ... All our sore areas began to discharge pus after a few days, and continued to discharge all the time. Many of us had salt-water sores, septic fingers and toes, and boils. I had lost my glasses, and the light was very strong, and my eyes became sore and discharged pus fairly freely from the end of the first week ... Daily we saw our companions growing weaker, [and] saw that they had not long to live ... One wondered how long one could remain sane ... Our tongues became hard and dry and our lips swollen and cracked ... No one who has not sat cramped in a small boat, with the sun beating mercilessly day after day, and tormented by thirst, can ever imagine the strain and tension through which these men went.[86]

Only sixteen, of the boat's original sixty-eight occupants, were still alive when it was finally beached in Liberia.

No matter how the survivors' reports might be analysed, and no matter how much they sometimes conflicted with one another in certain points of detail, the one issue on which there could be no difference of opinion was the importance of drinking water. The possibility of producing drinking water from seawater, either by stills or by chemical means, had been mentioned in Surgeon Rear-Admiral (later Vice-Admiral Sir) Sheldon Dudley's preliminary paper of 22 January 1942,[87] when, as chairman, he outlined the thinking of the Medical Research Council's Committee on the Care of Shipwrecked Personnel. The potential of distillation had been impressively demonstrated in a lifeboat from the *Macon*, torpedoed 460 miles west of Madeira on 24 July 1941. After survivors had passed a thirsty week in the lifeboat, the carpenter suggested trying to make a still, and some experimentation led to the construction of an apparatus from a one-gallon oil drum, a piece of tourniquet tubing out of the first aid kit and a bucket in which a small fire could be lit. On 1 August they managed to produce two gallons of drinkable water, but had to suspend operations because too much pressure caused the apparatus to blow up and the smoke from the fire became unbearable following a wind-shift. Next day, with a new can, they produced a further gallon.[88] In his report to the owners, the second officer recommended that boats ought to carry a primus stove, an empty can and a length of rubber tubing to make a still.

It took two years after that success with home-made apparatus, and eighteen months after Dudley's committee began looking into the merits of distillation, before the Ministry of War Transport could take a firm decision in favour of placing stills in all lifeboats. Since that was the period of heaviest merchant ship losses, it seems fair to conclude that merchant seamen were dying of thirst while apparatus which might have saved them was being developed with, apparently, no real sense of urgency. Interested Members of Parliament were fobbed off with anodyne phrases. On 24 June 1942, Noel-Baker told William Dobbie, the Labour MP for Rotherham, that the work on stills was 'being actively pursued';[89] Sir Robert Rankin, the Conservative MP for Liverpool Kirkdale, was assured on 14 October that Noel-Baker was hoping to have 'early information' about tests on experimental stills.[90]

The responsibility for the delay was widely shared. Civil servants, sailors and scientists threw themselves into detailed research and experiments to find the perfect lifeboat still, when men desperate for a few mouthfuls of water would gladly have swapped the prospect of future perfection for any gimcrack, cobbled-together device which was just 'good enough' to see them through the next day or two. There was also an element of inter-departmental and commercial rivalry. Stills, such as the 'Mulhearn', were being developed commercially and were being demonstrated in Liverpool in the spring of 1942.[91] The Ministry of War Transport developed a still called the 'Minimax' in association with a commercial manufacturer; the Admiralty favoured its own design, the 'MWD' invented by Lieutenant J. H. G. Goodfellow RNVR; and the Chemical Research Laboratory produced yet another version, named the 'Dirshel', for the Department of Scientific and Industrial Research. The authorities wrangled over whether the stills should be fuelled by paraffin, special solid fuel blocks, or driftwood and kapok from life-jackets – or burn just anything that came to hand. Disputes arose over claimed outputs varying between five and a half to eight pints of drinking water per hour: a rate produced using 'dry pitch pine' was unlikely to be replicated in a lifeboat![92]

In late 1942 and early 1943 some shipping companies which were concerned about the safety of their crews lost patience with the wrangling and began to install stills acquired commercially, some 200 to 250 British ships being equipped in this way. But, in the absence of official guidance, other companies hesitated to provide stills in case, as soon as they had incurred the expense, the Ministry of War Transport should reject the model they had adopted and insist on some other type, and some marine superintendents were reluctant to recommend stills for the same reason.[93] Eventually, in April 1943, the Ministry of War Transport officially approved the 'Minimax' and placed an order for five thousand.[94] An exhibition of the various types of still was staged on board HMS *Chrysanthemum* in London, and the ability of the still to make hot drinks and dry wet clothes was publicised as a bonus.[95] No wonder the journal of the National Union of Seamen headlined its report 'A FRESH WATER STILL AT LAST'.[96] At the same time a compact rain catcher made of white cambric, with its own tube to transfer rainwater to a lifeboat's tanks, was also introduced, somewhat belatedly, so that survivors would no longer be reduced to catching rain in the sail, with the attendant problems of pollution from salt spray and the revolting red dye used on the sails.

Even then, the various types of still were subjected to further testing at sea in lifeboats of the Outward Bound Sea School at Aberdovey. This organisation had been founded by Lawrence Holt and others to improve the training of merchant seamen in lifeboat handling, and it has been claimed that the training at the school enabled many lifeboats from ships of his Blue Funnel Line to sail to safety.[97] Over a period of several weeks, seamen undergoing courses were sent off in boats into the Irish Sea where they were required to operate the various stills under different conditions and using all types of possible fuel. The tests were not completed until 6 July 1943.[98] The inevitable delays in distribution meant that the time of heaviest casualties among merchant seamen was long past before many ships received their lifeboat stills. When the *Fort La Maune*, for example, was torpedoed in the Arabian Sea on 25 January 1944 her boats had no distillers and her third officer made one 'with empty cans and the burner from one of the lamps. With this he managed to distil about one ounce of water, which, although a good effort, was not much use among twenty-one men.'[99] That was two and a half years after the *Macon*'s carpenter had shown how it could be done, and two years after Surgeon Rear-Admiral Dudley's committee had begun to examine the question. The delays could hardly be laid at their door: Dudley's paper of 12 January 1942 had promptly, clearly and unequivocally emphasised the supreme importance of providing more drinking water in boats and rafts; and decisions about the technical specifications for a suitable still hardly fell within the province of medical men.

In addition to sifting information from reports made by survivors, the Medical Research Council's Committee on the Care of Shipwrecked Personnel, through its various sub-committees, initiated or inspired a great deal of empirical research into such matters as minimum nutrition requirements and protection against exposure. The Sorby Institute in Sheffield was one of the pioneering research centres where Dr Kenneth Mellanby investigated vitamin and water requirements.[100] Human volunteers were used as guinea-pigs. Some of them were servicemen, others conscientious objectors who recognised that the humanitarian value of the experiments involved no conflict with their strongly held beliefs. The courage and endurance of the volunteers who submitted themselves to the discomforts and deprivations of these experiments made a contribution to the Battle of the Atlantic which has been largely ignored, although something of their work was revealed when Richard Wodeman, a conscientious objector who had taken part in experiments on minimum water requirements, was arrested and jailed for failing to appear before a Tribunal.[101] In all of this empirical research it was accepted that there were ethical limits to the amount of suffering and danger to which volunteers could be legitimately exposed, a limitation not recognised in Germany, where Dr Rascher used selected inmates of Ravensbruck concentration camp for experiments on hypothermia by immersing them in freezing water and then observing the body temperature at which they died or their response to different resuscitation techniques.

The work of the Medical Research Council's Committee on the Care of Shipwrecked Personnel led to a number of significant publications. In 1943 Surgeon Captain Macdonald Critchley, one of the members, published his *Shipwreck Survivors: A Medical Study*,[102] an authoritative account of the medical problems encountered by survivors. This was a technical work intended mainly for those who were professionally involved. There was, however, an obvious need to set out the committee's findings in a form which would be read by merchant seamen and other interested laymen. This was published at the beginning of 1943 under the title *A Guide to the Preservation of Life at Sea after Shipwreck*.[103] In 1956 Dr R. A. McCance, who had served on the committee during the war, was to lead the team which wrote *The Hazards of Men Lost at Sea, 1940–44*.[104]

Waterproof copies of the 1943 guide were placed in lifeboats and rafts. The writers of the guide had clearly tried to relate their professional knowledge and research findings to the practical experiences described in survivors' reports; and it is a pity that it only appeared after the period of heaviest sinkings had passed. In 1943 the average monthly loss of British merchant shipping was to be almost 127,000 tons, less than half the 1942 figure, and with a further sharp reduction to an average of 34,000 tons over the last twenty months of hostilities.[105] A monthly average of almost 384 deaths among their merchant seamen and DEMS gunners in 1943 was again less than half the 1942 figure, and over the last twenty months of hostilities the average monthly losses fell to about ninety-two merchant seamen and DEMS gunners.[106]

Even so, the guide represented an important and very welcome, if belated, advance over an earlier, and necessarily briefer, advice leaflet produced by the Technical Committee of the Chamber of Shipping. Now survivors could consult a pretty comprehensive and authoritative work of reference instead of relying on such dubious sources as nautical folklore, old wives' tales, fo'c'sle hypochondriacs or uninstructed collective wisdom. Written in lucid and succinct language, it covered in about eighteen pages such matters as routine preparations on board ship, abandoning ship, lifeboat procedures, treatment of sick and wounded, common lifeboat ailments, rescue and treatment after rescue. Just occasionally, in its anxiety to cover everything and be intelligible to all, it offers some blindingly obvious advice, such as, if swimming through oil, 'keep your head and eyes high and your mouth closed',[107] or, when sharks are present, 'it is advisable to keep your hands and feet inside the boat'.[108] But in a 'poor man's guide' of this type it was probably wise to err on the side of underestimating the intelligence of possible readers.

The guide advised seamen to sleep fully clothed in danger areas so that they would not find themselves too lightly clad after abandoning ship, and they were told to memorise each day the ship's position and other navigational data that might prove useful. They were assured that most survivors could expect to be picked up within a few days and that lifeboat voyages of over three weeks were quite exceptional. 'Once a crew is safely away from the abandoned ship in a lifeboat it is three-quarters of the way to safety.'[109]

Fresh water was more important than food. While the common practice of using small quantities of seawater to wash out the mouth or soften food was acceptable, the drinking of seawater or urine was unreservedly condemned. Knowing that the great majority of survivors in boats and on rafts were picked up within a few days, the medical experts were critical of the way those in charge of boats had usually rationed drinking water at a rate of two to eight ounces per man per day in case their voyage turned out to be protracted. 'It is obviously foolish, if not indeed dangerous, to ration water on, say, a sixty-day basis when the chances of being picked up in ten days are good. Quite often men are picked up in poor condition owing to low water rations, with considerable stocks of water still in the boat.'[110] The recommendation was to manage without water for twenty-four hours if possible, then issue eighteen ounces per man per day until only about twenty ounces per man remained, and at that stage impose a very sharp reduction to two ounces per day. On that basis, in a fully manned boat, the water would have been exhausted in about sixteen or seventeen days. Statistically that would certainly have covered most cases, but it was not an attractive gamble for men adrift on the high seas. Those in charge of lifeboats usually continued a much stricter rationing policy with amounts such as nine or twelve ounces daily being at the more generous end of the scale.

Survivors were warned that, since the food rations were insufficient to replace lost energy, they should not waste their strength by singing, shouting or getting excited, and certainly not by continuous rowing 'as the trivial gain in distance will be far outweighed by the early exhaustion of the crew'.[111] The guide carefully explained the best ways of using the Methedrine or Benzedrine energy tablets which had been introduced in the previous year as a means of reviving an exhausted crew when some special physical effort or alertness was required.

In view of the many survivors' reports which mention some success in supplementing their food supplies by catching fish, sea birds and molluscs or crustaceans found in floating seaweed, it is rather surprising that the medical experts offered no guidance either on catching or consuming food of this type. They did, however, seek to allay the frequently reported anxiety about the reduction in the passage of urine and absence of bowel movements, neither of which was considered to give cause for concern, and laxatives were thought to be harmful. Mercifully, the guide did not take up the suggestion of the master of the *Peisander* that each boat should be equipped with the means of administering a seawater enema.[112]

The 1943 survival guide placed great emphasis on the importance of leadership in organising survivors and sustaining their morale. For that, it insisted, 'strict discipline must be maintained and if necessary vigorously enforced'.[113] It is, of course, easy to see why lifeboats needed to be run in an orderly fashion, but one wonders whether a committee dominated by officers of the Royal Navy and Royal Air Force really appreciated that discipline in the Merchant Navy was often very different from that in their own services. Although most of the reports made by surviving officers are couched in terms of authoritarian decision-making, there were some who clearly adopted a more democratic approach by encouraging, for example, those who had a knowledge of navigation to discuss the best course to steer, while the setting or changing of food and water rations was sometimes put to a vote.

No guidance was offered on one very thorny aspect of discipline – the difficulties which could be created, especially on long boat voyages, when significant numbers of seamen from different religious, linguistic and cultural backgrounds were present. In such circumstances, European survivors were often suspicious, resentful and critical of men from other races; but they never seemed quite sure whether the problems stemmed from idleness, lack of stamina, oriental fatalism or disaffection. The following comments were fairly typical:

> The Arabs did not attempt to help, but simply lay in the bottom of the boat like 'dead men', until meal times came, when they soon came to life.[114] (*Empire Wave*, 1941)

[In No. 5 boat,] 'the Chinese ... wanted to take charge, but after being threatened with an axe and the biscuit keg key we managed to restore some kind of order. Our position was not too secure.[115] [In two other boats there was also trouble, but in No. 8 boat the Chinese behaved well.] All the criticism was by people who were not competent to judge them ... The average Chinese mind is that of a child, and they must be led not driven. It is only to be expected that they will ask for more water etc., and shouting at them will not improve matters.[116] (*Calchas*, 1941)

I had trouble with the Chinese ratings, who seemed to be under the impression that the white men were going to claim all the food, and they announced their intention of throwing overboard all the white men in the boat. The situation became dangerous for a time; although the Chinese did not appear to have arms concealed anywhere we were considerably outnumbered. However, with diplomacy I managed to restore order, although there remained an undercurrent of dissatisfaction.[117] (*Thursobank*, 1942)

I called for everyone who could to take the oars ... but still these Arab firemen refused to help. I punished them by reducing their water ration, a terrible punishment for thirsty men after nearly nine days in a boat.[118] (*Bolton Castle*, 1942)

Most of the survivors in the boat were natives, and were absolutely useless, so I put them all in the bow leaving them more or less to themselves.[119] (*Shillong*, 1943)

There may well have been a tendency to criticise these Arab, Chinese or Indian seamen as a scapegoat group where similar unco-operative behaviour by British seamen would have been reported as a failure by particular individuals, if it were not simply shrugged off as a typical bit of traditional grumbling or looked on sympathetically as only to be expected from men at the limit of endurance. Many of the difficulties were probably exacerbated by language barriers, and others by the inability of some seamen from warmer countries to operate in the extremely cold and wet conditions experienced by, for example, the boats from the *Empire Wave*, *Bolton Castle* and *Shillong*. By way of contrast, some reports praised the behaviour of foreign seamen as a group, especially when they were given a good lead by their own petty officers, and there was sometimes warm praise for individuals. The chief officer of the *Clan MacWhirter*, for instance, reported that his lascars behaved extremely well, and he singled out the serang (bosun), two tindals (bosun's mates) and a lascar who kept strict discipline and obeyed orders unquestioningly.[120] The master of the *Manaar* reported that his lascars quickly recovered from their first fright and behaved very well thereafter,[121] while the chief engineer of the *Larchbank*, after a nineteen-day lifeboat voyage in the Indian Ocean, commented with great satisfaction that his crew had 'behaved extremely well throughout the long, trying ordeal, and actually made up a very happy party. The Asiatics recognised me as being in charge, and they all did as they were ordered.'[122]

In their reports to the Admiralty, senior survivors usually claimed that European seamen and gunners behaved well in the lifeboats, although there were also many references to such aspects of low morale as boredom, lethargy, despair, grumbling, and minor bickering brought about by physical discomfort. It seems likely that they tended to minimise the incidence of these features out of respect for shipmates with whom they had shared a terrible ordeal, and in some cases they may also have feared that any emphasis on problems of that kind would be seen as reflecting badly on their own powers of leadership. One suspects that a similar reticence was applied when speaking of techniques for sustaining morale. Cigarettes and alcohol were sometimes mentioned as having a calming or comforting effect, and a small increase in the food or water ration was sometimes given as a reward for some extra exertion like rowing or steering in bad weather. Occasionally survivors were uplifted by the influence of one of their number. Someone like Gunner Wilkinson of the *California Star* would lead prayers and talk to the men to keep up morale,[123] and the chief officer of the *Llanashe* praised the role of Hodder, the gunlayer, during an eleven-day raft voyage: 'This man had no intention of dying and he was always cracking jokes in an endeavour to cheer the others up.'[124] An engineer from the *Nebraska*, having already survived three previous sinkings in two years, helped to keep people cheerful by reciting humorous verses.[125]

In favourable weather conditions, there were various activities which could help to alleviate boredom and depression. The lifeboats of the *Medon*, for example, offered quite a range of activities. The third officer in No. 4 boat favoured an evening sing song, with a harmonised version of the 'Volga Boatman' instead of the actual rowing; the second officer organised a draughts tournament after a suitable board had been cut on one of the side benches of No. 3 boat; and the chief officer in No. 2 boat led physical exercises and deep breathing, which benefited the Europeans and raised amused smiles among the Chinese who did not join in. This last boat also held story-telling competitions and word games, and a pack of playing cards was made out of scraps of stiff paper in which biscuits had been packed.[126]

Those in charge of boats usually led by example in such matters as massaging feet, eating pemmican, taking seawater baths or avoiding sunbathing. Morale was helped if they arranged proper rotas for men to take turns sleeping in the most comfortable or sheltered spots in the boat. Ensuring sympathetic attention for sick or wounded men was also important. Fairness in allocating duties and issuing rations was absolutely essential. Even when they did not feel like it, those in charge needed to maintain an air of competence and confidence. This could take the form of not revealing the low level of drinking water that remained, or being over-optimistic about the distance which still had to be covered to reach safety, but that was a risky policy because, if the true state of affairs became known, the disappointment would be all the harder for men to bear and faith would not be restored easily.

The master of the *Celtic Star* set great store by 'pep talks' to keep his men informed. When his ship was sunk about 375 miles southwest of Freetown on 29 March 1943, he assured the survivors that there was no need to worry as they had enough supplies to last five weeks, and he cheerfully forecast that, if there was no wind at all, they would still be able to row ashore in eight days (an optimistic prediction with the risk of the prevailing currents sweeping the boats into the Gulf of Guinea). When they were lucky enough to be picked up after only two days he reminded them that they had had an easy time, urged them not to grumble or complain, and exhorted them 'to uphold the honour of the Merchant Navy', which evoked cheers and applause.[127]

Leadership in trying circumstances is always a difficult art and can never be reduced to a rigid formula. The nature of the problems to be faced, how long the ordeal was likely to last, the personalities involved, and previous relationships could all vary so much that an approach that produced cheers for one leader might easily produce jeers and catcalls – or even violence – in different circumstances. By whatever techniques the results were obtained, the fact that so many boatloads of survivors ultimately reached safety is eloquent testimony to the professional competence and leadership of those in charge.

9

Safe at Last

On 20 May 1942 the British cargo ship *Baron Semple* sighted two lifeboats some 210 miles southeast of Nantucket Island, USA. The boats were rowing hard to intercept the ship, and they were flying large yellow flags and burning red flares to attract her attention. They came from the Blue Funnel liner *Peisander*, torpedoed three days earlier in a position one hundred miles further to the southeast. In the best tradition of the sea, the master of the *Baron Semple* stopped and called one of the boats alongside so that the survivors could be plucked to safety before those in the other boat were rescued.

The second officer of the *Peisander* described what followed: 'On hearing that the *Baron Semple* was bound for South Africa I enquired of the crew if they wanted to be transferred. They unanimously agreed to stay with me. The master of the *Baron Semple* seemed surprised at my decision.'[1] The survivors in the second boat also declined to be rescued, so after topping up the boats' water supplies, and giving the men some hot tea, magazines and blankets, the rather bemused master of the *Baron Semple* got under way again and continued his voyage. The two lifeboats took four more days to reach Nantucket, where they were picked up by the coastguard and reunited with survivors from a third boat, commanded by the master of the *Peisander*, which had become separated from the others before the chance of rescue was so astonishingly declined. The master, for his part, had made every effort to get his boat into the path of another possible rescuer on 21 May, but had seen his hopes frustrated when the ship fled, broadcasting a U-boat warning after, presumably, mistaking the lifeboat in poor visibility for a submarine's conning tower. The cruel disappointment felt at the time was amply compensated when the survivors learned after landing that their potential rescuer, the American *Plow City*, had been herself torpedoed later that same day.[2]

The (possibly tongue-in-cheek) explanation offered by the master of the *Peisander* for his crew's decision not to board the *Baron Semple* was that they must have decided 'that it would be much more unpleasant being landed in South Africa than having an adventure in a lifeboat in the open sea with the hope of ultimately landing on the American Coast'.[3] Perhaps they thought that they had a good chance of meeting a ship that would whisk them quickly to somewhere like New York or Boston; perhaps they did not wish to risk being carried back through the area where their own ship had been sunk or through the dangerous waters between West Africa and Brazil.

Most survivors, however, would unhesitatingly have swapped the privations of a lifeboat voyage for the, perhaps illusory, safety and relative comfort of the *Baron Semple*, and thanked their lucky stars for the opportunity, even if she did belong to a company known throughout the Merchant Navy as 'Hungry Hogarths'. People who had spent day after day fruitlessly scanning the empty horizon for a rescue ship that never appeared or vainly searching the empty skies for non-existent reconnaissance aircraft would have found the decision of the *Peisander*'s crew utterly incredible, although one or two senior officers whose boats were picked up close to land sometimes expressed regret at being robbed of the professional satisfaction of reaching safety entirely by their own efforts.

The need to maintain a lookout for possible rescuers could be extremely wearing on the nerves. Men with rather pessimistic tempera-ments quickly became depressed when no rescuers appeared; optimists could irritate their shipmates each morning with their irrational fore-casts that something would be sighted that day; those who were exhausted or hysterical might identify a distant albatross as an aircraft, any far-off bit of floating timber as a ship, and some thin bank of cloud on the horizon as smoke or land. The deranged might leap overboard to swim or walk to a non-existent rescue ship. Even the most level-headed men could be misled by mirages, which can occur at sea as in the desert. These false reports of sightings invariably produced a roller-coaster effect on the emotions as rising hope turned into plunging despair.

Even when a real ship or aircraft was sighted, survivors often suffered the heartbreak of seeing it disappear without giving any indication of having spotted the boat or raft. Desperate men were naturally inclined to be bitterly critical of what looked to them like, at best, failure of lookouts to stay alert or, at worst, a callous and cowardly refusal to come to their assistance. This last interpretation was particularly common where a possible rescuer seemed to be heading directly towards them and then turned sharply away, although a more charitable explanation might well have been that the alteration of course arose simply from the timing of a particular zig-zag pattern or, with aircraft, a box search pattern. Survivors found it hard to accept that a ship or aircraft which they could see quite clearly, perhaps silhouetted against a light sky, might not be able to see a small boat or raft as it appeared and disappeared amid the waves and swell against the constantly changing disruptive visual pattern of the sea.

Because of this difficulty, survivors needed to keep a good lookout so that they could take some positive action to attract attention to their plight, and they needed to exercise considerable patience in not exhausting their strength and resources at an unrealistic distance from possible rescuers. At the beginning of the war, it was thought that the main problem was likely to be attracting attention at night. Pre-war regulations had required all lifeboats to carry an oil lamp, a tin containing a dozen self-igniting red flares and suitable matches.[4] An electric signalling torch was added at the beginning of 1940.[5] In daylight, presumably, the traditional shirt tied to a boathook was still available or, like the survivors from the *Truro* in 1939, vain attempts could be made to attract the attention of an aircraft five or six miles away by waving blankets.[6]

In October 1940 the Flag Officer, Belfast, wrote to the Commander-in-Chief, Western Approaches, concerning survivors' accounts which mentioned that even aircraft close to the boats had failed to spot them. He also expressed the view that the red flares carried in lifeboats were not an effective means of attracting attention in daylight. He had taken the matter up with the Royal Air Force in Northern Ireland, and in consultation with them offered four suggestions for new aids to improve the visibility of ships' lifeboats: a large yellow flag four feet six inches by eight feet, the canvas boat hood then being introduced to be painted yellow, each boat to have means of producing yellow smoke, and liferafts to be painted yellow.[7]

The ideas were passed to the Ministry of Shipping, who were also considering suggestions from other sources for the use of fluorescene powder to stain the sea, and for the use of balloons or kites to be flown from lifecraft.[8] After some correspondence with the Air Ministry, the Ministry of Shipping accepted that bright yellow was more easily visible from the air than red and white stripes, which had been adopted for such things as lifesaving rings, and a decision was made in January 1941 to begin introducing the yellow flag, yellow boat hood and smoke floats.[9] Yellow was also adopted for the exposure suits introduced in the autumn. The Air Ministry did not think that kites or balloons would be particularly helpful,[10] and the fluorescene and yellow liferafts do not seem to have been taken up for merchant vessels. Of course, while yellow rafts were housed on their launching ways they would have increased a ship's own visibility to an unacceptable extent.

The yellow flags and yellow paint for the boat hoods presented no problems, and became increasingly common during the summer of 1941. The value of the flag was well illustrated by the experience of the survivors from the *Hatasu* after she was torpedoed about 600 miles east of Cape Race on 2 October 1941. The carpenter took charge of a lifeboat with eight other men in it, and later reported:

> We all had periods when our minds seemed to wander, and we imagined that we could see destroyers and all sorts of good food, but after a time these illusions would pass and we came back to normal again. We were eventually picked up by an American destroyer, the *Charles F. Hughes* on 16 October at 1100. We were flying a yellow flag from the mast and the lookout from the destroyer sighted it and she came over and picked us up.[11]

The *Empire Wave*, a straggler from the same convoy as the *Hatasu*, was torpedoed on the same day, but her survivors had more difficulty on gaining attention. On the fifth day, they twice saw aircraft and burned red flares without success. Her chief officer commented wistfully: 'If we had had a rocket in the boat, I am sure that we should have been sighted ... A smoke float would also have been of assistance.' Another aircraft passed without seeing them on the fourteenth day, when they came within sight of Iceland. Next morning, when another aircraft appeared, they took to the oars, 'knowing that the splash from them would attract the attention of the aircraft', and they also 'used the tin lid of the medicine chest for flashing in the sun'.[12] The American aircraft directed the trawler *Surprise* to their rescue.

Arranging for the testing, manufacture and distribution of suitable smoke floats took up most of 1941, so the Merchant Ships' Technical Committee had to wait until November before they could be assured that the floats were coming off the production line. They were also told that a rocket for lifeboats was also being considered.[13] Under the Merchant Shipping (Life-Saving Appliances) Emergency Rules issued on 27 July 1942, each lifeboat was required to carry twelve red flares, six hand rockets and four buoyant smoke floats 'capable of giving off a volume of orange smoke'.[14] The usual wartime distribution problems meant that, even after that date, ships might still be sailing without smoke floats. For instance, the *Glendene* had none when she was sunk on 8 October 1942,[15] and the master of the *Ripley*, sunk on 12 December, complained that they had been unobtainable in Liverpool when he had sailed in September.[16]

The success or failure of these devices for making lifeboats and rafts more visible depended on such variables as wind and sea conditions, visibility, the number and alertness of lookouts in ships and aircraft, and how far equipment had suffered from damage or deterioration. Ships tended to use them in combination, and sometimes added one or two of their own, as shown by these examples from 1942:

> I sighted a ship on the port bow about half a mile distant and burned the remaining two flares, flashed my torch and ordered every man to switch on his life-jacket light. The ship altered course and steamed towards us.[17] (*Thursobank*)

> We burnt our smoke flares, and even in the very little wind the flares burnt with a crimson smoke rising about ten feet from the water. HMS *Fortune* reported very favourably on these flares when she picked us up.[18] (*Glenshiel*)

> We sighted a ship on the horizon. We immediately burned smoke floats, red flares and a life jacket soaked in oil. This ship, which proved to be the *City of Bermuda*, sighted our boat about ten miles away.[19] (*Empire Dryden*)

> I sighted a steamer steering in a southerly direction. I climbed up the mast and waved the yellow flag and the ship altered course and came towards us.[20] (*Stanbank*)

> At 2350 a star shell was sighted and we immediately set fire to some petrol in a tin and waved it about.[21] (*Ross*)

> Sighted a ship approaching from the east. We threw over a smoke float, after carefully following the instructions in detail, but it failed to function. Another one was tried which, after about four seconds, commenced spluttering, before any smoke started. This smoke only lay on top of the water to a depth of about three feet ... We set off a third smoke float ... There was no yellow flag in the boat ... so I climbed a mast and waved a shirt. The steamer then turned and headed towards us.[22] (*Aldington Court*)

Vessels encountering lifeboats or rafts by chance, or summoned to the rescue by aircraft, were usually cautious in approaching survivors. Before heaving to they generally tried to check that the sinking was not so recent that the enemy submarine might still be in the vicinity, and in poor visibility they sometimes mistook a lifeboat or raft for a U-boat's conning tower. On 4 May 1941, in the North Atlantic, the *Lycaon* opened fire at 0350 on a supposed U-boat, assuming it to be one that she had driven off by gunfire the previous evening. Fortunately the shell missed what was then correctly identified as a man standing on a raft. He was the sole survivor of the British ship *Henri Mory*,[23] and after eight days adrift he must have been rather disconcerted by the initial response of his rescuers.

A similar experience befell the five survivors from the *Tjisalak* on 28 March 1944 in the Indian Ocean. Two days after their shipmates had been massacred by the Japanese, they were relieved and delighted to see an American 'Liberty' ship approaching until, in the words of her second officer:

> suddenly we saw a flash and a shell whistled overhead. As this ship fired several shots, some falling over and some short, we thought she ... had been captured by the Japanese who were using her as a raider ... We took down the sail, and immediately she ceased fire, so we breathed again. However, she then opened fire with machine-gun tracers ... She finally ceased fire, so we pulled alongside, climbing on board at 1730 ... This vessel was the American *James O. Wilder*.[24]

It speaks volumes for the humane tradition of seafaring that, after initial caution, so many ships of all types and nationalities took the risk of stopping to pick up survivors. They ranged from the great British battleship *Rodney*, which saved a boatload of survivors from the *Chilean Reefer*, to the German blockade runner *Rhakotis*, which picked up three exhausted survivors from the *City of Cairo* who had been adrift for thirty-five days. The work of rescue involved sailing schooners in the Caribbean, Russian patrol boats in the Barents Sea, Liberian fishing canoes, Portuguese frigates and Spanish freighters; British and allied cargo liners, tramp steamers, coasters, corvettes and trawlers all played their part. It was truly a great international effort over the whole period of the war.

Vessels picking up survivors faced a tricky problem of ship handling in getting alongside the boats and rafts without capsizing them or drawing them into the propeller, but even survivors who had spent a long time in their lifecraft were usually so encouraged by the imminence of rescue that they could do much to help themselves, and some were rendered positively euphoric. Ten days after their ship had been sunk in July 1941, the *Macon*'s No. 3 lifeboat 'came alongside the *Clan MacPherson* in true naval fashion. The crew, although weak, insisting

[on] "tossing" the oars ... Every member came up the pilot ladder unaided [with one exception].'[25] Many other reports mention with obvious pride that all, or nearly all, of the survivors managed to climb onto the rescue craft unaided, although they sometimes collapsed on reaching the deck.

Where survivors were too exhausted or suffering too badly from immersion foot to climb on board the rescue ship, they might have to be hauled up on bowlines, or in cargo nets and Neil Robertson stretchers. Tragically some lost their lives at the very moment of rescue. Captain Batho of the *Mendoza*, sunk on 1 November 1942, had difficulty in climbing on board the US vessel *Cape Alava* because the lifeboat was surging up and down about twelve feet, and he fell from the ladder when his legs were crushed between the boat and the ship's side.

> He managed to grasp a rope net a little further aft and here the struggle for his life went on for some time. Three sailors from the *Cape Alava* went down the net and into the water, but Captain Batho was continually torn from their grasp as the sea rose and fell. They persevered until they were thoroughly exhausted and could not succeed in getting a rope round him and had to give up the attempt.[26]

Whatever their nationality, the crews of ships which picked up survivors almost always treated them with great kindness and generosity, a fact readily acknowledged in subsequent reports. Those ships which carried doctors were able to offer proper professional care. On the *City of Bermuda* the men from the *Empire Dryden* were given 'small drinks of water at fifteen minute intervals followed by apples, oranges and ice cream in small quantities and spread over a long period'.[27] The doctor of the German blockade runner *Rhakotis* could not save the life of a woman passenger from the *City of Cairo*, but he visited the two men three times a day and kept them 'on a strict diet of milk and light food for ten days', before gradually allowing a switch to normal ship's food.[28] The 1943 *Guide to the Preservation of Life at Sea after Shipwreck*, offered the advice that survivors could drink as much as they wished, hot or cold, without harm – but for a few days food should be limited to bread and milk or soup.[29]

On the many ships which carried no doctor, the fare offered could vary a great deal: ubiquitous corned beef sandwiches on British corvettes, hot coffee and vodka on a Russian minesweeper for survivors from the *Induna*, cooked fish from local fishermen for the *Rhexenor*'s survivors, bread and jam for the men of the *Point Pleasant Park*. Sometimes the temptation for hungry men proved too great. A survivor from

the *Mattawin*, picked up by the USS *General Greene* after five days in a
lifeboat in June 1942, recalled:

> After two cups of coffee we all felt fine. A meal was prepared for us.
> Some people ate rather a lot and were heartily sick. I ate just a little,
> slowly, as the ship's doctor recommended, and felt highly refreshed and
> my stomach was not in the least upset. During the time I was in the
> boat I did not pass a motion, nor did I feel any inclination to. After
> the meal on the rescue ship my bowels worked normally immediately
> without the taking of any laxative, though I believe that some members
> of the crew had difficulty at first.[30]

No doubt the experts of the Medical Research Council would have
been horrified at some of the food offered to survivors. After a record
133-day solitary raft voyage from November 1942 to April 1943, a
Chinese seaman from the *Benlomond* amazed his Brazilian rescuer by
eating very strong red peppers by the handful.[31] One of the survivors
from the *Fort Buckingham*, after sixteen days on a raft in the Indian
Ocean, recalled how they were entertained when picked up by the
Norwegian tanker *Ora* on 5 February 1944: 'We were given water, and
pork sandwiches, which we readily ate, although I knew we should really
only have taken a light diet for a time. However, it seemed to do us
no harm. We were all very thirsty for two or three days.'[32]

As well as food, cigarettes, hot baths and medical care, ships carrying
out rescues often had to find clothing for survivors. Torn, blood-stained
or oil-soaked garments fit only for destruction were replaced by the
rescuers' spare shirts, boiler suits, pyjama trousers, jumpers, odd bits
of shore-going rig, tennis shoes, seaboots, and whatever else would
approximate to an acceptable outfit. Since merchant seamen did not
usually travel with an extensive wardrobe, donations to survivors involved real sacrifice which they made gladly, even though many could
ill afford it.

Clothing survivors was an even bigger problem for the men of the
Royal Navy serving in convoy escorts. For them picking up survivors
became a frequent occurrence, and it was not unusual for a ship to
pick up so many survivors that they outnumbered the escort's own crew.
At times the men gave away so much of their kit that they only possessed
the clothes they stood up in.[33] In 1943 Walter Edwards, Labour MP
for Whitechapel and former able seaman, complained that, although
the men could claim for loss of kit, 'the rate of compensation is about
two-thirds of the actual value, and it probably comes some months
later, so that in the small ships it is not always easy for men to replace

the gear which they have given'.[34] He urged that escort vessels should be equipped with clothing for survivors, but by that stage of the war bags containing emergency kits were already being supplied on the North Atlantic and Arctic convoys. This valuable innovation sprang initially from the generosity of the people of Canada,[35] although even earlier some escort vessels had put together their own unofficial kits of cast-off clothing for emergency use.

For some survivors, relief and recuperation on the rescue ship and pleasant anticipation of the varied pleasures to be enjoyed on dry land could be dramatically interrupted by the sinking of the rescue ship herself. After their ship was torpedoed on 8 October 1942, the crew of the *Glendene* sailed sixty miles in their lifeboat before being picked up by the *Agapenor* at 1330 on the 10th. Only eleven hours later they abandoned ship again when their rescuer was torpedoed, but by 1000 on the 11th they were all safely on board HMS *Petunia* and reached Freetown that evening.[36] In December, nineteen survivors from the *Teesbank* spent ten days in their lifeboat before being rescued by the *East Wales* on the 15th. She, in turn was torpedoed the following day, losing seventeen of her crew, but all of the men from the *Teesbank* again abandoned ship successfully to spend another six days in a lifeboat before being rescued by the Swedish ship *Ginnaren* which landed them at Natal, Brazil on the 23rd.[37] The two survivors from the *City of Cairo* who had been so carefully nursed back to health by the doctor of the German blockade runner *Rhakotis* after their thirty-five-day ordeal in a lifeboat, were sufficiently restored to health to survive that ship's sinking by HMS *Scylla* on 1 January 1943. One was rescued by a U-boat and became a prisoner-of-war; the other spent another four days in a lifeboat before being rescued by Spanish fishermen on 5 January.[38] In addition to cases such as these, where the rescue ship became a victim, there were many other examples where merchant seamen became survivors for a second time when vessels on which they were being repatriated, after being landed abroad, were sunk before they could reach a home port.

Aircraft played an important role in many of the rescues, especially in the later years of the war when more and more sea areas were regularly reconnoitred by more numerous aircraft capable of greater range and endurance. When a single boat was sighted by more than one aircraft, with slight variations in the reported position, there was sometimes uncertainty about whether to search for a single boat or several adrift in roughly the same area. To eliminate this confusion, early in 1943 the Ministry of War Transport accepted an Air Ministry request for each lifeboat to carry large white identification marks on its red lugsail. Usually the first and last letter of the ship's name and the boat's number were used for that purpose.[39] As a further aid to attracting attention, in mid 1943 the Ministry began supplying at government expense a four-inch square stainless steel signalling mirror for use in lifeboats and rafts.[40] No doubt this was a response to reports of the successful use of tin lids or ordinary glass mirrors for that purpose.

The main role for aircraft was locating rafts or boats so that ships could be directed to pick them up. Signalling between aircraft and lifecraft was always difficult because of differences in equipment and skill, and the high speed of the aircraft, but the simple knowledge that they had been spotted was a tremendously important psychological boost for survivors. As soon as he was sure that a Sunderland aircraft had sighted his lifeboat at 1245 on 31 March 1943, the master of the *Celtic Star* gave up his attempt to reach the West African coast. 'I told my men that they were all right now, that there was no need to row any more; I gave them extra water, telling them to sit back and take it easy.'[41] His optimism was justified. Within six hours they were safely aboard HMS *Wastwater*, where they were saddened to learn that, in trying to direct the ship towards the *Celtic Star*'s boats, the Sunderland had crashed killing six of her crew, and the rescue had only been made possible by information supplied by one of three injured airmen who were picked up from the sea.

In the early part of the war, airmen were sometimes so moved by the plight of survivors that they improvised ways of dropping their own food, drink, cigarettes, first aid kits and items of clothing, perhaps wrapped in a lifejacket or sleeping bag, for the boats to recover. In the later years of the war maritime reconnaissance aircraft frequently carried essential supplies packed in specially prepared containers for dropping in this way.

Although the possibility of survivors being rescued by flying boats landing on the open sea had been widely publicised by the picking up of the crew of the *Kensington Court* in 1939, this type of rescue was uncommon. The RAF did not encourage pilots to incur the many obvious risks of striking wreckage, encountering bigger waves than expected, damage from lifeboats coming alongside, or inability to restart engines. Some rescues of this kind were, however, carried out despite the difficulties. On 6 March 1942, a Sunderland landed in the sea 230 miles out from Freetown to take on board all fifty-six survivors from the *Benmohr*, sunk the previous day. The ship's master estimated that the pilot had to taxi for between five and seven miles before he could persuade the overloaded plane to take to the air again.[42] A Catalina flying boat which attempted to pick up survivors from the US merchant ship *Montana* on 8 June 1943 flooded, and the airmen had to take to their dinghies and join the Americans.[43] Three survivors from the *City of Canton* were picked up by a British civilian passenger flying boat in the Mozambique Channel on 19 July,[44] and two Catalina flying boats picked up twenty survivors from the *Congella* near the Maldive Islands on 27 October 1943.[45]

When the *Clan Ferguson* was sunk on 12 August 1942 during the 'Operation Pedestal' convoy to Malta, a large German flying boat landed in the sea next day to pick up thirty-two survivors from rafts, twelve more than the pilot initially calculated he could fit in. Handling the injured with great tenderness, they promised to return for the remainder, but a second rescue was prevented by the quantity of wreckage floating in the area. The following day an Italian Red Cross seaplane managed to alight on the water to pick up another seven men.[46]

In the absence of rescuing vessels or succour from the air, some lifeboats had no alternative but to battle on until they made a landfall by their own unaided efforts. The relief on reaching land can be imagined, especially when some fishing port or settlement offered a safe place to land: Ireland, the Cape Verde Islands, the Canary Islands, the Azores and the Caribbean all offered plenty of suitable landing places, usually with local boats to offer help if required. But when a landing had to be attempted on an open beach, especially in darkness, the survivors had to face the risk of being wrecked on an offshore reef or broaching-to in heavy surf. Coping with these conditions called for strong and skilled oarsmanship which could well be beyond the capability of an exhausted crew.

After the *Athelqueen* had been torpedoed on 15 March 1942, the master navigated his three lifeboats to Abaco Island in the Bahamas, arriving about midnight of 16/17 March. Appreciating the risks of trying to land on a lee shore, even with a relatively fresh crew, he set course to pass round the north of the island to find a more sheltered spot when, in his own words,

> suddenly the boat began pitching and rolling and then grounded on a reef. I shouted to the other boats to pull away out to sea and wait until daylight when I would try and rejoin them. We pulled hard to get the boat free, but the tide kept sweeping us in more and more on the reefs. The crew were becoming very tired so I decided to turn and pull as hard as we could towards the shore and risk the boat being capsized.

The boat suddenly freed herself and we landed without damaging the boat to any great extent. Meanwhile the third officer's boat had also reached the edge of the reef, and the first they knew was the boat pitched and hit the reef, violently throwing the third officer right out of the boat. The crew, thinking that the boat had been holed and that the third officer had jumped for it, got panicky and five of the men jumped overboard and started swimming for the shore. The third officer managed to climb back into the boat, which was undamaged, but owing to the darkness was unable to see these five men and after searching round ... pulled out to sea and remained until dawn in company with the chief officer's boat. Two of the men who had jumped overboard managed to reach the island, but the other three were drowned or eaten by sharks. As soon as it was light the other two boats rowed in and landed safely on the beach.[47]

Groups of survivors who came ashore in remote and isolated places did not usually have to wait long before they were able to make contact with local people who would report their plight to the authorities. In the case of the men from the *Athelqueen*, small boys carried news of their arrival to the local commissioner and a priest. Survivors might still have to face a fifteen-mile hike along a Liberian beach, a ten-mile trek through the undergrowth to reach the nearest road in Mozambique, or a canoe trip up an Indian river, but they had the satisfaction of knowing that they were on the first stage of a journey home.

For some survivors, however, reaching the shore turned out to be merely an extension of their ordeal. Five lifeboats from the *Chilka*, torpedoed off Padang by the Japanese submarine *I–2* on 11 March 1942, succeeded in reaching some small islands off the west coast of Sumatra, where they were cared for by the Dutch authorities. Increasingly alarmed by reports that the Japanese would soon land on the islands, most of the *Chilka*'s crew resigned themselves to becoming prisoners-of-war, but the master and some of his officers decided to sail for Ceylon in a lifeboat which had originally belonged to the *Jalarajan*. They set out on 31 March but, lacking the means of accurate navigation, they were well off course when rescued thirty-five miles northeast of Madras by the Greek ship *Pipina* on 4 May.[48]

A boatload of survivors from the *Chulmleigh* faced a terrible ordeal of a different kind. After running aground on a reef south of Spitzbergen on the night of 5/6 November 1942, she was bombed by German aircraft the next day. In bitterly cold weather, two boats set sail for Barentsburg, a distance of about 150 miles. One boat disappeared without trace.

The other was washed over a reef and cast ashore in the early hours of the 12th. They found some uninhabited huts, where they were able to shelter and light a fire, and they also found some food in the deserted settlement, but repeated efforts to find a way to Barentsburg failed.

It was such a rock-strewn, barren place, broken up by ravines, with large stretches of snow and ice, and they returned each time completely exhausted. Thirteen men died during the first three or four days from frost-bite, gangrene having set in, and from exhaustion and exposure. They seemed to give up hope and then died.[49]

Others died later, and the survivors were all in a bad way, their 'clothes soaked with pus from gangrenous limbs which caused a horrible stench',[50] when they were found by two Norwegians on 2 January 1943. Sledges were fetched from Barentsburg, where the men from the *Chulmleigh* were all safely in hospital by the 4th. They were kept in hospital for two months. They had to remain at Barentsburg until 10 June, when they were picked up by HMS *Bermuda* and HMS *Cumberland* and eventually landed at Thurso on the 15th.

A very different location became the refuge of fifty-five (mostly Chinese) survivors from the *Radbury*, torpedoed in the southern entrance to the Mozambique Channel on 13 August 1944. They landed from rafts on the tiny, waterless Europa Island, but they managed to stay alive by catching wild chickens, goats, fish and turtles to eat. The Chinese chief engineer produced drinking water with a still improvised from buoyancy tanks and piping. After being marooned for ten weeks, they were sighted on 26 October by a Catalina flying boat from 265 Squadron, based at Diego Suarez. The airmen's report brought HMS *Linaria* to the rescue two days later.[51]

When survivors had managed to reach a place of safety they might still require a great deal of assistance. The DEMS gunners, being members of the Royal Navy or the Army, were clearly the responsibility of the government, but the care of merchant seamen, as civilian employees of commercial firms, might rest with the shipping companies or their agents. Where they could not immediately meet that responsibility various seamen's charities, such as the Shipwrecked Mariners' Society or the Missions to Seamen, took on the task. In the opening months of the war, this divided responsibility did not always work well. There were too many cases of survivors being kept waiting while someone tried to sort out who would pay for their accommodation, supply a bare-footed man with a pair of shoes or issue a gas mask to a man whose identification papers were at the bottom of the Atlantic. At its meeting on 14 December

1939, the National Executive Committee of the National Union of Seamen approved a resolution from the North Shields branch urging the government to set up a chain of depots to care for survivors at government expense.[52] Public appeals for donations of clothing to fit out survivors angered Members of Parliament representing port constituencies. In February 1940 the government announced that the responsibility rested with county and borough councils, and that the issue of cast-off clothing was not thought appropriate.[53]

From time to time protests continued about the way Merchant Navy survivors were being cared for in the United Kingdom. A former Liberal MP, Margaret Wintringham, complained that local authorities were not aware of their responsibilities, and appealed for spare clothing to be sent to the Queen Mary Hostel in Grimsby, which had cared for 708 shipwrecked people of all nationalities in the first six months of the war.[54] Bridget Talbot complained that survivors on their way home were being refused refreshment at canteens for the armed forces.[55] Mary Mathew, of the Officers' Kit Replacement Organisation, protested that the compensation paid to Merchant Navy officers to replace their clothing and equipment was totally inadequate. She suggested, with a hint of sarcasm, that if the Minister of Shipping could manage it on the money allowed he had missed his vocation.[56] The extent of voluntary effort was indicated by the fact that, by July 1940, the Shipwrecked Mariners' Aid Society had already cared for 8899 survivors of all nationalities from 401 different ships.[57]

Nevertheless, as experience was gained of what was required, a loose alliance of government ministries, local authorities, charitable bodies, shipping companies and philanthropic individuals produced a network of hostels, clubs, convalescent homes, clothing depots, charitable funds, travel warrants, visits to dependants and whatever else was needed. It would not have looked very neat and tidy on an organisation diagram, there was certainly some duplication of effort, and it lacked a clear central direction and chain of command, but by and large it came to work quite well.

One grievance which seems to have been stamped indelibly on the collective memory of merchant seamen was that their pay stopped from the day their ship was sunk. This apparently heartless practice arose from the long-established legal agreement between a seafarer and the vessel's master. That agreement usually related to a specific voyage and terminated with the end of that voyage. In commercial law, sinking undoubtedly brought an end to both voyage and pay; and in due course survivors would receive a pay slip calculated on that basis. Apart from the first few months of the war, however, it is not correct to suppose that survivors received no payment for the time they spent in lifeboats or awaiting repatriation. In December 1939 the Ministry of Shipping accepted a proposal from the shipowners that the pay of survivors should continue for one month after the loss of the ship or until they returned to the United Kingdom, whichever was the longer. The additional expense was shared equally between the government and the owners. The compensation to which injured survivors were entitled was topped up to the equivalent of full wages for a second month at the expense of the shipowners.[58] After the establishment of the Merchant Navy Reserve Pool in 1941, a survivor would receive wages while he was waiting to sign on his next ship.

Of course, there were tedious wrangles about the precise amounts due to survivors and whether particular special allowances were or were not to be included in the calculations; sometimes, no doubt, there were needless delays in the payment of agreed allotments from wages to the families of survivors, especially if there was uncertainty about their fate; but survivors were certainly paid for a period after their ship sank, even if the money came from a different source and arrived some time after the payment relating to service prior to the sinking.

Another grievance, arising from the early months of the war, was the expense which survivors incurred in replacing clothing and equipment before they could return to sea. By March 1940 the Ministry of Shipping had established a government-financed compensation scheme for officers and men.[59] A letter pleading for generous compensation, written by Admiral of the Fleet Sir Reginald Tyrwhitt and Field Marshal Lord Milne, appeared in *The Times* on 22 June 1940.[60] Three days later Ronald Cross, then Minister of Shipping, replied that masters could receive up to a maximum of £100 and certificated officers up to £50.[61] By October 1943 the maximum payments ranged from £150 to cover the kit and personally-owned equipment of masters, through £90 for certificated officers and £50 for carpenters, down to £25 for seamen, greasers and firemen and £20 for boys.[62] Those amounts were by no means generous when one considers that all seamen needed a variety of clothing suitable for all the variations in the world's climate. In addition, masters and deck officers had to buy such items as new sextants, while a carpenter might have to replace a treasured set of tools which he had built up over many years. No doubt the cash amounts were fixed after a calculation of the likely second-hand value of the possessions lost by survivors, and some proof of what had been lost was required before a claim could be met. Having to buy replacement kit at current market prices and arguing with Ministry of War Transport accountants about the value of what had been lost – and how one might prove the existence of articles then lying on the ocean floor – left many survivors with feelings of bitterness.

As the war spread to more distant waters, survivors were often landed in places where no organisation had been set up. They could find themselves being cared for by the spontaneous generosity of local communities at the places where they landed, and many survivors' reports reveal how touched they were by the way they were received by people of many different races and religions. The master of the *Weirbank* obviously found the reception he and his crew received on 29 July 1942 at a village on the island of Tobago quite overwhelming after two days in their lifeboats:

> About ten native surf boats came out to meet us ... They brought us a bottle of rum, coffee and sandwiches, and insisted on towing us, however, they were not used to towing boats and at the finish we were towing them. [Charlettville] is a very small place ... The whole village turned out to greet us including the ARP and VAD squads, in fact every local organisation possible including the Fire Brigade, and there was much obvious disappointment amongst the thirty native nurses at finding there were no broken legs or other ailments to be attended to. I allowed them to rub my legs as compensation; as a matter of fact my knees and thighs were stiff and skinned from sitting in the overcrowded boat in one position. We were given as much food as we could eat and were sent by buses to Scarborough where we were quartered in private houses.[63]

At other places survivors might find themselves in the care of foreign governments, local charities, British consulates or embassies, local agents of British shipping companies, ad hoc groups of expatriate British residents, colonial administrations of varying levels of competence, or assorted military and naval establishments. Occasionally they might find that their needs were lost sight of amid confusion, red tape, bureaucratic procedures, interminable buck-passing and staggering indifference or incompetence. When this happened, the gratitude which survivors felt for their immediate rescuers quickly turned to blistering criticism of the arrangements on shore.

The master of the *Aldergrove* described the reception at Gibraltar in 1941: 'We were received by Mr Tamplin of the Ministry of War Transport. He took us to the Shipping Office – some of the men had to walk through the streets in bare feet – and it was arranged for some of the men to go to the Sailors' Home and some of us to the Victoria Hotel.

He stated that he had no funds at his disposal and could not do anything else for us ... There were about 134 survivors at Gibraltar, and clothing was very costly and very scarce.'[64]

Of conditions in Iceland in 1941, the master of the *Baron Pentland* complained: 'The sanitary arrangements were not at all good ... The food was very bad indeed ... It was almost thrown at us ... There was not sufficient accommodation for officers. I went to the Naval Authorities and complained about the conditions, but they said they could do nothing about it, as the Officer in Charge was away, and would not be back until the end of the week. I then went to the Consul, who merely told me that he considered that the conditions were satisfactory.'[65]

Survivors from the *Clan MacPherson* found little to their satisfaction when they reached Freetown in 1943. The master reported: 'It is no exaggeration to say that the [Grand Hotel] was absolutely filthy ... The sanitary arrangements were appalling ... For breakfast we were given half a sausage and a small piece of fried bread ... There were numerous rats running about at night. [Lascars] had been placed in "boarding houses", but had had to sleep on the floor ... The general feeling seemed to be that no one cared what happened to survivors, so long as they were not bothered by them.'[66]

The master of the *Birchbank*, on arrival in Algiers in 1943, found that his 'officers were accommodated in a third-rate hotel ... in which the accommodation was both poor and dirty. They had to walk to the Merchant Navy Club, which took thirty-five minutes, for their meals. At this club there were drunken Arabs, coloured seamen, and all had to scramble for their food in a most disgusting manner.'[67]

Other complaints referred to the inadequate medical care provided for survivors by the Russians at Murmansk.[68] Survivors often felt aggrieved at the long delays which could occur before the authorities found ships which could repatriate them under the traditional arrangements for 'distressed British seamen', and accommodation on some of those vessels was both uncomfortable and overcrowded. No doubt many of these criticisms were quickly remedied, and they were probably the result of quite temporary local difficulties brought about by a sudden influx of survivors with which local officials could not cope. Some criticisms may have been exaggerated by frustrated masters who had been under intolerable strain. It has to be said that most survivors' reports refer warmly to the kindness and consideration they received, and the efficiency with which they were kitted out and accommodated by officials of the Ministry of War Transport, British consuls and shipping company agents.

It would have been unreasonable to expect that arrangements for the reception of survivors could reach a uniformly high standard wherever they might be required anywhere in the world. But it would be equally unreasonable to expect men who had struggled to stay alive in boats and on rafts, while they dreamed of the drink, food and comfort they would enjoy ashore, to view any shortcomings with either meek submission, pathetic gratitude or an historian's detachment. They naturally resented any delay in arranging for them to be shipped home, and they were rightly angered if they detected any hint of indifference about their welfare on the part of government officials, 'office wallahs', foreigners or brass-bound naval officers. They were delighted to feel safe at last; but on their own behalf, and on behalf of their dead shipmates, they also wanted to feel that merchant seamen were valued, respected, and entitled to civilised and considerate treatment.

10

The Cost

No truly definitive figure has ever been produced for the total number of British merchant seamen who lost their lives as a result of enemy action during the Second World War. One obvious problem is the difficulty, or even propriety, of applying a term such as 'British' to a multinational population of seamen drawn not only from all parts of the United Kingdom but also from many colonies and protectorates, the self-governing dominions, allied countries under enemy occupation, Eire, Goa, some other neutral countries, and even individuals from such diverse groups as Spanish republicans, White Russians and refugees from the Baltic States. Attempts to calculate the number of fatal casualties have generally concentrated, therefore, on the nationality of the ships rather than the nationalities of the individual seamen, but that approach also produces problems where British crews sailed in foreign vessels hired by Britain under 'bareboat' charters or where British seamen served in allied vessels which were short-handed.

In March 1946 Sir William Elderton, statistical adviser to the Ministry of War Transport, produced a report which subsequently formed the basis of a paper presented by him to the Institute of Actuaries.[1] He took as his starting point the 34,018 deaths reported to the Registrar-General of Shipping and Seamen as having occurred on British registered vessels, vessels under 'bareboat' charter, or on shore outside the United Kingdom between September 1939 and the end of 1945. That figure could be broken down into 27,790 (including 4903 lascars) who had died from enemy action, and 6228 (including 1237 lascars) from other causes. The distinction drawn between the two categories must have entailed some fairly arbitrary and subjective judgements. When a ship struck a mine, for example, there must sometimes have been doubt whether it was one laid by the enemy or just an unfortunate accident with a British mine; and when ships simply disappeared, even research in enemy records after the war could not always determine whether they had been sunk as a result of enemy action or as a result of marine accident or stress of weather. Again, some of the deaths from other causes, although not brought about by direct enemy action, would certainly have been attributable to war conditions such as accidents on blacked out ships, collisions in convoy, dangerous cargoes, and strandings arising from the extinguishing of lighthouses and lightbuoys.

Elderton accepted that the deaths reported to the Registrar-General of Shipping and Seamen needed to be adjusted upwards to take account of such categories as 165 men reported to have died while prisoners in the Far East but where the full details had not yet been established, 110 men known to have been prisoners-of-war but not yet accounted for, and 443 men missing from ships sunk in the Far East. Some of these men might have made their own way to homes in foreign countries or settled among local communities for reasons of their own, but he estimated that at least 600 (including 110 lascars) must have died, of whom 440 (including ninety lascars) might be attributable to enemy action. Thus he arrived at a total of 28,230 deaths (including 4993 lascars) from enemy action.[2]

That figure did not include the missing crews of many small vessels, mainly lost in Southeast Asia, because neither the vessels nor their crews came under the jurisdiction of the Registrar-General. An estimate based on tonnage suggested that the crews of those vessels would have totalled approximately 4537 (including 3600 lascars). Elderton chose to omit them from his calculations for lack of evidence and because they would have invalidated his statistical comparisons with pre-war figures. In the absence of detailed crew lists, the fate of this group must be a matter for conjecture. Some of them would have deserted their ships in the face of the Japanese advance. They, and others who survived the loss of their ships, might have simply settled into local communities. Others, happy to earn a living irrespective of the flag displayed on the employer's vessel, might have taken service under the Japanese. Some would certainly have lost their lives, but Elderton was inclined to think that possibly the proportion was not very high.[3]

Another category which did not figure in reports to the Registrar-General were deaths which occurred in the United Kingdom after seamen had come on shore. Up to the end of 1945, the Ministry of Pensions knew of 1078 merchant seamen who had died in the United Kingdom 'from wounds or from such illnesses as were regarded as consequent on the war',[4] but no attempt was made to identify how many of those would have fallen within the Registrar-General's criteria for 'deaths from enemy action'. Elderton's figures also excluded almost 900 deaths which occurred on British registered fishing vessels.[5]

Elderton mentions that 2465 men from the Royal Navy and the Army lost their lives while manning the defensive armament on merchant ships.[6] These casualties are generally included in the figures for their respective services, but they signed the articles of the ship in which they sailed, and they were, therefore, technically a part of the crew under the orders of the master. Their combatant status was hidden, as far as possible, in neutral ports in case they should find themselves interned. They shared the same dangers as their shipmates from the Merchant Navy; they were dependent on the same safety equipment; when ships were sunk they shared a common struggle for survival; and in all too many cases they shared the same tragic fate. In retrospect, it seems a pity that men who sailed together, fought alongside one another against both the enemy and the perils of the sea, and eventually died together, should have been separated by the compilers of statistical tables and the erectors of national war memorials. The same might be said of convoy commodores and their staffs who were killed.

If one makes allowances for slightly differing criteria, official figures produced after the end of the war do not seem inconsistent with the figures drawn up by Sir William Elderton. In a written reply to a question in the House of Commons on 29 November 1945, the Prime Minister (then Mr Attlee) cited a figure of 30,189 deaths (excluding natural causes but including deaths in captivity or internment) of merchant seamen of all nationalities in British registered ships and fishing boats and of British subjects in foreign vessels chartered or requisitioned by the British government.[7] At that time 5264 were still listed as missing, presumably most of these were those considered by Elderton as falling outside the jurisdiction of the Registrar-General of Shipping and Seamen. A government White Paper in 1946, apparently using the same criteria, quoted 30,248 killed and 4654 missing.[8] Those figures have continued to be used in official publications up to the present day.

Costello and Hughes list figures derived from the records of the Admiralty Trade Division.[9] They total 30,132 crew lost from all enemy causes but, since that figure includes DEMS gunners from the Royal Navy and the Army, it might appear rather low until one takes account of the fact that it covers only the casualties in ships which were actually sunk. Presumably men who lost their lives in ships which survived, or were killed on shore abroad (and possibly some other peripheral categories) are excluded. In the official history, C. B. A. Behrens also focused on the number of fatal casualties among crews whose ships were sunk. She used information from the Registrar-General of Shipping and Seamen to arrive at a total of 25,864 deaths, but excluding

DEMS gunners, and merchant seamen who lost their lives in rescue ships or while being carried as passengers.[10]

Writing in 1968, Vice-Admiral Schofield and Lieutenant- Commander Martyn quoted an estimate of 32,952 deaths of British merchant seamen from enemy action, although they did not give any detailed explanation of how the figure was calculated.[11] In particular, it is unclear whether men lost in fishing vessels were included.

In a more recent publication, Gabe Thomas, a former post-war Registrar-General of Shipping and Seamen, states that the records of that department show that 32,076 merchant seamen (excluding DEMS gunners) are recorded as having died through enemy action.[12] If that figure is accepted, and the fishermen and DEMS gunners who lost their lives are added, total deaths among the crews of British merchant vessels and fishing boats would amount to over 35,000. John Terraine has given a figure of 35,000 for Merchant Navy dead,[13] a figure first quoted in 1946 by Sir David Maxwell-Fyfe, one of the British prosecuting counsel at the Nuremberg war crimes trial.[14]

It may be asked how a multiracial body of civilians with an average age of thirty-two, drawn mainly from underprivileged backgrounds, and lacking the disciplinary framework of the armed forces, could have continued to go down to the sea in ships despite all the casualties and suffering which they had to face. In the official history, Dr Behrens suggested that a psychological explanation might be found in 'the spirit ... that dominates the group and that may cause people in general to behave either with less or, in this case, with more courage than human nature usually shows'.[15] A possible alternative explanation might be that some merchant seamen had a tendency to respond with abusive language, obscene gestures, truculent defiance, and possibly violence, to any attempt by shipping office clerks, dock police, publicans, marine superintendents, mothers-in-law or other figures of authority to lay down what they should or should not do. If Adolf Hitler, Erich Raeder, Karl Doenitz and the entire Kriegsmarine chose to put obstacles in the way of honest merchant seamen earning their living they were likely to meet with very similar responses – and so would Benito Mussolini and Hideki Tojo.

In addition to the merchant seafarers, the sinking of British ships also involved heavy casualties among both civilian and military passengers. From the ocean liners specifically designed to carry large numbers, it seems likely that something of the order of 11,000 passengers were lost through enemy action. To this one would need to add losses from vessels designed for carrying passengers in the short sea trades, such as the

Irish Sea ferry *St Patrick* which was sunk by German aircraft on 13 June 1941. It might also be asked whether one should also add those lost from foreign passenger liners which were essentially operating under British control. The total would be increased considerably if one included cases such as the Dutch *Slamat* and the Belgian *Leopoldville*. The Dutch ship lost over 800 of her mainly military passengers and crew when first the ship herself and then two Royal Navy destroyers engaged in rescuing survivors were sunk by aircraft during the evacuation of Greece in 1941. The Belgian ship also lost over 800, mainly US troops, when she was torpedoed five miles off Cherbourg in 1944.[16]

One would certainly need to add people who lost their lives in the sinking of vessels which were not primarily designed for carrying passengers. With every berth at a premium, cargo ships were often required to carry a small number of passengers with valid reasons for travelling to out of the way destinations even in wartime. They present a special problem for the compiler of statistics in that, to avoid the medical regulations concerning the carriage of passengers, they were often signed on a ship's articles in the same way as DEMS gunners and were thus, technically, part of the crew.

Any attempt to arrive at a figure for fatalities among passengers is defeated by the conditions under which, in the first half of the war, hazardous evacuations had to be hastily improvised from places such as Norway, Holland, Belgium, Dunkirk, other French ports, Greece, Crete, Singapore, Sumatra, Java and various islands in the Dutch East Indies, the Solomons and Polynesia. Given the motley assortment of vessels pressed into service and the conditions under which they were loaded, no one can say with any certainty how many passengers were on board those which were subsequently sunk before they could reach safety.

One is forced to the conclusion that, if one cannot write with any degree of confidence about the precise number of merchant seamen who lost their lives as a result of enemy action, there are even more formidable uncertainties about the number of passengers lost while travelling in British ships, and there is little point in suggesting a figure which could amount to little more than a rather ill-informed guess.

Although this book has focused on the survival problems of merchant seamen, the authors would not wish it to be thought that they are unmindful of the many officers and men of the Royal Navy who lost their lives, often in actions directly or indirectly arising from the need to defend merchant shipping. Without the courage and self-sacrifice of men serving under the white ensign, the cost in merchant seamen's lives would have been far higher.

A sinking ship presents a very similar range of basic survival problems irrespective of the ensign she flies or the uniform worn by her crew. Explosions, fire, scalding steam, choking fuel oil, predatory fish, drowning, exposure, thirst and starvation all take their toll without regard to rank, service or nationality. To that extent ideas for improving the chances of survivors could arise from the experience of men from either service and might well have an application to both; but their survival problems were not identical. For example, the Merchant Navy provides few, if any, parallels with the particular risks faced by men flying with the Fleet Air Arm or serving in the Royal Navy's submarines, minelayers, minesweepers, light coastal forces and landing craft.

To enable warships to perform their primary function they usually had to carry large quantities of explosive materials in their magazines. Those explosives constituted an ever-present threat to all on board, no matter how skilfully naval architects sought to minimise the risks of direct hits by the enemy and of subsequent blast effect or fire, no matter how well-drilled crews were in damage control, and no matter how well-disciplined they were in guarding against accidents. Massive explosions in magazines produced two of the Royal Navy's most costly disasters of the war: the loss of the great battlecruiser HMS *Hood* in the North Atlantic on 24 May 1941 as the result of five salvoes from the main armament of the *Bismarck*, and the sinking of the battleship HMS *Barham* by a torpedo from *U–331* in the Eastern Mediterranean on 25 November 1941. From the *Hood*'s entire ship's company there were only three survivors to mourn over 1400 of their comrades who had lost their lives; from the *Barham* about 450 survivors were picked up by accompanying destroyers but over 860 men died as a mighty explosion caused their ship to disintegrate, an awesome event captured for posterity on cinefilm by a cameraman on one of the other ships in company.

The sinking of individual merchant vessels did not produce casualties on that scale among merchant seamen because, in general, merchant vessels usually carried smaller – often very much smaller – crews than warships of comparable size. Within the broad categories of their traditional deck, catering and engine-room departments, merchant seamen rather prided themselves on being 'jacks of all trades', but ships of the Royal Navy had to carry many more men trained for highly specialised roles handling technically sophisticated equipment. The action stations of most of those men would be below decks in confined spaces, separated from other parts of the warship by watertight doors designed to ensure that even a badly damaged ship could be kept afloat and capable of remaining in action as long as possible. Thanks to that feature of their design some warships were able to survive damage which would certainly have finished off a merchant ship but, when a warship did have to be abandoned, men in compartments far below deck might never receive the order to leave, while the watertight doors might prove impossible to operate if, perhaps, they had been warped by fire or structural stresses, or if they were too heavy to move against an adverse list, or if the handles were covered in fuel oil. Many accounts by Royal Navy survivors describe difficulties of this kind as they struggled to reach the open deck where they could set about abandoning ship.[17]

The sinking of any major warship was likely, therefore, to involve a very heavy loss of life. Over 500 men died in the torpedoing of the aircraft carrier HMS *Courageous* by *U–29* southwest of Ireland on 17 September 1939; close on 800 more lost their lives when the battleship HMS *Royal Oak* was torpedoed at anchor in Scapa Flow by *U–47* the following month; and more than 1400 men died on 8 June 1940 when the aircraft carrier HMS *Glorious* and her escorting destroyers *Ardent* and *Acasta* were sunk by the *Scharnhorst* and *Gneisenau* during the Norwegian campaign. From over 700 men in the cruiser HMAS *Sydney* there were no survivors when she was sunk in action with the German auxiliary cruiser *Kormoran* on 19 November 1941; over 800 died when Japanese aircraft sank HMS *Prince of Wales* and HMS *Repulse* off the east coast of Malaya on 10 December 1941; while on 19 December there was only one survivor from a complement of 746 when the cruiser HMS *Neptune* was sunk by mine north of Tripoli.

Between the Merchant Navy and the Royal Navy there were important differences in tradition and expectations when it came to abandoning ship. In the Merchant Navy, when a vessel had sustained damage which made it unlikely that ship and cargo could be saved or when it became clear that she lacked the means to resist a vastly stronger enemy, the master's overriding duty was to provide for the survival of his crew and passengers by whatever means were open to him. Generally that called for a decision to abandon ship with all possible speed, or it might require surrender in the face of *force majeure*. In the Royal Navy, on the other hand, tradition required that the ship should be fought as long as there was the slightest chance that she might be able to inflict damage on the enemy or render some assistance, however slight, to her consorts. She had to be almost on the point of sinking before her captain would order his men over the side.

That readiness to fight on to the bitter end led to many gallant and heart-stirring battles against enormous odds, such as the ramming of the heavy cruiser *Admiral Hipper* by the sinking destroyer HMS *Glowworm*, the sacrifice of the armed merchant cruiser HMS *Jervis Bay* in attempting to defend convoy HX84 against the vastly superior pocket battleship *Admiral Scheer*, and the dogged determination of the crippled destroyer HMS *Achates* to lay a smoke-screen between the Murmansk convoy JW51B and the heavy guns of the *Lützow* and *Admiral Hipper*. Actions such as these bear eloquent witness to the fine fighting tradition of the Royal Navy, but they inevitably involved a very high price in killed and wounded which might have been avoided by a more timely abandonment or more circumspect decisions when faced with impossible odds.

Unlike their comrades aboard merchant ships, the men of the Royal Navy were not protected by legislation requiring the provision of sufficient lifeboats to accommodate everyone on board. Vessels specifically designed as warships did carry a number of boats, but they were intended for functions other than lifesaving and, even if all of them could be launched in the heat of action, they could only hold a fraction of the ship's full complement. Survivors from warships were, therefore, heavily dependent on personal lifebelts of various designs, some inflatable and some stuffed with kapok, or on large oval Carley floats. These floats were canvas-covered oval rings, filled with cork or kapok, the largest capable of supporting up to fifty survivors hanging on to ropes around the side or sitting within the oval on a netting or wooden grid floor through which the sea could wash. They were relatively light and easily thrown overboard, but they provided little protection from the elements and they were not designed or equipped for the kind of prolonged survival voyages which merchant seamen sometimes had to endure.

Survivors from warships might hope to be rescued relatively quickly because they often had other warships sailing in company. One of them might actually be laid alongside the stricken vessel to evacuate survivors, or they might have the speed, manoevrability and low freeboard to pluck survivors from the water. Even when sailing alone, a warship's whereabouts would usually be known with reasonable accuracy on board a flagship or at headquarters on shore so that, if her powerful radio transmitter failed to raise the alarm, others would usually be able to order a search as soon as it was appreciated that she was overdue. If, however, survivors were not rescued quickly, their lifebelts and Carley floats would not bear comparison with a merchant ship's lifeboats and rafts in providing for survival over a longer period. For instance, over 300 men were lost when *U–124* sank the cruiser HMS *Dunedin* on lone patrol 900 miles west of Freetown on 24 November 1941. The one boat which she managed to launch was swamped as far more men than it was designed to carry tried to clamber on board. Seventy-two men survived on seven Carley floats to be rescued three days later by a US merchant ship. Six of those floats had no food or water; the seventh carried one gallon and a few biscuits. During their three days adrift, the survivors had seen many of their comrades die, sometimes after first being driven insane, from sunstroke, thirst and savage attacks by dogfish which could bite men through the lattice floor of the floats. Over half the men who survived were suffering from serious bites of this kind, and all were in very poor physical shape when rescued.[18]

Between 1939 and 1945 the Royal Navy lost 51,578 men listed as killed or missing as a result of enemy action. That total was about 35–40 per cent greater than the total of dead and missing in the Merchant Navy, and the figures may be compared with 177,850 in the Army and 76,342 in the Royal Air Force.[19] Speaking in the House of Commons on 21 September 1943, Winston Churchill paid tribute to the Merchant Navy's contribution to the national war effort. *En passant* he mentioned that their losses had been 'in greater proportion even than those of the Royal Navy'.[20] That remark has frequently formed the basis of a claim that the men of the Merchant Navy faced greater dangers than men in other services and suffered the heaviest casualties.

From time to time attempts have been made to quantify the casualty rates of merchant seamen as compared with the armed forces, by looking at deaths from enemy action in relation to the total enlistment in a particular service, the average number in service, or the peak number enlisted at any one time.[21] Although such comparisons may serve to enliven arguments in ex-servicemen's clubs towards 'closing time', when old men tend to recall bygone inter-service rivalries, they serve little purpose because they are not comparing like with like. The total enlistment in the armed forces necessarily included large numbers of administrators, clerks, storekeepers, medical staff, intelligence operatives, chaplains, signallers, instructors and other specialists who all served in uniform. Those who provided similar support services for the Merchant Navy were not classified as merchant seamen: they were usually civilians carrying out their normal jobs in Mercantile Marine Offices, shipping company offices, cargo agencies, ship chandlers, seamen's missions, port health authorities, marine radio stations and so on. In any fair comparison, all of these people would need to be added to the total size of the Merchant Navy, and one would need to make a similar adjustment to take account of those members of the armed forces in such branches as the Admiralty Trade Division and Defensively Equipped Merchant Ships whose primary role was also in support of the Merchant Navy. Of course, one would then need to add to the figure for Merchant Navy casualties all deaths from enemy action among the personnel of these support services. It is difficult to disagree with Sir William Elderton's conclusion 'that it is impracticable to set out the relative risks run by men of the Royal Navy and by men of the Merchant Service from the statistics available'.[22] In any case, where all served in a great common cause, those who died and those who survived deserve to be remembered for better reasons than the invidious comparisons of a 'league table of risks' compiled by statisticians, even if the figures available were more reliable and comprehensive.

In addition to those merchant seamen who are known (or presumed) to have died as a result of enemy action, and those whose fate was never satisfactorily determined, the health of many others was seriously damaged either by enemy action or through the general stress of serving at sea in wartime. The average *monthly* discharges on physical grounds from the Merchant Navy Reserve Pool rose from 467 in 1943, to 660 in 1944, and 768 in the first eight months of 1945.[23] The discharges are classified into various medical categories, but no indication is given of whether, for example, men discharged on account of ear or eye problems were suffering from normal deterioration or accident, or whether they had been deafened or blinded by enemy action. Other categories such as digestive disorders and nervous disorders do not, and probably could not, distinguish between natural defects and wartime stress. It seems likely that discharges through fractures and deformities (including amputations, frostbite and burns) would have included many examples directly attributable to enemy action, but the average monthly figures of forty-two (1943), sixty-one (1944) and forty (January to August 1945) would also have included the normal accidents to be expected in employment regarded as dangerous even in peacetime. Elderton expressed the opinion that, among the men discharged on physical grounds, 'there is a considerable proportion that consists of permanently damaged lives and some who can have had only a few months to live ... Probably over 60 per cent of those discharged in 1943 ... and about 40 per cent of those discharged in 1945 would be regarded as uninsurable or insurable only on special terms.'[24]

Two further categories of casualty need to be considered. The British White Paper of 1946 classified 5720 merchant seamen as internees or prisoners-of-war, and 4707 as wounded, out of a grand total of 45,329 casualties of all types (killed, missing, wounded and prisoners).[25] Thus, of the total Merchant Navy casualties, internees and prisoners-of-war made up 12.6 per cent and wounded made up 10.4 per cent. Of the total casualties for men in the armed forces of the United Kingdom, however, prisoners made up 22.9 per cent and wounded 36.7 per cent. If one combines the figures for killed and missing, on the other hand, they made up 77 per cent of all Merchant Navy casualties compared with 40.5 per cent of all casualties to men in the armed forces of the United Kingdom. No doubt these differences arose out of variations in the types of risk to which merchant seamen were exposed as compared with the risks faced by men in the other services. For example, merchant seamen were less likely to find themselves made prisoner in large capitulations such as that at Singapore, and their main enemy was the U-boat which by its construction and mode of operation could only accommodate a small number of prisoners. It seems likely that, as compared with men wounded on land, wounded merchant seamen were more likely to die through the violence of the sea or because there was no skilled medical assistance on hand.

There may still be a tendency in some quarters to suggest that the high percentage of deaths among merchant seamen can be explained as an outcome of the enemy's complete disregard of both international law and the traditional humanity of seafarers towards those whose lives are in peril. From Oberleutnant Lemp's tragic error in sinking the *Athenia* on the first day of the war, and the subsequent sinking of neutral vessels, British propaganda was able to establish a widespread public assumption that all attacks on merchant ships were illegal. Press reports of certain questionable incidents and of the appalling suffering of civilian merchant seamen after their ships had been sunk continued to reinforce that assumption, which was spelled out in many wartime speeches. For instance, Lord Winster, a former naval officer and MP, was reported as saying in 1944:

> In the plan of campaign which [Hitler] had formed to starve us he felt that the one great thing he had to do was to break the nerve of the officers and men of the Merchant Navy so that they would refuse to go to sea. With that end in view, he gave his orders for a campaign of cold-blooded terrorism and brutality towards those men. Again words are useless to describe all the tortures and brutalities which have been inflicted upon the officers and men of our Merchant Navy. It is a story which will stain for all time the traditions of the sea. I cannot forget that the German navy made itself the willing instrument of this campaign

of brutality and terrorism, and I hope that no Englishman will ever again shake hands with a German naval officer.[26]

At the principal war crimes trial of German leaders before the International Military Tribunal at Nuremberg in 1946, the two leading German admirals, Erich Raeder and Karl Doenitz, were numbered among the accused. Along with most of the other prisoners in the dock, they were charged with conspiracy and with crimes against peace by waging an aggressive war; and, more specifically, the two admirals were also accused of authorising, directing and participating in war crimes, 'particularly crimes against persons and property on the high seas'.[27] On this last charge, the prosecution case relied mainly on evidence concerning three aspects of the war at sea: the failure by the Germans to keep to the letter of international law, especially the rules laid down in the London Submarine Agreement of 1936; a small group of sinkings of named vessels such as the *Athenia, City of Benares, Peleus, Sheaf Mead, Noreen Mary* and *Antonico*; and Doenitz's intentions concerning the rescue of survivors in his Order 154 of 1939–40 and the '*Laconia* Order' of 1942.

The defence claimed that the British Admiralty – by arming merchant vessels, ordering them to use radio or attempt to ram when attacked, equipping them with depth charges, and sailing them in convoys – had made it impossible to operate under the 1936 rules without endangering the U-boats in a way that no combatant nation could accept. In German eyes, merchant vessels were seen as auxiliaries of the Royal Navy operating under Admiralty orders. Although British merchant seamen were legally civilians throughout the war – and were frequently referred to in British speeches and newspapers as 'unarmed' civilians – Doenitz told the court: 'Germany considered the crews of merchantmen as combatants, because they fought with the weapons which had been mounted aboard the merchant ships in large numbers.'[28] Ample justification for this assessment can be found in war-time newspaper reports and films about merchant seamen manning guns, in awards for gallantry in action, and in Admiralty instructions concerning the recruitment of gun crews.[29] Indeed, British merchant seamen took a pugnacious pride in their ambiguous status – able and willing to shoot back when facing the enemy but enjoying the better pay, war risk money and trade union representation appropriate to civilian employees who were free from the irksome uniforms, saluting, 'bull' and all-pervading discipline of the armed forces of the Crown. Of course, whether they were technically regarded as combatants or non-combatants should not have affected their right to expect humane treatment once they had abandoned ship.

Concerning the deaths which occurred during the sinking of certain named vessels, the defence argued that they were genuine accidents or errors arising from the conditions under which all who took part in the war at sea had to fight or, alternatively, they resulted from the actions of stressed individuals acting on their own initiative in breach of the orders they had received.

In response to questioning by Dr Kranzbühler, his defence counsel, Doenitz explained the precise circumstances under which he had issued the two orders of which the prosecution complained. He emphasised that their purpose had been to stop U-boat commanders from putting their boats at risk by attempting to rescue survivors from sunken ships.

> During a war the necessity of refraining from rescue may well arise. For example, if your own ship is endangered thereby, it would be wrong from a military viewpoint and, besides, would not be of value to the one to be rescued; and no commander of any nation is expected to rescue if his own ship is thereby endangered.[30]

Doenitz rejected totally, however, the charge that the '*Laconia* Order' was intended to authorise the murder of survivors:

> [When] members of the crew ... after the sinking of their ship, are not able to fight any longer and are either in lifeboats or other means of rescue or in the water ... firing upon these men is a matter concerned with the ethics of war and should be rejected under any and all circumstances. In the German Navy and U-boat force this principle, according to my firm conviction, has never been violated, with the one exception of the affair Eck.[31] No order on this subject has ever been issued, in any form whatsoever.[32]

Sir David Maxwell-Fyfe, the British prosecuting counsel, tried hard to shake Doenitz on this point, but the admiral consistently claimed that the U-boats had fought fairly. To a question about whether the deaths of so many British merchant seamen was a source of pride to him, Doenitz replied: 'Men are killed during wars and no one is proud of it ... It is a necessity, the harsh necessity of war.'[33] On the sinking of some neutral vessels without warning the admiral claimed: 'If one or two instances of mistakes are found in the course of five and a half years of clean submarine warfare, it proves nothing.'[34] Asked how his men would have reacted if they had been given an order to annihilate survivors, Doenitz asserted confidently: 'As I know my U-boat forces, there would have been a storm of indignation against such an order. The clean and honest idealism of these [men] would never have allowed them to do it; and I would never have given such an order or permitted it to be given.' [35]

Among witnesses called by the prosecution was Oberleutnant Heisig, who testified that, while on a training course, he had heard Doenitz make a speech in which he explained that crews as well as ships were legitimate targets to prevent the Allies manning the new tonnage being built in America. Another witness, Korvettenkapitän Moehle, who had commanded the Fifth U-boat Flotilla at Kiel from June 1941 to the end of the war, testified that in his briefing of commanding officers he had indicated that the '*Laconia* Order' could be interpreted as author-ising attacks on survivors.

The prosecution's case was weakened by the fact that Heisig's original deposition was probably made with the intention of helping a friend among the accused officers of *U–852* in their separate earlier trial for attacking survivors from the *Peleus*, and Moehle's own defence at his forthcoming trial might be helped if Doenitz could be shown to have intended the '*Laconia* Order' to lead to attacks on survivors. The most serious weakness, however, lay in the very small number of specific accusations concerning named ships. If Doenitz had intended that his U-boats should annihilate survivors as a deliberate policy, one would have expected to see from him a clear and unequivocal order to that effect, and one would surely have expected to see a greater number of clear-cut examples of that policy's having been carried out in respect of survivors after the sinking of named vessels.

In their final addresses to the court, the two admirals were both defiant and confident. Doenitz told the judges: 'You may judge the legality of German submarine warfare as your conscience dictates. I consider this form of warfare justified and I have acted according to my conscience. I would have to do the same all over again.' [36] For his part, Raeder insisted:

On the basis of the evidence the German Navy's cleanness and decency in battle were fundamentally confirmed. The German Navy stands before this Court and before the world with a clean shield and an unstained flag ... The Naval Operations Staff and its chief ... made an honest endeavour from the first to the very last moment to bring the conduct of modern naval warfare into harmony with the requirements of inter-national law and humanity, on the same basis as our opponents.[37]

When the International Military Tribunal delivered its judgement, on 1 October 1946, Doenitz was found not guilty of the charge of conspiracy but guilty of waging aggressive war. On the specific charges relating to the deaths of survivors, the Tribunal was 'not prepared to hold [him] guilty for his conduct of submarine warfare against British armed merchant ships',[38] and it considered that the 'evidence did not show with the certainty required that [he] deliberately ordered the killing of shipwrecked survivors'.[39] His War Order No. 154 and the '*Laconia* Order' were, however, held to be undoubtedly ambiguous on the latter point and deserving of the strongest censure. In a rather confusing judgement, the Tribunal held that failure to rescue survivors and the sinking of neutral vessels without warning in certain specified sea areas were clear breaches of the London Submarine Agreement of 1936. The Tribunal went on to argue that, Germany having signed without reservations, the provisions of that agreement ought to have had priority over any considerations about the safety of the attacking U-boats. But in view of evidence about orders issued to British submarines in May 1940, and Admiral Nimitz's admission that the United States had pursued a policy of unrestricted submarine warfare in the Pacific Ocean, the Tribunal explained that Doenitz's sentence of imprisonment for ten years had not been 'assessed on the ground of his breaches of the international law of submarine warfare'.[40] His was the lightest sentence passed on any of the accused found guilty.

Presumably in anticipation of the guilty verdict, and possibly fearing that it might lead to the death penalty, a plea for revision of the sentence had already been drawn up by a group of Germany's leading submarine commanders, many with high decorations for bravery. They asserted that there had never been any order to kill survivors, and that anybody who had interpreted the '*Laconia* Order' in that way must have been 'prompted to do so by personal psychological inclination'. They pleaded that they had fought fairly and that their commander-in-chief ought not to be branded a criminal. Among the signatories appeared such names as Albrecht Brandi (*U–617, U–380, U–967*), Otto Buelow (*U–404*), Peter 'Ali' Cremer (*U–333*), Carl Emmermann (*U–172*), Ulrich Heyse (*U–128*), Georg Lassen (*U–160*), Heinrich Lehmann-Willenbrock (*U–96*), August Maus (*U–185*), Victor Oehrn (*U–37*), Hermann Rasch (*U–106*), Adalbert Schnee (*U–6, U–60, U–201, U–2511*), Victor Schuetze (*U–103*), Otto Schuhart (*U–29*), Wilhelm Schulz (*U–124*), Reinhard Suhren (*U–564*), and Erich Topp (*U–552*). By the end of the war, many of these officers had been commanding U-boat flotillas or serving at U-boat headquarters.[41]

The Tribunal found Raeder guilty on all three counts of the indictment and sentenced him to life imprisonment. He was, presumably, considered the more culpable for his part in the Nazi conspiracy to wage an aggressive war; but with regard to the specific accusations concerning the conduct of U-boat warfare the Tribunal indicated that its judgement on his conduct was identical to the decision reached in Doenitz's case.[42] In fact, Raeder gained early release in 1955, a year before Doenitz completed his sentence.

Since the end of the war, many novels, films and boys' picture story books have tended to depict the principal maritime enemy, especially the German U-boat commanders, as arrogant, blood-thirsty Nazis steeped in sadistic cruelty and completely indifferent to the sufferings of merchant seamen on those occasions when they deigned to desist from murdering them out of hand. Certainly war is a cruel and bloody business in which participants on both sides – members of the armed forces and civilians alike – are frequently subjected to terrifying ordeals, appalling injuries, prolonged suffering and excruciatingly painful deaths. For those who serve at sea, there are always the additional dangers from the sea itself and from exposure to extreme weather conditions. Despite the compassionate yearnings of common humanity, and the best efforts of international jurists to enshrine them in the law of nations, war cannot be conducted painlessly and it cannot be conducted with all the nicely modulated courtesies and consideration of a state ball or a formal debate at the Oxford Union. Forced to make life or death decisions in fog, smoke, darkness, and agonising uncertainty, men will sometimes make tragic mistakes; and their opponents will place the worst possible construction on those mistakes. Amid the fear and exhilaration of battle, normally considerate men may behave in ways quite alien to their natural character, as may those who have been traumatised by some dreadful experience. Similarly, when whole nations feel they are fighting for their very existence against implacable foes, they and their leaders are unlikely to accept restraints of custom and law when it can be persuasively argued that changes in the technology of war, the enemy's own practices, or overriding operational considerations have already rendered custom and law archaic and inoperative.

Even so, there was no shortage of examples of how men of the German and Italian navies, at least, often gave such help as lay in their power to survivors from sunken ships.[43] Seamen from Axis as well as Allied ships were, however, frequently left to struggle for their own survival because neither their attackers nor their own ships could break off from the continuing battle to effect a rescue,[44] or they could not accept the risk of being attacked during rescue operations. In addition, submarines and small craft simply could not accommodate large numbers of survivors; weather and sea conditions could impede or prevent rescue; and rescue by attacking aircraft was totally impracticable except, occasionally, for a flying boat in very favourable circumstances. Inability to help survivors is, clearly, a very different matter from deliberately setting out to slaughter them. If one makes adequate allowances for the harsh and inescapable realities of naval warfare, the great weight of evidence from war-time survivors' reports, post-war memoirs and oral reminiscences of survivors does not support the accusation that the Germans, Italians or even Japanese, apart from a few atypical incidents, routinely and deliberately set out to murder British merchant seamen when they had been compelled to abandon their ships.

Certain individuals were, however, successfully prosecuted for war crimes committed against British merchant seamen on the high seas. Even before the trial of the major war criminals at Nuremberg, Kapitän-leutnant Heinz Eck and four other members of the crew of *U–852* had been put on trial at Hamburg in October 1945. Before a court martial composed of British and Greek officers, they were charged with murdering survivors from the Greek ship *Peleus* on 13 March 1944 by firing machine-guns and throwing hand grenades.[45] The British Admiralty hoped that Eck would incriminate Doenitz by pleading that he had acted under orders to kill survivors, but he resolutely refused to adopt that line of defence: he loyally maintained that he knew of no such order.[46] An experienced U-boat commander who had been a staff officer at U-boat headquarters, Korvettenkapitän Adalbert Schnee, gave evidence that he had briefed captains of the danger that wreckage from sunken ships would reveal their presence to patrolling aircraft, but added that the stress of command in difficult circumstances must have caused Eck to lose his nerve. Schnee claimed that, in similar circumstances, he personally would not have acted as Eck had done; he would have tried to save lives.[47] All five of the accused were found guilty. Eck and two of his officers were sentenced to death, another officer to life imprisonment and a leading seaman to fifteen years imprisonment.[48] The death sentences were carried out by shooting, but the imprisoned men were released in 1952 and 1951 respectively.

Korvettenkapitän Karl-Heinz Moehle, who had given evidence against Doenitz, was tried on 15 and 16 October 1946 for briefing U-boat commanders of his Fifth Flotilla at Kiel that the ambiguity of Doenitz's '*Laconia* Order' could be interpreted as authorising attacks on survivors.

He pleaded that he was only passing on the orders of his superior officer, and had advised his listeners: 'You must yourselves decide as your own consciences dictate. The safety of your own boat must always remain your prime consideration.' [49] Rejecting the plea of superior orders, the court sentenced Moehle to five years imprisonment, although his defence counsel, Dr Zippel, pointed out a few days after the trial that 'not one single case of unlawful killing of shipwrecked survivors could be proved as a result of this order', and it was absurd 'to convict the subordinate who passed the order down through the chain of command while the originator of the order who conceived it and is responsible for its contents is acquitted by the International Military Tribunal'.[50]

In a trial held at Hamburg in May 1947, Helmuth von Ruckteschell, captain of the German auxiliary cruiser *Widder*, was found guilty of continuing to fire on the *Davisian* after she had signalled that she was complying with his orders, and of failing to provide for the safety of survivors from the *Anglo Saxon* and the Norwegian vessel *Beaulieu*, but he was acquitted of firing at survivors on rafts from the *Anglo Saxon* and of continuing to fire on the *Empire Dawn* after the master had signalled by torch that the vessel was being abandoned. The evidence in these cases underlined the difficulties of signalling between ships during an action when the glare from fires or gun flashes could combine with darkness or smoke to obscure an answering pennant or a desperate signal made with a feeble hand torch. It also illustrated the tendency for fearful survivors to assume that shots aimed at their ship were actually aimed at rafts or lifeboats. Von Ruckteschell was sentenced to ten years imprisonment. Both the Judge Advocate and the British prosecuting counsel were surprised at the severity of the sentence on a fifty-seven-year-old man who had been seriously ill since 1943,[51] and the reviewing officer eventually reduced the sentence to seven years, presumably on the grounds that, in voting to evade capture by pulling away under cover of darkness, the survivors from the *Beaulieu* had effectively prevented von Ruckteschell from providing for their safety. Von Ruckteschell died in prison just before he was due for early release on health grounds.

The evidence that survivors were deliberately massacred was much clearer in the case of atrocities committed by the Japanese. For ordering the murder of survivors from the British vessel *Behar*, Rear-Admiral Sakonju was sentenced to death, and Captain Mayazumi of the cruiser *Tone*, on whose deck the killings took place, was sentenced to seven years imprisonment, this much lighter sentence recognising his repeated efforts to persuade his superior to countermand the order about disposing of the survivors.[52]

Others clearly guilty of vile crimes against survivors could not be put on trial. Lieutenant-Commander Kazuro Ebato, who had directed *RO–110*'s attack on the survivors of the *Daisy Moller*, had been lost when his submarine was sunk some two months later, and Captain Tatsunoseke Ariizumi, who had ordered the massacre of survivors from the *Tjisalak*, committed suicide rather than surrender to the Americans at the end of the war.[53] It seems likely that more cases would have been brought to trial, both in Europe and the Far East, if the accused or key witnesses for the prosecution had survived to the end of the war.

One further question remains to be considered: could the British government and shipowners have done more to improve the chances of survival for the crews of merchant ships? Describing conditions in the early days of the war, the acting general secretary of the National Union of Seamen, Charles Jarman, alleged that inadequate life-saving equipment had cost the lives of hundreds of men because 'all the improvements put into ships during the last war had been discarded because of the cost'.[54] At that period of the war, the union had had to plead and fight for improvements because, in his view, nothing had changed since the *Titanic* had gone down in 1912. Merchant seamen would have found nothing strange in that accusation: it would merely have confirmed their deeply ingrained prejudice against 'penny-pinching shipowners' who, in the collective memory of seafarers, had always valued a healthy balance sheet and their own prosperity above the dangers, discomforts, welfare and safety of the men who manned their ships. The speed with which a relieved and grateful nation after 1918 had forgotten its wartime debt to the merchant seamen, the bitterness aroused by the imposition of a 10 per cent wage cut leading to the seamen's strike of 1925, and the unemployment and deprivation of the years of depression between the wars, had done nothing to soften the average seaman's opinion of either his employers or his government.

Jarman was also critical of the way his members had been exposed to danger in convoys which could not be given an adequate escort and in ships, some newly constructed, which were so slow that they could easily be overtaken by surfaced U-boats. At the height of the Battle of the Atlantic in 1943, he accused the government of treating these matters as aspects of policy which it was 'willing to handle without much regard to conserving the precious lives of the men of the Merchant Navy'.[55] By that stage Jarman had decided that the union needed to

apply pressure to government departments where he was far from
convinced that everything possible was being done, but he went out
of his way to emphasise that he was making no reflection on the
shipowners: 'I refuse to believe that any shipowner has deliberately
refrained from meeting the statutory requirement in respect of lifeboats
and other life-saving equipment.' [56]

With the wisdom of hindsight, it is obvious that more merchant seamen
would have survived the war if, in the inter-war years, shipowners had
phased out all the older, slower ships fitted with radial davits and
replaced them with new, faster vessels, generously equipped with life-
saving aids and fitted with quadrant or gravity davits. It would be
unreasonable, however, to criticise the shipowners for their reluctance
to embark on such a policy at a time when world trade was beset by
economic depression, cut-throat competition with foreign shipowners
was rife, and the League of Nations was expected to prevent any further
wars. Shipowners and shareholders were – very understandably – mainly
concerned with operating vessels which were adequate for the commercial conditions of the 1920s and 1930s, and supplying their ships with
those life-saving appliances required by law to meet what were regarded
as normal peacetime risks. They could not be expected to foresee the
conditions which were to prevail in the early 1940s, and it certainly
would not have been in Britain's interest when the crisis came if many
of her shipping companies had gone out of business ten or fifteen years
earlier through trying to operate faster and more lavishly equipped
ships than could be employed economically under the trading conditions
then prevailing.

Now hindsight also suggests that merchant seamen could have been
better protected if, in the inter-war years, successive British governments
had maintained in commission a far larger number of ships suitable
for escorting merchant convoys in any future war – but the expense
would have been prohibitive for a nation impoverished by the cost of
the First World War, and it would have been politically unacceptable
to a democratic and largely pacifist electorate which was convinced that
only a few years earlier it had won a war to end all wars. In any case,
the government could hardly have envisaged that war would entail the
collapse of France and the opening up of the French Biscay ports for
use as enemy U-boat bases at a time when many potential escort vessels
would have to be sacrificed while engaged in evacuating British troops
from Norway, Belgium, France, Greece and Crete.

The suggestion that culpable and short-sighted policies adopted
by shipowners and governments in the 1920s and 1930s led to

unnecessarily high wartime casualties among merchant seamen might, perhaps, be persuasively argued at an abstract and theoretical level, especially if one believes that no expenditure would have been too great if only it could have diminished the seamen's appalling ordeal. The charge of culpability is, however, difficult to sustain if one makes adequate allowance for the harsh practical commercial and political realities which affected policy-making during those years. Admittedly, it would have been disgraceful if, as Stephen Roskill has claimed, not one exercise involving the defence of merchant convoys was conducted between 1919 and 1939,[57] but more recent research has indicated that some exercises were conducted in the use of ASDIC in defence of convoys, although the lessons were not widely disseminated.[58] In other important respects neither the shipping companies nor the Admiralty can be said to have been completely unprepared in 1939.[59] In the immediate prelude to war the arrangements for setting up the Naval Control Service for merchant shipping, for introducing the convoy system, for supplying ships with stiffening, armament and other war equipment, for preparing code books and instructions to masters and shipowners, and for training merchant seamen in gunnery, all made an important contribution to protecting not only the ships themselves but also their crews once war had begun.

Throughout the war there was widespread recognition of the important role of merchant ships and their crews. No one would have dissented from the assessment that they were vital both for the defence of an island nation under siege conditions and for supporting any offensive action to bring the war to a successful conclusion. An enormous effort was put into building corvettes and frigates to escort convoys, providing them with support from both ship-based and land-based aircraft, discovering the enemy's intentions through traditional intelligence gathering and the Enigma code-breakers at Bletchley Park, and developing such devices as Asdic, radar, degaussing, Snowflake, Leigh lights, HF/DF, Hedgehog, Squid and various anti-aircraft weapons. Finding the raw materials, the manpower and the means of production under wartime conditions was a tremendous achievement when one considers the competing claims of other sections of the armed forces and civilian organisations. Of course, one might debate whether trade protection should have been given an even greater priority by, for example, transferring long-range aircraft from the RAF's bombing offensive to maritime reconnaissance, or by reducing the resources devoted to the heavier warships, or by using steel to build better protected ships rather than tanks for the army. But the decisions taken at the time, often in conditions of recurrent crises, competing demands and inadequate data, could hardly be expected to provide perfect and unchallengeable solutions to every problem: it was sufficient that they turned out to be 'good enough' at the time and were implemented with energy and ingenuity.

The primary purpose of those innovations was the preservation of merchant ships and their cargoes, rather than the safety of their crews. As such, a detailed account of their development has been considered to lie outside the scope of this book but, even if their contribution was largely incidental and unquantifiable, they must have improved the merchant seamen's chances of survival. Aircraft or escorts forced U-boats to submerge before they could attack; more effective weapon systems discouraged some enemy commanders from pressing home attacks at close range; code-breakers sometimes gave timely warning of U-boat concentrations so that convoys could be diverted away from danger areas; RAF and USAF bombing raids disrupted the work of building and supplying U-boats and training their crews; and, decisively, over 700 German U-boats and many of their most experienced commanders and crews were destroyed. As a result of these types of operation, many merchant seamen reached their destination completely unscathed.

The fate of those who were not so fortunate received a great deal of attention. No doubt it was accepted by those responsible for the higher direction of the war that, so long as ships had to put to sea, some – probably very many – merchant seamen would lose their lives. It would be grossly unfair, however, to suggest that possible measures to help crews survive the sinking of their ships were viewed with either callous indifference or fatalistic resignation by those in authority. Given the worldwide scope of the shipping industry, the multiplicity of ships in service, changing operational conditions, and the multitude of different shipowners, there was no possibility of introducing rapid across-the-board solutions to survival problems. But there was no lack of effort on the part of the Admiralty and the shipowners in gathering information about the practical experiences of survivors; there was no lack of interest on the part of medical researchers, inventors, civil servants, businessmen and seamen in devising additional survival equipment or improving existing equipment; and there was no lack of pressure for enhanced safety provision from philanthropic individuals and organisations, a number of MPs, the press and the maritime unions.

Improvements in safety equipment introduced during the war deserve to be regarded as something of a triumph for government Ministers, civil servants, Ministry surveyors and shipping company marine and engineering superintendents. They faced much criticism, frequent disappointments and daunting wartime problems at every stage in such matters as consultation, evaluation, decision-making, acquiring materials and arranging production in adequate quantity. Distribution and installation were necessarily piecemeal, and seamen could be both tantalised and infuriated by the knowledge that other ships had more up-to-date equipment than their own. Every improvement took time, and lives were lost which might have been saved if better equipment could have been made available sooner, but bit by bit the safety arrangements were improved until, eventually, Charles Jarman of the National Union of Seamen was prepared to concede that the provision of lifesaving equipment on British ships 'was second to none in the world'.[60]

Early in 1943, Jarman had even felt moved to complain that the press was causing relatives of merchant seamen needless anxiety by paying far too much attention to sensational stories about the perils and privations of protracted voyages in lifeboats and rafts and largely ignoring the more frequent occasions when survivors were rescued very quickly.[61] He was supported in that criticism by the Minister of War Transport, Lord Leathers, who claimed at a luncheon in London on 22 March 1943 that with the methods then employed, 'eighty-seven out of every hundred merchant seamen were saved when cargo vessels were attacked and sunk ... Once away from the sinking ship a man was well on the way to safety, and in five cases out of six the survivors were picked up within twenty-four hours'.[62] Possibly the claim that 87 per cent of crew members were being rescued referred to a limited period in very favourable circumstances; possibly it was intended to reassure the seamen's families at a critical time in the Battle of the Atlantic; or it may have been deliberately intended to mislead the enemy. It certainly did not give the full picture. Admiralty Trade Division figures suggest that the percentage of crew (merchant seamen and DEMS gunners) rescued when merchant ships were sunk in 1943 was about 74 per cent, which was also the average rescue rate for the whole war. The worst year of the war was 1941, when 69 per cent were rescued.[63] A detailed postwar study involving a sample of ships with a total of 27,000 crew calculated that, in fact, only 68 per cent were rescued.[64]

No matter how generous the provision of survival aids, no matter how efficient the arrangements for rescuing survivors, no matter how reassuring the statistics, all who sailed under the red ensign between

1939 and 1945, whatever their nationality, were well aware that they were engaged in a very hazardous occupation. Survival could ultimately depend on an unpredictable combination of luck, skill, courage, resourcefulness, determination and fortitude. Without the merchant seamen's willingness to face up to that knowledge and their readiness to continue sailing their ships in spite of all risks, victory would not have been possible and Britain would not have survived as an independent state.

From time to time correspondents to certain newspapers engage in a sporadic debate about the need for an additional statue to complete the grand design for London's Trafalgar Square. There is never any lack of ideas about who might be commemorated in this way, but perhaps a life-size bronze group of Merchant Navy survivors on a raft would be a fitting reminder of some important, but largely unsung, contributors to the long history of British seapower. It might even touch the conscience of an island nation which has spent the last fifty years indifferent to the decline of its merchant fleet and the gradual disappearance of a once proud seafaring tradition.

Notes

Preface

1. Atle Thowsen, 'The Norwegian Merchant Navy in Allied War Transport', in Stephen Howarth and Derek Law, *The Battle of the Atlantic, 1939–1945* (London, 1994), p. 61.
2. Geoffrey Till, 'The Battle of the Atlantic as History', in Howarth and Law, *The Battle of the Atlantic*, p. 587.

Chapter 1: The German Threat to British Merchant Shipping

1. *Parliamentary Debates* (Commons), hereafter cited as *PD(C)*, vol. 351, col 371, W. S. Churchill, oral answer, 4 September 1939.
2. Ibid.
3. Ibid., col. 372.
4. Ibid., A. V. Alexander.
5. Ibid., col. 374, W. S. Churchill.
6. *Daily Mirror*, 5 September 1939, p. 1.
7. *Manchester Guardian*, 7 September 1939, p. 6, *The Guardian* ©.
8. *Observer*, 10 September 1939, p. 6, *The Guardian* ©.
9. *Daily Telegraph*, 5 September 1939, p. 6, leading article, © Telegraph Group, London, 1939.
10. Ibid., 6 September 1939, p. 6.
11. Lord Lee of Fareham, speech, 22 December 1921, reported in US Congress (Senate), 67th Congress, session 2, document 126, *Conference on the Limitation of Armament* (Washington DC, 1922), p. 269.
12. Article 4 of 'Draft Treaty on the Use of Submarines and Noxious Gasses', ibid., p. 888.
13. Admiral Doenitz, *Memoirs: Ten Years and Twenty Days* (London, 1959), p. 54.
14. This figure is quoted by such writers as Winston Churchill, John Terraine and Peter Kemp, but other sources give slight variations.
15. *The Times*, 9 September 1939, p. 10, citing report by Commander Hitchcock, an assistant US naval attaché who interviewed survivors landed in Galway.
16. ADM 199/2130, report of interview with Chief Officer Copeland. ADM 199/2130–2148 inclusive consist of reports of interviews with survivors. In subsequent references the words 'report of interview with' are omitted.
17. Ibid.
18. J. A. H. Hopkins, compiler, *Diary of World Events* (Baltimore, 1942), ii, item 20, from *Baltimore Sun*, 14 September 1939, report by James F. King, Associated Press, after interviewing survivors at Halifax, Nova Scotia.

19. Ibid., item 31, from *Baltimore Sun*, 7 September 1939, article by Doris Kent, survivor landed in Galway.
20. Ibid., item 17.
21. ADM 199/2130, Chief Officer Copeland.
22. Hopkins, *Diary of World Events*, passim.
23. *Daily Telegraph*, 6 September 1939, p. 1.
24. Fred Taylor (trans. and ed.), *The Goebbels Diaries, 1939–1941* (London, 1982), entry for 31 December 1939, p. 79.
25. Doenitz, *Memoirs*, quoted on p. 57.
26. IWM 11393/4, transcript of interview by Tony Lane with Paddy Bryan, a survivor.
27. ADM 199/2130, Captain Barnetson.
28. Admiralty, 'Defence of Merchant Shipping Handbook', 1938, DMS 3 3 65, quoted as evidence to the International Military Tribunal (IMT), vol. 40, p. 88.
29. ADM 199/2130, Captain T. Georgeson.
30. Ibid., Captain Thomas Prince.
31. *PD(C)*, vol. 351, cols 1243–44, 26 September 1939.
32. Ministry of Information general press release. See, for example, *The Times*, 26 September 1939, p. 8.
33. ADM 199/2130, Chief Officer Norman Hartley. Surprisingly, writing in 1948 in the first volume of his memoirs, p. 331, Churchill was still alleging that there had been no survivors from the *Royal Sceptre* and *Bosnia*.
34. ADM 199/2075, memorandum, 21 September 1939.
35. *Manchester Guardian*, 11 September 1939, p. 3, *The Guardian* ©.
36. ADM 199/2130, Captain W. Trowsdale.
37. *The Times*, 2 October 1939, comment by Captain McAlpine of the *Blairlogie*, p. 15.
38. ADM 199/2130, Captain Hugh Kerr.
39. *Manchester Guardian*, 16 September 1939, interview with John Atkinson, survivor from the *British Influence*.
40. ADM 199/2130, Captain J. E. Egner.
41. Hopkins, *Diary of World Events*, ii, item 61, *New York Herald Tribune*, 24 September 1939.
42. Ibid., item 40, *Baltimore Evening Sun*, 19 September 1939.
43. Admiralty, 'Defence of Merchant Shipping Handbook', 1938, DMS 3 1 55, quoted as evidence in *IMT*, vol. 40, p. 88.
44. ADM 199/2130, Captain J. Busby.
45. Ibid.
46. *The Times*, 22 September 1939, pp. 8 and 12; 23 September 1939, pp. 8 and 10; ADM 199/2130, Captain Schofield.
47. Order suggested by Doenitz and approved by Hitler, quoted in Günther Hessler, *The U-Boat War in the Atlantic, 1939–1945* (London, 1992), p. 42.
48. *The Times*, 2 October 1939, p. 8.
49. IMT, document C–191, vol. 13, p. 356.
50. ADM 199/2074, Anti-Submarine Report for October 1939.
51. *Manchester Guardian*, 11 January 1940, p. 6, *The Guardian* ©.
52. Order cited in *IMT*, document 642-D, vol. 35, p. 270.

53. *The Times*, 15 November 1939, p. 8.
54. ADM 199/2130, Chief Officer J. H. Casson.
55. *Lloyds List and Shipping Gazette*, 19 February 1940, p. 3, quoting German News Agency report of 17 February 1940.
56. Hopkins, *Diary of World Events*, iii, item 282, *Baltimore Sun*, 4 March 1940, text of broadcast.
57. Winston Churchill, speech to secret session of the House of Commons, 25 June 1941, in Charles Ede (ed.), *Secret Session Speeches* (London, 1946), pp. 26–27.

Chapter 2: Meeting the Threat

1. *PD(C)*, vol. 343, cols 1553–54, Llewellin, oral answer, 14 February 1939.
2. Ibid., vol. 345, col. 653, Shakespeare speaking on Naval Estimates, 16 March 1939.
3. Ibid., col. 654.
4. *The Times*, 14 October 1939.
5. *PD(C)*, vol. 353, col. 80, 7 November 1939, Sir John Gilmour, written answer.
6. *The Seaman*, October 1941, p. 33.
7. National Maritime Board (Sailors', Firemen's and Catering Department Panel) minutes, 29 January 1942.
8. *Lloyds List and Shipping Gazette* of 13 and 18 May 1940 reports the case of a ship's fireman from Liverpool sentenced to one month's imprisonment for revealing information in Laurenço Marques.
9. *PD(C)*, vol. 358, cols 1761–62, 18 March 1940, speech by Salter.
10. Ibid., vol. 357, col. 432, 8 February 1940. Salter told Emmanuel Shinwell that, up to 31 January, 431 merchant seamen had been killed.
11. Ibid., vols 351–57 passim.
12. ADM 199/2075, Admiralty circular, 15 September 1939.
13. *PD(C)*, vol. 358, col. 1678, 18 March 1940, speech by Gilmour.
14. See, for example, the quarterly reprints of General Minutes to Superintendents, 1935–40, Marine Safety Agency, Southampton.
15. Figures, rounded to nearest thousand, from annual census by the Registrar-General of Shipping and Seamen and quoted in Sir William Elderton, 'Merchant Seamen during the War', *Journal of Institute of Actuaries*, 83 (1946), p. 254.
16. C. B. A. Behrens, *Merchant Shipping and the Demands of War* (London, 1955), appendix 27, p. 179.
17. Elderton, 'Merchant Seamen during the War', p. 255.
18. *PD(C)*, vol. 357, col. 1, oral question to Minister of Shipping, 6 February 1940.
19. Ministry of Information (for Ministry of War Transport), *Merchantmen at War: The Official Story of the Merchant Navy, 1939–1944* (London, 1944), p. 13.
20. Admiral Sir Bertram Ramsay, report on 'Operation Dynamo', 18 June 1940, Churchill Archives Centre, Ramsay Papers, RMSY 8/5.
21. Kenneth Poolman, *Focke-Wulf Condor: Scourge of the Atlantic* (London, 1978).
22. ADM 205/7, paper on Protection of Trade in the Western Approaches, Dunbar-Nasmith to First Sea Lord, 22 December 1940.

23. Authors' calculations based on *BMVL*, and Jürgen Rohwer, *Axis Submarine Successes, 1939–1945* (Cambridge, 1983).
24. Authors' calculations from Admiralty Trade Division figures reproduced in John Costello and Terry Hughes, *The Battle of the Atlantic* (London, 1977), p. 304.
25. W. S. Churchill, *The Second World War*, ii, p. 639.
26. Ibid., p. 529

Chapter 3: The Battle for National Survival

1. Winston S. Churchill, *The Second World War* (London, 1952), iii, p. 609.
2. Adolf Hitler, Fuehrer Directive No. 23, 6 February 1941, in *Fuehrer Conferences on Naval Affairs, 1939–1945* (London, 1990), p. 179.
3. Churchill, *The Second World War*, iii, p. 100.
4. Hobhouse to Brocklebank, 12 February 1941, Brocklebank MSS in Merseyside Maritime Museum Archives.
5. Churchill, *The Second World War*, iii, pp. 105–7.
6. Ibid., p. 108.
7. Robert Rhodes James (ed.), *'Chips': The Diaries of Sir Henry Channon* (London, 1993), p. 302.
8. Churchill, *The Second World War*, iii, pp. 126–27.
9. Behrens, *Merchant Shipping and the Demands of War* (London, 1955), figure from appendix 28, p. 183; quotation from appendix 30, p. 186.
10. *The Times*, 9 May 1941, p. 4.
11. Behrens, *Merchant Shipping and the Demands of War*, p. 170 n. 2.
12. F. H. Hinsley et al., *British Intelligence in the Second World War: Its Influence on Strategy and Operations* (London, 1979–84), vol. 2, p. 169.
13. Churchill, *The Second World War*, iii, p. 609.
14. Erich Raeder, Report of C-in-C Navy to the Fuehrer, 17 September 1941, in *Fuehrer Conferences on Naval Affairs 1939–1945*, p. 235.
15. Ibid., Report of 13 November 1941, p. 240.
16. Ibid., Report of 12 December 1941, p. 245.
17. Stephen Roskill, *War at Sea* (London, 1954), vol. 1, p. 614; and John Costello and Terry Hughes, *The Battle of the Atlantic* (London, 1977), p. 304.
18. Jürgen Rohwer, *War at Sea 1939–1945* (London, 1996), p. 53.
19. Authors' calculation.
20. Authors' calculations based on *BMVL*, and Jürgen Rohwer, *Axis Submarine Successes, 1939–1945* (Cambridge, 1983).
21. Authors' calculations from Admiralty Trade Division figures reproduced in Costello and Hughes, *The Battle of the Atlantic*, p. 304.
22. See *Manchester Guardian*, 1 November 1940, p. 8; *New York Herald Tribune*, 10 November 1940; and the Radio Officers' Union journal *Signal*, December 1940, p. 321 (reprint of an article in the *Hull Weekly Chronicle*).
23. Guy Pierce Jones, *Two Survived* (London, 1941), p. 12.
24. *PD(C)*, vol. 368, col. 811, 4 February 1941.
25. Ibid., vol. 373, col. 1423, 30 July 1941.
26. Ibid., col. 1790, 5 August 1941.
27. *Shipbuilding and Shipping Record*, 5 June 1941, p. 545.

28. *Salt Spray Reporter*, journal of the Mercantile Marine Service Association, 66 (1941), p. 87.
29. *The Times*, 2 July 1941, p. 2.
30. *Shipbuilding and Shipping Record*, 27 November 1941, p. 509.
31. *Motor Boat and Yachting*, November 1941, p. 275.
32. *Shipbuilding and Shipping Record*, 18–25 December 1941, p. 599.
33. Authors' calculations based on *BMVL*, and Jürgen Rohwer, *Axis Submarine Successes*.
34. Churchill, *The Second World War*, iv, p. 860.
35. Anthony J. Watts, *Axis Submarines* (London, 1977), pp. 19–20.
36. Costello and Hughes, *The Battle of the Atlantic*, p. 304.
37. Admiralty Trade Division figure in Costello and Hughes, *Battle of the Atlantic*, p. 304.
38. Correlli Barnett, *Engage the Enemy More Closely: The Royal Navy in the Second World War* (London, 1991), p. 463.
39. Ibid., p. 464.
40. Winston S. Churchill, *The Second World War*, v, p. 551.
41. See Jürgen Rohwer, *The Critical Convoy Battles of March 1943* (London, 1977).
42. Authors' calculations based on *BMVL*, and Jürgen Rohwer, *Axis Submarine Successes*.
43. Roskill, *War at Sea*, vol. 3, pt 2, p. 472.
44. Ibid., iii, pt 2, p. 289.
45. Watts, *Axis Submarines*, pp. 18 and 20.
46. Admiral Doenitz, *Memoirs: Ten Years and Twenty Days* (London, 1959), pp. 116–17.

Chapter 4: From Fire and Foe

1. See, for example, Correlli Barnett, *Engage the Enemy More Closely: The Royal Navy in the Second World War* (London, 1991), p. 252.
2. R. A. McCance, C. C. Ungley, C. C. W. Crosfill and E. M. Widdowson, *The Hazards to Men in Ships Lost at Sea, 1940–44*, Medical Research Council Special Report Series No. 291 (London, 1956), p. 6.
3. *Manchester Guardian*, 11 January 1940, p. 3, *The Guardian* ©.
4. *Lloyds List and Shipping Gazette*, 19 February 1940, p. 3.
5. IWM 82/5/1, Captain E. Terrell; entries in *Who's Who* (1974).
6. BMVL, see list on pp. 64–72.
7. *PD(C)*, vol. 369, col. 937, 5 March 1941, A. V. Alexander speaking on the Navy Estimates.
8. ADM 199/2139, 3rd Engineer A. T. Greene.
9. ADM 199/2141, Captain J. Pascoe.
10. R. J. Scarlett, compiler, *Under Hazardous Circumstances: A Register of Awards of Lloyds War Medal for Bravery at Sea, 1939–1945* (Dallington, 1992), p. 85.
11. Ibid., p. 88.
12. Robert Seamer, *The Floating Inferno: The Story of the Loss of the Empress of*

Britain (Wellingborough, 1990), p. 40. Set on fire by the bombs, the ship was torpedoed two days later by *U–32*.

13. Ibid., p. 42.
14. ADM 199/2135, J. D. Edwards.
15. Richard Baker, 'Sequel to a Sea Battle', *Sea Breezes*, 67 (1993), pp. 878–81.
16. ADM 199/2138, Third Officer A. H. Bird.
17. Karl August Muggenthaler, *German Raiders of World War II* (London, 1980), pp. 207–209, 230–31.
18. ADM 199/2148, Second Officer C. B. Skinner.
19. ADM 199/2138, Captain G. Kinnell.
20. ADM 199/2140, Captain T. J. Williamson.
21. ADM 199/2145, Captain S. Wilson.
22. ADM 199/2148, Captain J. Errett, interview with the Athel Line's marine superintendent.
23. ADM 199/2130, Captain J. Busby.
24. ADM 199/2142, Captain J. Dodds.
25. ADM 199/2143, Chief Officer J. G. Swanson.
26. See, for example, ADM 199/2140, Captain A. Henney of the *Melpomene*.
27. Houlder Brothers and Co., *Sea Hazard, 1939–1945* (London, 1947), pp. 73–74, quoting report to the company by First Officer J. Allerton.
28. ADM 199/2131, Chief Officer H. Thompson.
29. ADM 199/2138, Captain J. C. Cooke.
30. ADM 199/2147, Captain W. L. Taylor.
31. ADM 199/2132, Second Officer V. P. Wills-Rust.
32. Scarlett, *Under Hazardous Circumstances*, passim.
33. David Williams, *Wartime Disasters at Sea* (Sparkford, 1997), pp. 104–105.
34. Ibid., pp. 193–94.
35. Brian James Crabb, *Passage to Destiny: The Sinking of the SS Khedive Ismail in the Sea War against Japan* (Stamford, 1997), pp. 114–32.
36. Williams, *Wartime Disasters*, pp. 135, 182 and 122–23.
37. ADM 199/2148, Sapper E. Munday.
38. Williams, *Wartime Disasters*, pp. 157, 173 and 169.
39. *The Times*, 4, 5, and 10 July 1940; David Williams, *Wartime Disasters*, pp. 106–7.
40. Léonce Peillard, *U-Boats to the Rescue: The Laconia Incident* (London, 1976), p. 211.
41. The significance is discussed below at pp. 120–22 and pp. 220–26.
42. David Williams, *Wartime Disasters*, pp. 170–71.
43. ADM 199/2144, Captain G. Goold
44. Doris M. Hawkins, *Atlantic Torpedo* (Bath, 1969), pp. 7–8.
45. ADM 199/2147, Second Officer C. H. R. Munday.
46. ADM 199/2133, Captain D. Gillies.
47. ADM 199/2138, Bosun S. J. Bramich.
48. ADM 199/2139, 2140 and 2143.
49. Jordan Vause, *U-Boat Ace: The Story of Wolfgang Lüth* (Shrewsbury, 1992), pp. 105–6 and 160.
50. See Glenn Infield, *Disaster at Bari* (London, 1974).
51. ADM 199/2140, Captain W. J. Gray.
52. *BMVL*, pp. 78–81.

Chapter 5: Abandon Ship!

1. R. A. McCance, C. C. Ungley, C. C. W. Crosfill and E. M. Widdowson, *The Hazards to Men in Ships Lost at Sea, 1940–44*, Medical Research Council Special Report Series No. 291 (London, 1956), p. 7.
2. Authors' calculations.
3. ADM 199/2138, Captain P. A. Wallace.
4. Ibid., Captain E. L. Hughes.
5. Ibid., Captain G. Kinnell.
6. Ibid., Captain A. B. Campbell.
7. Ibid., Chief Officer S. Miller.
8. ADM 199/2165, Admiralty Merchant Ships' Technical Committee, minutes, 24 October, 14 November and 5 December 1941.
9. Ibid., 17 April 1942.
10. ADM 199/2143, Captain W. J. Slade.
11. PD(C), vol. 356, col. 434, 23 January 1940, written answer.
12. *Merchant Navy Journal*, March 1941, p. 59.
13. PD(C), vol. 357, col. 1375, 21 February 1940, question.
14. Ibid., vol. 358, cols 186–87, 5 March 1940, oral answer.
15. Ibid., vol. 365, col. 84, 17 September 1940, oral answer.
16. Ministry of War Transport Notice M.202, December 1941.
17. ADM 199/2140, Captain A. Henney.
18. ADM 199/2141, Captain F. J. Hewlett.
19. ADM 199/2142, Chief Officer R. W. Thomson.
20. ADM 199/2143, Chief Officer I. S. McLean.
21. ADM 199/2139, Third Engineer A. T. Greene.
22. ADM 199/2143, Captain A. G. Williams.
23. ADM 199/2140, Captain D. Anderson.
24. ADM 199/2138, Chief Engineer F. Ellis.
25. ADM 199/2135, Captain J. W. Kemp.
26. Len Fifield, 'To Archangel', *Sea Breezes*, 71, (1997), p. 955.
27. ADM 199/2142, Captain R. Brown.
28. ADM 199/2145, Captain J. Kerr.
29. ADM 199/2148, Captain A. Ellis.
30. ADM 199/2140, Captain R. Brown.
31. Merchant Shipping (Life-Saving Appliances) 1938, SR & O 1938, No. 1375.
32. Charles H. Brown, *Nicholls's Seamanship and Nautical Knowledge* (18th edn, Glasgow, 1938), p. 83.
33. Notice to Owners and Skippers of Fishing Vessels, M.175, January 1940; Notice to Owners and Ship Masters, M.182, February 1940.
34. MT 9/3266, Chamber of Shipping to T. E. Metcalfe, 24 April 1940.
35. Merchant Shipping (Additional Life-Saving Appliances) No. 2 Rules 1940, SR & O 1941, No. 1304. See also *PD(C)*, vol. 365, col. 576, 15 October 1940, oral answer by Sir Arthur Salter.
36. Ocean Archives, Merseyside Maritime Museum, file OA 1132/1.
37. Ibid., file OA 89/2a.
38. ADM 199/2138, examples from 1941.

39. Brown, *Nicholls's Seamanship*, p. 85.
40. ADM 199/2140, Captain R. Brown of the *Glenshiel*.
41. See, for example, J. H. Drew, 'An Alternative Method of Breasting-Out Ships' Lifeboats in Lieu of Booms', *Merchant Navy Journal*, April 1942, p. 69.
42. MT 9/3812, report to the Minister of War Transport.
43. *Merchant Navy Journal*, July-September 1943, p. 69.
44. ADM 199/2133, Chief Officer H. W. Chadd.
45. ADM 199/2138, Second Officer R. S. Walker.
46. ADM 199/2143, Captain C. R. Aitken.
47. ADM 199/2145, Captain E. Gough.
48. ADM 199/2136, *Simnia*, 15 March 1941.
49. ADM 199/2138, *Tahchee*, 10 September 1941.
50. Ibid., *Inverlee*, 19 October 1941.
51. ADM 199/2140, *British Resource*, 14 March 1942.
52. Ibid., *Caspia*, 16 April 1942.
53. ADM 199/2141, *Bolton Castle*, 5 July 1942.
54. ADM 199/2142, *Sheaf Mount*, 24 August 1942.
55. Ibid., *Ross*, 29 October 1942.
56. ADM 199/2143, *Polydorus*, 27 November 1942.
57. ADM 199/2144, *Inverilen*, 3 February 1943.
58. Ibid., *Nailsea Court*, 9 March 1943.
59. ADM 199/2145, *Aymeric*, 16 May 1943.
60. McCance et al., *The Hazards to Men in Ships Lost at Sea*, pp. 7–8.
61. 'An Emergency Liferaft', *Motor Boat and Yachting*, 16 December 1939, p. 511.
62. James Linklater, letter to the editor, *Shipbuilder and Marine Engine-Builder*, January 1940, p. 12.
63. Ministry of Shipping Notice M.174, 'Emergency Rafts', December 1939. Notice M.175, January 1940, suggested similar, but smaller, rafts for fishing vessels.
64. MT 9/3168, note of a meeting with Miss Talbot.
65. *PD(C)*, vol. 356, col. 397, oral answer, 23 January 1940.
66. MT 9/3204, minute by Mr Boyd, 16 February 1940.
67. MT 9/3168, survey and minutes, January-February 1940.
68. *PD(C)*, vol. 357, col. 1872, oral answer, 27 February 1940.
69. Ibid., vol. 358, col. 187, oral answer, 5 March 1940.
70. ADM 199/2138, *Ciscar*; ADM 199/ 2139, *Grelhead*.
71. *Lloyds List and Shipping Gazette*, advertisement, 31 January 1940, p. 7; *Shipbuilder and Marine Engine-Builder*, March 1940, pp. 95–96.
72. *Lloyds List and Shipping Gazette*, 11 April 1940, advertisement, p. 3, and special lifesaving supplement, p. iii; *Motor Ship*, October 1940, p. 235.
73. *Lloyds List and Shipping Gazette*, 11 April 1940, special lifesaving supplement, advertisement, p. xx; *Shipbuilder and Marine Engine-Builder*, June 1940, article, p. 244.
74. *Shipbuilding and Shipping Record*, 26 February 1942, p. 275, and 19 March 1942, p. 352; *Shipbuilder and Marine Engine-Builder*, April 1942, p. 85.
75. ADM 199/2140, Captain P. W. Savery.
76. ADM 199/2143, Captain W. J. Slade.
77. *Signal*, January 1940, p. 12.

78. Ministry of Shipping Notice M.182, February 1940.
79. ADM 199/2138, Chief Officer S. Miller.
80. ADM 199/2142, Third Officer J. R. Mitchell.
81. ADM 199/2143, Captain C. S. Clutterbuck.
82. Ibid., Captain A. G. Williams.
83. MT 9/2964, 'Merchant Shipping (Life-Saving Appliances) Rules', 14 November 1938; see also Brown, *Nicholls's Seamanship*, p. 111.
84. *Observer*, 10 December 1939, p. 12.
85. MT 9/3168, senior surveyor, Glasgow, to Ministry of Shipping, 31 January 1940.
86. Ibid., various reports from surveyors, late January 1940.
87. National Union of Seamen, MSS 175/1/1/9, in University of Warwick, Modern Records Centre.
88. MT 9/3204, draft of Notice M.182 to ship owners and ship masters, February 1940; see also *Lloyds List and Shipping Gazette*, 23 March 1940.
89. *Lloyds List and Shipping Gazette*, 28 February 1940, p. 5.
90. *Daily Telegraph*, 18 December 1939, advertisement, p. 9.
91. *Lloyds List and Shipping Gazette*, advertisement, 20 February 1940.
92. Ibid., special supplement, 11 April 1940, p. xxvii.
93. *Merchant Navy Journal*, July/August 1942, p. 151.
94. *Manchester Guardian*, 22 July 1940, p. 5; see also MT 9/3266, Merchant Shipping (Additional Life-Saving Appliances) No. 2 Rules, 18 July 1940.
95. MT 9/3266, Chamber of Shipping to Metcalfe, 24 April 1940.
96. MT 9/3718, memorandum on lifejackets and lifesaving waistcoats, n.d. but circa late August 1942.
97. Ibid., minute by Metcalfe, 11 September 1942.
98. *Lifesaving at Sea*, Crown Film Unit, 1944.

Chapter 6: Face to Face with the Enemy

1. *The Times*, 23 October 1939, p. 10.
2. ADM 199/2130, Captain C. S. Tate.
3. *Manchester Guardian*, 31 January 1940, p. 12.
4. *Lloyds List and Shipping Gazette*, 7 June 1940, p. 2.
5. Ibid., 10 June 1940, p. 3.
6. Ibid., 3 August 1940.
7. *The Times*, 18 September 1940, p. 3.
8. ADM 199/2133, Captain R. G. Hammett.
9. Jordan Vause, 'Victor Otto Oehrn: The Ace with No Name', in Theodore P. Savas (ed.), *Silent Hunters: German U-Boat Commanders of World War II* (Campbell, California, 1997).
10. IMT, vol. 13, p. 275, evidence of Doenitz, 9 May 1946.
11. IWM 002723/01, post-war interview with Kretschmer.
12. ADM 199/2134, Second Officer of the *Invershannon*.
13. ADM 199/2135, Third Officer P. Jones.
14. *The Times*, leader, 5 October 1940, p. 5.
15. Winston Churchill, BBC broadcast, 27 April 1941.
16. *Lloyds List and Shipping Gazette*, 15 July 1940, p. 5.

17. ADM 199/2140, Captain C. J. R. Roberts.
18. ADM 199/2143, Captain C. S. Clutterbuck.
19. ADM 199/2165, Merchant Ships Technical Committee, minutes, 29 January 1943.
20. ADM 199/2134, Captain T. Fraser.
21. ADM 199/2144, Chief Officer S. P. Lloyd.
22. ADM 199/2140, Captain G. A. Niddrie.
23. Ibid., Second Officer D. Crook.
24. ADM 199/2141, Captain D. J. Williams.
25. ADM 199/2142, Chief Officer R. W. Thomson.
26. ADM 199/2137, Captain R. C. Loraine.
27. ADM 199/2140, Captain J. Kennedy.
28. ADM 199/2141, Apprentice K. F. Hancock.
29. Baron Burkhard von Müllenheim-Rechberg, *Battleship Bismarck: A Survivor's Story* (London, 1981), p. 262.
30. H. J. Brennecke, *Ghost Cruiser HK 33* (London, 1954), p. 108.
31. Theodor Detmers, *The Raider Kormoran* (London, 1961), p. 64.
32. Kurt Weyher and Hans Jürgen Ehrlich, *The Black Raider* (London, 1955), p. 42.
33. Kurt Weyher, personal postscript to Weyher and Ehrlich, *The Black Raider*, p. 199.
34. Detmers, *The Raider Kormoran*, p. 60.
35. Bernhard Rogge, *Under Ten Flags* (London, 1960), p. 120.
36. Ibid., p. 6.
37. ADM 199/2130, Captain P. G. G. Dove.
38. ADM 199/2135, Fourth Officer E. A. Gilham.
39. ADM 199/2136, Captain T. W. Morris.
40. ADM 199/2130, Captain C. Pottinger.
41. *Manchester Guardian*, 15 January 1940, p. 2, *The Guardian* ©.
42. Weyher and Ehrlich, *The Black Raider*, pp. 37–42, 69–71; *The Times*, 7 September 1940, p. 3.
43. Rogge, *Under Ten Flags*, pp. 80–81; Ulrich Mohr and A. V. Sellwood, *Atlantis: The Story of a German Surface Raider* (London, 1955), pp. 91–98.
44. ADM 199/2135, Fourth Officer E. A. Gilham.
45. IWM 89/3/1, Fifth Engineer R. Bellew.
46. Rogge, *Under Ten Flags*, p. 85; see also Mohr and Sellwood, *Atlantis*, pp. 110–17.
47. Weyher and Ehrlich, *The Black Raider*, pp. 139–40; see also *The Times*, 2 January 1941, pp. 3 and 4.
48. *The Times*, 30 June 1941, p. 3.
49. Brennecke, *Ghost Cruiser HK 33*, pp. 196–206.
50. IMT, vol. 5, document D–423, p. 219.
51. Fuehrer Conferences on Naval Affairs, 1939–1945 (London, 1990), p. 283.
52. IMT, vol. 13, p. 277.
53. H. R. Trevor Roper (ed.), *Hitler's Table Talk* (London, 1953), pp. 696–97.
54. Samuel Eliot Morison, *History of United States Naval Operations in World War II*, i, *The Battle of the Atlantic, 1939–1943* (Boston, 1947), p. 130.
55. ADM 199/2140, Captain F. J. Stirling.

56. ADM 199/2141, Second Officer B. M. Metcalfe.
57. Doenitz, *Memoirs*, p. 261.
58. IMT, vol. 13, p. 278.
59. *Fuehrer Conferences on Naval Affairs*, 1939–1945, p. 294.
60. ADM 116/5549, translation of written statement by Moehle, 19 July 1945.
61. IMT, vol. 13, p. 294.
62. ADM 199/2142, Captain H. Burgess.
63. Fred Sheehan, 'The Last Voyage of the *St Usk*', *Sea Breezes*, 72 (1998), pp. 145–50.
64. ADM 199/2142, Chief Officer J. Lee.
65. Ibid., Captain J. Dodds.
66. ADM 199/2143, Apprentice B. W. Whitty.
67. Ibid., Captain S. B. Davis.
68. Ibid., Second Officer A. Fell-Dunn.
69. ADM 199/2145, Captain S. Wilson.
70. Ibid., Captain J. Kerr.
71. *The Seaman*, February/March 1943, p. 217.
72. Ibid., September/October 1943, p. 294, and July/August 1944, p. 110; also *The Times*, 20 July 1943, p. 2.
73. *Manchester Guardian*, 25 March 1942, p. 8; *The Times*, same date, p. 3.
74. Bernard Edwards, *Blood and Bushido* (London, 1991), pp. 83–91.
75. Kenneth Hudson and Ann Nicholls, *The Book of Shipwrecks* (London, 1979), p. 111.
76. ADM 199/2147, Chief Officer P. Payne.
77. Ibid., Chief Engineer R. H. Rees.
78. Ibid., Cadet H. M. Fortune.
79. Edwards, *Blood and Bushido*, pp. 172–78.
80. ADM 199/2147, Second Officer J. Decker. In July a very similar massacre was perpetrated by the same submarine commander on survivors from the American ship *Jean Nicolet*.
81. FO 371/51050.
82. WO 311/564, statement of Captain Mayazumi, 17 March 1947, and other evidence; see also Edwards, *Blood and Bushido*, pp. 156–63.
83. J. Cameron (ed.), *The Peleus Trial* (London, 1948). See also WO 235/5 for transcript of the trial; and Dwight R. Messimer, 'Heinz-Wilhelm Eck: *Siegerjustiz* and the *Peleus* Affair', in Theodore P. Savas (ed.), *Silent Hunters*.
84. Heinz Eck, quoted in *The Times*, 19 October 1945, p. 3.
85. ADM 116/5549 includes a list of the vessels whose loss was investigated.

Chapter 7: *Vessel Abandoned!*

1. ADM 199/2138, Captain E. L. Hughes (*Ciscar*).
2. Ibid., Second Officer H. F. Jowett (*Cingalese Prince*).
3. ADM 199/2142, Chief Officer R. W. Thomson (*Empire Arnold*).
4. ADM 199/2145, Captain S. Wilson (*Hopetarn*).
5. ADM 199/2140, Third Officer S. W. Taylor.
6. ADM 199/2141, Apprentice K. F. Hancock.
7. R. A. McCance, C. C. Ungley, C. C. W. Crosfill and E. M. Widdowson, *The*

Hazards to Men in Ships Lost at Sea, 1940–44, Medical Research Council Special Report Series, 291 (London, 1956), p. 32.

8. OA 89/2, Captain A. M. Caird.
9. Ibid. Dr F. W. Mathews.
10. ADM 199/2144, Captain G. Goold.
11. E. C. B. Lee and Kenneth Lee, *Safety and Survival at Sea* (London 1989), p. 77.
12. *Navy News*, November 1996, p. 9.
13. G. W. Molnar, 'Survival of Hypothermia by Men Immersed in the Ocean,' *Journal of the American Medical Association*, 131 (1946) p. 1046, cited in McCance et al., *The Hazards to Men in Ships Lost at Sea*, p. 9.
14. Bernard Robin, *Survival at Sea* (London, 1981), p. 189, citing US Navy figures.
15. Lee and Lee, *Safety and Survival at Sea*, p. 54.
16. ADM 199/2138, Chief Engineer R. H. Wilson.
17. ADM 199/2140, Captain D. Anderson.
18. OA 89/2, Junior Wireless Operator V. B. Harrison.
19. OA 1132/1, Chief Officer W. C. Bird.
20. ADM 199/2144, Chief Officer W. H. Kell.
21. ADM 199/2143, Captain D. M. Williams.
22. *PD(C)*, vol. 358, col. 187, 5 March 1940.
23. *Lloyds List and Shipping Gazette*, 21 March, 30 April, 20 June, 3 September 1940, respectively.
24. *Shipbuilder and Marine Engine-Builder*, February 1943, p. 53.
25. MT 9/3266, notes of meeting, 23 May 1940.
26. Ibid., memorandum by Plumb, 21 June 1940.
27. MT 9/3251, 3266, correspondence.
28. *The Times*, 21 September 1940, p. 5, Talbot to the Editor.
29. *PD(C)*, 22 October 1940, vol. 365, col. 926.
30. MT 9/3521, Metcalfe to Principal Officers and Surveyors, 10 March 1941.
31. Ibid., Oldham and Son to Ministry of Shipping, 26 March 1942.
32. ADM 199/2140, Captains D. Anderson (*Benmohr*) and J. Collier (*Hertford*).
33. ADM 199/2144, Captain G. Goold.
34. National Maritime Board, Sailors', Firemen's and Catering Department Panel, minutes, 29 January 1942.
35. ADM 199/2138, Captain E. L. Hughes.
36. ADM 199/2142, Cadet J. L. Oliver.
37. ADM 199/2146, Captain F. H. Parmee.
38. Ibid., Captain T. A. Kent.
39. MT 9/3880, lecture by Metcalfe on lifesaving at sea.
40. *Motor Boat and Yachting*, 25 November 1939, advertisement, p. 2.
41. Ibid., editorial, 25 November 1939, p. 433.
42. Ibid., editorial, 6 January 1940, p. 1.
43. See, for example, *Motor Ship*, February 1940, p. 391.
44. *PD(C)*, 14 February 1940, vol. 357, cols 745–46.
45. 'Motor Lifeboats for New Merchant Ships: Satisfactory Outcome of "The Motor Boat" Campaign', *Motor Boat and Yachting*, 24 February 1940, p. 132.
46. Ibid., 11 May 1940, p. 350, and 25 May 1940, p. 401.
47. Ibid., 11 May 1940, p. 21.
48. *PD(C)*, written reply, 23 July 1940, vol. 363, col. 629.

49. *Motor Boat and Yachting*, August 1940, p. 53.
50. *PD(C)*, vol. 365, col. 16, 5 September 1940, Ronald Cross, oral answer.
51. *Motor Boat and Yachting*, October 1940, p. 105.
52. MT 9/3361, minutes of meeting, 14 October 1940.
53. *Motor Boat and Yachting*, November 1940, editorial, p. 133, and article, pp. 138–39.
54. *Shipbuilding and Shipping Record*, 9 January 1941, p. 47.
55. *Motor Ship*, March 1941, p. 416.
56. *Shipbuilder and Marine Engine-Builder*, May 1942, p. 151.
57. McCance et al., *The Hazards to Men in Ships Lost at Sea*, p. 8.
58. ADM 199/2140, Third Officer R. Johnson.
59. ADM 199/2142, Captain J. Dodds.
60. ADM 199/2143, Chief Engineer A. C. B. Watson.
61. ADM 199/2145, Captain J. Kerr.
62. ADM 199/2146, Captain F. H. Parmee.
63. ADM 199/2147, Chief Officer H. F. Tennant.
64. *PD(C)*, vol. 379, col. 756, 23 April 1942, Noel-Baker, oral answer.
65. Merchant Shipping (Life-Saving Appliances) Emergency Rules, 27 July 1942.
66. *PD(C)*, vol. 381, col. 966, 9 July 1942, Noel-Baker, written answer.
67. ADM 199/2142, Chief Officer W. Gibb.
68. ADM 199/2141, Captain D. W. Hughson.
69. ADM 199/2144, Carpenter K. Cooke.
70. MT 9/3204, draft of Notice M.182, February 1940.
71. ADM 199/2138, Chief Officer J. Cameron and Captain C. J. Evans.
72. *The Times*, 10 July 1941, p. 9; *Shipbuilder and Marine Engine-Builder*, May 1942, p. 151; *Merchant Navy Journal*, advertisement, July-August 1942, p. 149.
73. *Shipbuilding and Shipping Record*, 25 September 1941, p. 289.
74. *The Seaman*, July-August 1944, pp. 118–21.
75. ADM 199/2141, Second Officer D. L. M. Evans.
76. Ibid., Captain J. Pascoe.
77. ADM 199/2142, Captain S. R. Evans; ADM 199/2143, Chief Engineer A. C. B. Watson.
78. ADM 199/2142, Third Officer A. D. Howe; ADM 199/2143, Chief Officer I. S. McLean.
79. Ministry of War Transport notice M.6237/41; *The Times*, 13 August 1941, p. 2; *Merchant Navy Journal*, August 1941, p. 215.
80. *PD(C)*, vol. 393, col. 972, 5 November 1943, Noel-Baker, written answer.
81. *Motor Ship*, February 1943, p. 371; *Shipbuilder and Marine-Engine Builder*, July 1943, pp. 243–45.
82. *Shipbuilding and Shipping Record*, 21 October 1943, pp. 400–1.
83. *The Times*, 22 April 1944, p. 5.
84. *Shipbuilding and Shipping Record*, 24 June 1943, pp. 579, 587.
85. *Shipbuilder and Marine Engine-Builder*, July 1943, p. 245.
86. *PD(C)*, vol. 393, col. 972, 5 November 1943.
87. W. E. Stanton Hope, *Tanker Fleet: The War Story of the Shell Tankers and the Men Who Manned Them* (London, 1948), pp. 93–95.
88. *The Times*, 15 May 1943, p. 2.
89. *Shipbuilding and Shipping Record*, 24 June 1943, pp. 576–78.

90. Ibid., 3 February 1944, p. 104.
91. McCance et al., *The Hazards to Men in Ships Lost at Sea*, pp. 10, 12.
92. OA 89/2, Third Engineer W. Graham.
93. ADM 199/2144, Captain S. Foulkes.
94. OA 89/2, Third Engineer W. Graham.
95. IWM 89/5/1, Fourth Officer W. Close.
96. McCance et al., *The Hazards to Men in Ships Lost at Sea*, pp. 13–14.
97. ADM 199/2140, Captain W. Ewing.
98. Ibid., Captain R. Brown.
99. ADM 199/2132, Captain W. J. Calderwood.
100 ADM 199/2135, Chief Engineer G. H. Armstrong.
101 ADM 199/2138, Captain E. L. Hughes.
102 Ibid., Captain H. M. McLean.
103 Paul Lund and Harry Ludlam, *Night of the U-Boats* (London, 1974) gives a full account of convoy SC7.
104 Dan van der Vat, *The Atlantic Campaign: The Great Struggle at Sea, 1939–1945* (London, 1988), p. 151.
105 Donald Macintyre, *The Battle of the Atlantic* (London, 1969), p. 50.
106 B. B. Schofield and L. F. Martyn, *The Rescue Ships* (Edinburgh, 1968), letter of 22 September 1940, quoted p. 6.
107 ADM 199/2145, Captain S. Morris.
108 ADM 199/2151, proceedings of the *Copeland* during the passage of convoy ONS7.
109 J. W. McNee, 'Convoy Rescue Ships', *Journal of the Royal Naval Medical Service*, 31 (January 1945), pp. 1–7, quotation pp. 5–7.
110 For a 1942 example see Robert C. Fisher, 'Group Wotan and the Battle for Convoy SC 104', *Mariner's Mirror*, 84 (February 1998), pp. 64–75.
111 Schofield and Martyn, *The Rescue Ships*, pp. 164–65.

Chapter 8: Lifeboat and Raft Voyages

1. *The Times*, 6 January 1940, p. 3; *Manchester Guardian*, 6 January 1940, p. 9, and 19 January 1940, p. 9.
2. ADM 199/2131, Chief Officer H. Thompson.
3. ADM 199/2133, Captain R. G. Hammett.
4. Ibid.
5. Geoffrey Shakespeare, *Let Candles be Brought in* (London, 1949), pp. 272–74.
6. Dan van der Vat, *The Atlantic Campaign: The Great Struggle at Sea, 1939–1945* (London, 1988), p. 150.
7. *The Times*, 2 October 1940, p. 5, letter to the Editor from Basil Hall.
8. *PD(C)*, 15 October 1940, vol. 365, cols 575–76.
9. Ibid., cols 572–74.
10. *Manchester Guardian*, 1 November 1940, p. 8.
11. *The Times*, 22 January 1941, p. 2.
12. *Manchester Guardian*, 16 June 1941, p. 6. See also F. West, *Lifeboat Number Seven* (London, 1960).
13. *Shipbuilding and Shipping Record*, 31 July 1941, p. 111.
14. S.R. & O., 1941, No. 781.

15. *Signal*, September 1941, p. 209.
16. OA 1132/1/3, Captain A. English.
17. ADM 199/2138, Captain W. A. Shute.
18. Ibid., Captain G. F. Dobson.
19. Ibid., Captain C. J. Evans.
20. OA 89/2A, Captain A. Shaw.
21. ADM 199/2140, Captain A. Shaw.
22. ADM 199/2142, Captain H. Burgess.
23. ADM 199/2143, Captain C. S. Clutterbuck.
24. ADM 199/2141, Captain F. J. Hewlett.
25. MWT notice M.202, December 1941.
26. MWT notice M.202 (Revised), May 1943.
27. *Signal*, September 1943, p. 100.
28. ADM 199/2145, Captain S. Wilson.
29. ADM 199/2147, Captain J. W. Binns.
30. ADM 199/2144, Carpenter K. Cooke.
31. ADM 199/2165, minutes, 23 May 1941.
32. OA 89/2, Major W. F. Boylin to Lawrence Holt, 19 June 1941.
33. MT 9/3377, Horlicks Ltd to Board of Trade, 9 September 1940.
34. Ibid., Minute by Dr Tinker, 8 May 1941.
35. *Shipbuilding and Shipping Record*, 17 July 1941, p. 71; *Merchant Navy Journal*, July 1941, pp. 183–84.
36. *Merchant Navy Journal*, July 1941, p. 180.
37. *The Seaman*, October 1941, p. 34.
38. Medical Research Council papers in the PRO, FD 1/6079–6084,
39. Authors' calculations based on *BMVL* and Jürgen Rohwer, *Axis Submarine Successes, 1939–1945* (Cambridge, 1983).
40. Authors' calculations from Admiralty Trade Division figures reproduced in John Costello and Terry Hughes, *The Battle of the Atlantic* (London, 1977), p. 304.
41. Ministry of Food, Food Facts No. 133, *Daily Express*, 19 January 1943, p. 4; and No. 134, *Daily Telegraph*, 27 January 1943, p. 3.
42. *Daily Mirror*, 26 February 1942, p. 3.
43. Ibid., 6 March 1942, p. 3.
44. *PD(C)*, vol. 378, col. 1668, 19 March 1942.
45. Daily Express, 18 March 1942, p. 3.
46. OA 89/2, Second Steward S. Curtis (*Calchas*) ; OA 1132/1/3, Second Officer H. Butler (*Macon*).
47. *PD(C)*, vol. 391, col. 391, 15 July 1943, Noel-Baker, written answer.
48. ADM 199/2147, Captain J. W. Binns (*Fort La Maune*) and Chief Officer P. Payne (*British Chivalry*).
49. ADM 199/2140, Third Officer R. Johnson.
50. ADM 199/2142, Chief Officer R. W. Thomson.
51. ADM 199/2140, Captain A. Shaw.
52. Ibid., Captain G. A. Niddrie.
53. ADM 199/2142, Third Officer A. D. Howe.
54. ADM 199/2141, Second Officer D. L. M. Evans.
55. Ibid., Captain D. A. Reid.

56. ADM 199/2142, Chief Officer R. W. Thomson.
57. Ibid., Chief Officer J. Lee.
58. Ibid., Captain J. Dodds.
59. ADM 199/2143, Chief Officer I. S. McLean. (When one of the authors joined the *Olivebank* later in the war he found that her lifeboats carried tinned pork sausages and bacon in addition to the officially approved foods. He was told that they would be extra food for the Europeans, as the lascars would not touch such food. Was this a company or individual initiative arising from the experience of the *Teesbank's* survivors?)
60. R. A. McCance, C. C. Ungley, C. C. W. Crosfill and E. M. Widdowson, *The Hazards to Men in Ships Lost at Sea, 1940–44*, Medical Research Council Special Report Series, 291 (London, 1956), p. 19.
61. Ibid., p. 20.
62. ADM 199/2140, Second Officer D. Crook and Chief Officer D. J. Davis respectively.
63. ADM 199/2144, Captain S. Foulkes.
64. Ibid., Carpenter K. Cooke.
65. Authors' calculations based on McCance et al., *The Hazards to Men in Ships Lost at Sea, 1940–44*, p. 21.
66. ADM 1/12193, Surgeon Rear-Admiral S. F. Dudley, 22 January 1942.
67. McCance et al., *The Hazards to Men in Ships Lost at Sea, 1940–44*, p. 13.
68. *Merchant Navy Journal*, March 1942, p. 46.
69. Ibid., pp. 43–46; April 1942, p. 65; June 1942, pp. 116–17.
70. ADM 199/2142, Chief Officer D. I. Spencer.
71. *Manchester Guardian*, 19 December 1942, p. 4, *The Guardian* ©.
72. OA 89/2, Fourth Officer E. W. Casson.
73. Ibid., A. Cooper.
74. OA 1132/1/23, Third Officer G. H. Griffiths.
75. ADM 199/2142, Chief Officer R. W. Thomson.
76. OA 89/2a, Chief Officer G. Edge.
77. *Merchant Navy Journal*, July-September 1943, p. 71.
78. ADM 199/2138, Chief Officer J. Cameron.
79. ADM 199/2140, Second Officer E. Rowlands.
80. Ibid., Captain G. A. Niddrie.
81. ADM199/2142, Chief Officer R. W. Thomson.
82. MT 62/108, Taylor to Sir Arthur Salter, 27 July 1942.
83. ADM 199/2140, Second Officer E. Rowlands.
84. ADM 199/2145, Apprentice D. E. Clowe.
85. ADM 199/2142, Chief Officer R. W. Thomson.
86. Doris M. Hawkins, *Atlantic Torpedo*, pp. 24–29.
87. ADM 1/12193, Surgeon Rear-Admiral S. F. Dudley, 22 January 1922.
88. OA 1132/1/3, Second Officer H. Butler and Third Officer R. S. Catherall.
89. *PD(C)*, vol. 380, cols 1999–2000, oral answer, 24 June 1942.
90. Ibid., vol. 383, col. 1619, oral answer, 14 October 1942.
91. ADM 199/2165, Merchant Ships' Technical Committee, minutes, 17 April 1942.
92. *Shipbuilding and Shipping Record*, 20 May 1943, p. 453, and 27 May 1943, pp. 475–76; *Shipbuilder and Marine Engine-Builder*, June 1943, pp. 214–15.

93. ADM 199/2165, Merchant Ships' Technical Committee, minutes, 12 March 1943.
94. Ibid., minutes, 30 April 1943.
95. *The Times*, 12 May 1943, pp. 2 and 6.
96. *The Seaman*, May-June 1943, p. 252.
97. IWM 89/5/1, post-war memoir of Fourth Officer W. Close of the *Macon*.
98. *The Times*, 7 July 1943, p. 2.
99. ADM 199/2147, Captain J. W. Binns.
100 K. Mellanby, *Human Guinea Pigs* (London, 1973).
101 Ibid., pp. 98ff.
102 M. Critchley, *Shipwreck Survivors: A Medical Study* (London, 1943).
103 Medical Research Council, *A Guide to the Preservation of Life at Sea after Shipwreck* (London, 1943); *The Times*, 13 January 1943, p. 8.
104 McCance et al., *The Hazards to Men in Ships Lost at Sea*.
105 Authors' calculations based on *BMVL*, and Rohwer, *Axis Submarine Successes* (Cambridge, 1983).
106 Authors' calculations from Admiralty Trade Division figures reproduced in Costello and Hughes, *The Battle of the Atlantic*, p. 304.
107 MRC (1943), *A Guide to the Preservation of Life at Sea after Shipwreck*, p. 7.
108 Ibid., p. 9.
109 Ibid., p. 5.
110 Ibid., p. 10.
111 Ibid., p. 20.
112 OA 89/2A, Captain A. Shaw.
113 MRC (1943), *A Guide to the Preservation of Life at Sea after Shipwreck*, p. 5.
114 ADM 199/2138, Chief Officer J. Cameron.
115 OA 89/2, Second Steward S. Curtis.
116 Ibid., Third Engineer W. Graham.
117 ADM 199/2140, Third Officer R. Johnson.
118 ADM 199/2141, Captain J. Pascoe.
119 ADM 199/2145, Apprentice D. E. Clowe.
120 ADM 199/2142, Chief Officer J. V. Findlay.
121 ADM 199/2145, Captain R. Mallett.
122 Ibid., Chief Engineer J. D. Ford.
123 ADM 199/2144, Captain S. Foulkes.
124 Ibid., Chief Officer S. P. Lloyd.
125 ADM 199/2147, Second Officer J. Allason-Jones.
126 OA 89/2A, Third Officer Painter, Second Officer Fuller and Chief Officer Edge.
127 ADM 199/2144, Captain J. H. A. Mackie.

Chapter 9: Safe at Last

1. OA 89/2A, Second Officer W. M. Thomas.
2. ADM 199/2140, Captain A. Shaw.
3. Ibid.
4. Charles H. Brown, *Nicholls's Seamanship and Nautical Knowledge* (18th edn, Glasgow, 1938), p. 106.

5. MT 9/3204, Ministry of Shipping notice M.182, February 1940.
6. ADM 199/2130, Captain J. E. Egner.
7. MT 9/3436, copy of Flag Officer, Belfast to Commander-in-Chief Western Approaches, No. 11765/40/A9, 7 October 1940.
8. Ibid., copy of Ministry of Shipping (W. Carter) to Air Ministry, 20 November 1940.
9. Ibid., copy of Ministry of Shipping (T. E. Metcalfe) to Air Ministry, 10 January 1941.
10. Ibid., copy of Air Ministry to Ministry of Shipping, S. 6428/S.6, 20 January 1941.
11. ADM 199/2138, Carpenter W Manning. This was his second boat voyage in four months. Injuries caused by immersion foot ended his employment at sea.
12. Ibid., Chief Officer J. Cameron.
13. ADM 199/2165, Merchant Ships' Technical Committee, minutes, 14 November 1941.
14. *Shipbuilding and Shipping Record*, 7 January 1943, p. 22, reporting a reply by Noel-Baker.
15. ADM 199/2142, Chief Officer J. Lee.
16. ADM 199/2143, Captain S. B. Davies.
17. ADM 199/2140, Third Officer R. Johnson.
18. Ibid., Captain R. Brown.
19. Ibid., Chief Officer C. T. V. Rixham.
20. Ibid., Captain G. A. Niddrie.
21. ADM 199/2142, Captain J. Dodds.
22. Ibid., Third Officer J. R. Mitchell.
23. S. W. Roskill, *A Merchant Fleet in War: Alfred Holt and Company, 1939–1945* (London, 1962), p. 132.
24. ADM 199/2147, Second Officer J. Dekker.
25. OA 1132/1/3, Second Officer H. Butler.
26. OA 89/2A, Chief Engineer G. N. Crossley.
27. ADM 199/2140, Chief Officer C. T. V. Rixham.
28. ADM 199/2143, Third Steward J. C. Edmead.
29. Medical Research Council, *A Guide to the Preservation of Life at Sea after Shipwreck* (London, 1943), p. 20.
30. OA 1132/1/23, Midshipman J. Scragg.
31. ADM199/2143, HM Consul, Belem, to BNSO, Rio de Janeiro.
32. ADM 199/2147, Chief Engineer E. Greenway.
33. S. A. Kerslake, *Coxswain of the Northern Convoys* (London, 1984), p. 130.
34. *PD(C)*, vol. 387, col. 597, speech, 3 March 1943.
35. Kerslake, *Coxswain of the Northern Convoys*, p. 63.
36. ADM 199/2142, Chief Officer J. Lee.
37. ADM 199/2143, Chief Officer I. S. McLean (*Teesbank*) and Second Officer A. Fell-Dunn (*East Wales*).
38. Ibid., Third Steward J. C. Edmead.
39. ADM 199/2165, Merchant Ships' Technical Committee, minutes, 8 and 29 January and 19 February 1943.
40. *Merchant Navy Journal*, July-September 1943, p. 72.

41. ADM 199/2144, Captain J. H. A. Mackie.
42. ADM 199/2140, Captain D. Anderson.
43. Arthur Banks, *Wings of the Dawning: The Battle for the Indian Ocean, 1939–1945* (Malvern Wells, 1997), p. 148.
44. Ibid., pp. 128–29.
45. ADM 199/2148, Second Officer C. B. Skinner.
46. ADM 199/2142, Second Officer A. H. Black.
47. ADM 199/2140, Captain C. J. R. Roberts.
48. Ibid., Captain W. Bird.
49. ADM 199/2143, Captain D. M. Williams.
50. Ibid.
51. Banks, *Wings of the Dawning*, pp. 300–302.
52. University of Warwick Modern Records Centre, National Union of Seamen Archive, MSS 175/1/1/13 (agenda) and 175/1/1/9 (minutes), 14 December 1939.
53. *PD(C)*, vol. 357, cols 991–92, 15 February 1940, Sir John Gilmour, written answer.
54. *The Times*, 26 February 1940, p. 4, letter to the Editor.
55. Ibid., 16 April 1940, p. 4, letter to the Editor.
56. Ibid., 4 July 1940, p. 9, letter to the Editor.
57. *Lloyds List and Shipping Gazette*, 20 July 1940, p. 3.
58. Ibid., 12 February 1940, p. 2.
59. Ibid., 11 March 1940, p. 2.
60. *The Times*, 22 June 1940, p. 4, letter to the Editor.
61. Ibid., 25 June 1940, p. 4, letter to the Editor.
62. *The Seaman*, September-October 1943, p. 305.
63. ADM 199/2141, Captain D. A. Reid.
64. ADM 199/2138, Captain H. M. McLean.
65. Ibid., Captain A. B. Campbell.
66. ADM 199/2145, Captain E. Gough.
67. ADM 199/2148, Captain A. Ellis.
68. G. H. G. McMillan, 'Care of World War II Convoy Casualties in the Kola Area of North Russia', *Journal of the Royal Naval Medical Service*, 81, pp. 221–30; and 82, pp. 61–79.

Chapter 10: The Cost

1. Sir William P. Elderton, 'Merchant Seamen during the War', *Journal of the Institute of Actuaries*, 83 (1946), pp. 250–84.
2. Ibid., p. 252.
3. Ibid., p. 268.
4. Ibid.
5. Commonwealth War Graves Commission, introduction to the *Register for the Merchant Navy Memorial, Tower Hill, London*, p. 10.
6. Elderton, 'Merchant Seamen during the War', p. 268.
7. *The Times*, 30 November 1945, p. 3.
8. H. M. Government, *Strength and Casualties of the Armed Forces and Auxiliary*

Services of the United Kingdom, 1939–1945, White Paper Cmd 6832 (London, 1946).

9. John Costello and Terry Hughes, *The Battle of the Atlantic* (London, 1977), p. 304.

10. C. B. A. Behrens, *Merchant Shipping and the Demands of War* (London, 1955), p. 178.

11. B. B. Schofield and L. F. Martyn, *The Rescue Ships* (Edinburgh, 1968), p. xix.

12. Gabe Thomas, *Milag: Captives of the Kriegsmarine* (Pontardawe, n.d.), p. ix n. 2.

13. John Terraine, *Business in Great Waters: The U-Boat Wars, 1916–1945* (London, 1989), p. 673.

14. IMT, vol. 13, p. 356.

15. Behrens, *Merchant Shipping and the Demands of War*, p. 176.

16. David Williams, *Wartime Disasters at Sea: Every Passenger Ship Loss in World Wars I and II* (Sparkford, 1997), pp. 130 and 223–24.

17. See, for example, the account by Marine Ronald Healiss of the sinking of the aircraft carrier HMS *Glorious* in John Winton, *The War at Sea, 1939–1945* (London, 1994), pp. 36–40

18. Baltimore Sun, 19 December 1941, reporting comments by the chief engineer of the rescuing vessel.

19. W. Franklin Mellor (ed.), *Medical History of the Second World: Casualties and Medical Statistics* (London, 1972), pp. 838–39.

20. *PD(C)*, vol. 392, col. 77, speech by Winston Churchill.

21. See, for example, Schofield and Martyn, *The Rescue Ships*, p. xix, and Gabe Thomas, *Milag: Captives of the Kriegsmarine*, p. ix.

22. Elderton, 'Merchant Seamen during the War', p. 267.

23. Ibid., p. 260.

24. Ibid., pp. 260–61.

25. Cmd 6832, *Strength and Casualties of the Armed Forces*, p. 7.

26. Lord Winster, reported in *The Seaman*, December 1944, p. 24.

27. IMT, vol. 1, p. 78.

28. Ibid., vol. 13, pp. 267–68.

29. See, for example, the film *Western Approaches* (1944), and B.R. 282, *D.E.M.S. Pocket Book* (Admiralty, 1942), pp. 52–53, 'Selection of Control Officer, Guns' Crews and Supply Party'.

30. IMT, vol. 13, p. 271.

31. A reference to the sinking of the Greek vessel *Peleus* by Kapitänleutnant Eck's *U–852*.

32. IMT, vol. 13, p. 272.

33. Ibid., p. 356.

34. Ibid., p. 363.

35. Ibid., p. 369.

36. Ibid., vol. 22, p. 390.

37. Ibid., p. 391.

38. Ibid., p. 558.

39. Ibid., p. 559.

40. Ibid.

41. FO 1060/1388, petition to the Allied Control Commission, dated September 1946.
42. IMT, vol. 22, p. 563.
43. For a German historian's views on this issue see Helmut Schmoeckel, *Menschlichkeit im Seekrieg?* (Herford, 1987).
44. See, for example, Donald Macintyre, *The Battle of the Atlantic* (London, 1961), p. 169.
45. *The Times*, 18 October 1945, p. 3.
46. WO 309/565, Admiralty Military Branch to Colonel Haldane, Headquarters, British Army of the Rhine, November 1945.
47. *The Times*, 20 October 1945, p. 3.
48. Ibid., 22 October 1945, p. 3. See also WO 235/5 for a transcript of the trial.
49. WO 235/209, summary of case prepared by Lord Russell of Liverpool, Deputy Judge-Advocate General, for Commander-in-Chief, British Zone of Germany, 31 May 1949.
50. Ibid., Dr O. Zippel, 28 October 1946, petition to have the sentence quashed.
51. WO 309/293, Major A. E. E. Reade, prosecutor, to Officer i/c War Crimes Group (NWE), HQ BAOR, 26 May 1947.
52. Lord Russell of Liverpool, *Knights of the Bushido* (Bath, 1989), p. 185.
53. Carl Boyd and Akihiko Yoshida, *The Japanese Submarine Force and World War II* (Shrewsbury, 1996), p. 179.
54. *The Seaman*, January 1944, pp. 15–16.
55. Ibid., February-March 1943, p. 202.
56. Ibid.
57. S. W. Roskill, *Naval Policy between the Wars* (London, 1968), p. 536.
58. G. D. Franklin, 'A Breakdown in Communication: Britain's Over Estimation of ASDIC's Capabilities in the 1930s', *Mariner's Mirror*, 84, (1998), pp. 204–14.
59. Martin Doughty, *Merchant Shipping and War: A Study in Defence Planning in Twentieth-Century Britain* (London, 1982), pp. 41–66.
60. *The Seaman*, January 1944, p. 16.
61. Ibid., February-March 1943, pp. 201–2, and April 1943, pp. 222–23.
62. *Manchester Guardian*, 23 March 1943, p. 3, *The Guardian* ©.
63. Authors' calculation from Admiralty Trade Division figures listed in Costello and Hughes, *The Battle of the Atlantic*, p. 304.
64. McCance et al., *The Hazards to Men in Ships Lost at Sea*, p. 6.

Bibliography

Unpublished Sources

British Government Records at the Public Record Office, Kew

Admiralty: ADM 1, ADM 116, ADM 199, ADM 223.
Foreign Office: FO 371, FO 1060.
Medical Research Council: FD 1.
Transport: MT 9, MT 25, MT 62.
War Office: WO 235, WO 309, WO 311.

Imperial War Museum

Private Papers

Gibson, Sir John, 89/5/1; Lamb, John, 91/5/1; Terrell, Captain E., 82/5/1.

Documents Written by Seamen and Others

Baxter G., 87/35/1; Bayly, R. E., 87/2/1; Bellew, R., 89/3/1; Burley, C., 91/31/1; Cardale, P., 90/23/1; Casson, E., 89/5/1; Close, W., 89/5/1; Fyrth, P., 88/42/1; Johnson, P., 89/5/1; Lee, A., 88/47/1; McDermott-Brown, L., 88/59/1; Turner, E., 91/21/1; Wilson, R., 91/31/1.

Oral History Recordings

Ashton, W., 12110; Blint, B., 13291; Birch, W., 12723; Boocock, P., 19299, Bryan, P., 11393; Caine, R., 11394; Clarke, W., 2728; Cooper, J., 11397; Cua, N., 11485; Dalgleish, J., 11401; Dove, C., 12275; Elliot, E., 2409/D/A; Evans, E., 11921; Fallon, J., 2446/E/D; Gorrie, J., 11407; Hopper, W., 10800; Hoyer, W., 11410; Hulse, N., 15332; Inglis, A., 11411; James, R., 11882; Liley, B., 11771; Lucia, W., 11334; Maxwell, D., 14823; Morris, J., 12272; Nielsen, L., 11424; Sheridan T., 10787; Short, W., 11276; Smith, B., 11327; Uren, R., 12717; Wright, H. A., 14928.

Shipping Company Records

Merseyside Maritime Museum
Alfred Holt
T. and J. Brocklebank
Elder Dempster
Glen Line
William Cory

University of Glasgow Business Records Centre
Ellerman

Trades Union Records

Warwick University Modern Records Centre
National Union of Seamen archives

NUMAST, Wallasey
National Maritime Board minutes

NUMAST, London
Unions in the Merchant Navy Officers Federation

Conversations and Correspondence

Bredow, H. (*Stiftung Traditionsarchiv Unterseeboote*)
Brookes, F. W. (*Allende*)
Burton, W. (*Margot*, DEMS)
Clifton, Dr G. (National Maritime Museum)
Collis, C. (DEMS)
Condon, Captain M. (NUMAST)
Doctor, B. (*Athenia*)
Fletcher, R. J. J. (HMS *Wolverine*)
Fyson, J. (*Empire City*)
Garside, M. (NUMAST)
Hill, D. (*Ousebridge*)
Hope, F. (*Anglo Canadian*)
Hughes, E. (*Speybank*)
Hunt, K. (DEMS)
Knight, G. (merchant seaman)

Leach, R. A. (*Teesbank*)

Legge, A. J. (*Olivebank*)

Pryke, A. (*Olivebank*)

Reaveley, Mrs C.

Shuttleworth T. (R.N. escort vessels)

Tanner, A. (R.N. escort vessels)

Thornley, D. W. (HMS *Hyperion*)

Watts, Captain A. S. (*Ile de Batz*)

Zestermann, G. (*U 533*)

Published Sources

Newspapers and Periodicals, 1939–1945

Daily Express
Daily Mirror
Daily Telegraph
Lloyd List and Shipping Gazette
Manchester Guardian
Merchant Navy Journal (Navigators' and Engineer Officers' Union)
Motor Boat and Yachting
Motor Ship
News Chronicle
Observer
Parliamentary Debates (Commons), 5th Series
Salt Spray Reporter (Mercantile Marine Service Association)
Seaman (National Union of Seamen)
Shipbuilder and Marine Engine-Builder
Shipbuilding and Shipping Record
Signal (Radio Officers' Union)
Star
The Times

Crown Films

Merchant Seamen (1941)
Lifesaving at Sea (1944)
Western Approaches (1945)

Books

(Paperback editions indicated by (p) after publisher's name.)

Anon., *The Ben Line: The Story of a Merchant Fleet at War, 1939–1945* (Thomas Nelson, London, 1946).

Bailey, Chris Howard, *The Battle of the Atlantic: The Corvettes and their Crews: An Oral History* (Sutton Publishing, Stroud, 1994).

Banks, Arthur, *Wings of the Dawning: The Battle for the Indian Ocean, 1939–1945* (Harold Martin and Redman, Malvern Wells, 1997).

Barker, Ralph, *Goodnight, Sorry for Sinking You: The Story of the SS City of Cairo* (Collins, London, 1984).

Barnett, Correlli, *Engage the Enemy More Closely: The Royal Navy in the Second World War* (Hodder and Stoughton, London, 1991).

Beaver, Paul, *U-Boats in the Atlantic* (Patrick Stephens, Cambridge, 1979).

Becker Cajus, *Hitler's Naval War* (Corgi (p), London, 1976).

Becker, C. D., *Swastika at Sea: The Struggle and Destruction of the German Navy, 1939–1945* (William Kimber, London, 1953).

Behrens, C. B. A., *Merchant Shipping and the Demands of War* (HMSO and Longmans Green, London, 1955).

Binning, A. J., *Survivors: The Story of U–188 and her Sinking of the SS Fort La Maune and SS Fort Buckingham in the Arabian Sea* (Norman Gibson, Essex, 1995).

Blake, G., *The Ben Line, 1825–1955* (Thomas Nelson, London, 1956).

Blond, Georges, *Convois vers l'URSS* (Artheme Fayard (p), Paris, 1950).

Bonwick, George J., *Lifeboat Handbook* (Maritime Press, Wokingham, 1955).

Boyd, Carl, and Akihiko, Yoshida, *The Japanese Submarine Force and World War II* (Airlife, Shrewsbury, 1996).

Brennecke, H. J., *Ghost Cruiser HK 33* (William Kimber, London, 1954).

Brennecke, Jochen, *The Hunters and the Hunted* (Corgi (p), London, 1960).

Brice, Martin, *Axis Blockade Runners of World War II* (Batsford, London, 1981).

Broome, Jack, *Convoy is to Scatter: The Story of PQ17* (Futura (p), London, 1974).

Brown, Charles H., *Nicholls's Seamanship and Nautical Knowledge* (Brown, Son and Ferguson, Glasgow, 18th edn 1938).

Brown, David, *Warship Losses of World War Two* (Arms and Armour Press, London, revised edn 1995).

Buchheim, Lothar-Gunther, *U-Boat War* (Collins, London, 1978).

Bushell, T. A., *Eight Bells: Royal Mail Lines War Story, 1939–1945* (Trade and Travel, London, 1950).

Cameron Ian, *Five Days to Hell* (Panther (p), London, 1961).

Campbell, Ian, and Macintyre, Donald, *The Kola Run: A Record of the Arctic Convoys, 1941–1945* (Futura (p), London, 1975).

Cameron J., *The Peleus Trial* (William Hodge, London, 1948).

Caulfield, Max, *A Night of Terror: The Story of the Athenia Affair* (Frederick Muller, London, 1958).

Chalmers, Rear-Admiral W. S., *Max Horton and the Western Approaches* (Hodder and Stoughton (p), London, 1957).

Churchill, Winston, *The Second World War*, 6 vols (Cassell, London, 1948–54).

Clissold, Peter, *Elementary Seamanship* (Brown, Son and Ferguson, Glasgow, 2nd edn 1939).

Costello, John, and Hughes, Terry, *The Battle of the Atlantic* (Collins, London, 1977).

Course, Captain A. G., *The Merchant Navy: A Social History* (Frederick Muller, London, 1963).

Crabb, Brian James, *Passage to Destiny: The Sinking of the SS Khedive Ismail in the Sea War against Japan* (Paul Watkins, Stamford, 1997).

Creighton, Rear-Admiral Sir Kenelm, *Convoy Commodore* (Futura (p), London, 1976).

Cremer, Peter, *U333: The Story of a U-Boat Ace* (Triad Grafton (p), London, 1986).

Critchley, M., *Shipwreck Survivors: A Medical Study* (J. and A. Churchill, London, 1943).

Dennis, Owen, *The Rest Go On* (John Crowther, London, n.d.).

Detmers, Captain Theodor, *The Raider Kormoran* (Kimber Pocket Edition, London, 1961).

Doenitz, Admiral, *Memoirs: Ten Years and Twenty Days* (Weidenfeld and Nicolson, London, 1959).

Doughty, Martin, *Merchant Shipping and War: A Study of Defence Planning in Twentieth-Century Britain* (Royal Historical Society, London, 1982).

Duffus, L., *Beyond the Laager* (Hurst and Blackett, London, n.d.).

Dyer, Jim, and Edwards, Bernard (eds), *Death and Donkeys' Breakfasts: War beyond Lundy* (D and E Books, Newport, Gwent, n.d.).

Edwards, Bernard, *The Merchant Navy Goes to War* (Robert Hale, (p) London, 1990).

Edwards, Bernard, *Blood and Bushido: Japanese Atrocities at Sea, 1941–1945* (Bernard Edwards, London, 1991).

Edwards, Bernard, *Dönitz and the Wolf Packs* (Arms and Armour Press, London, 1996).

Foss, Denis, and Entwistle, Basil, *Shoot a Line: A Merchant Mariner's War* (Linden Hall, Yeovil, 1992).

Frank, Wolfgang, *Enemy Submarine: The Story of Gunther Prien, Captain of U–47* (New English Library (p), London, 1977).

Franks, Norman, *Search, Find and Kill: The RAF's U-Boat Successes in World War Two* (Grub Street, London, revised edn 1995).

Gannon, Michael, *Operation Drumbeat: The Dramatic True Story Of Germany's First U-Boat Attacks Along the American Coast in World War II* (Harper and Row, New York, 1990).

German, Commander Tony, *The Sea is at Our Gates: The History of the Canadian Navy* (McLelland and Stewart, Toronto, 1990).

Gibson, Charles, *Death of a Phantom Raider: The Gamble that Triumphed and Failed, Atlantic, 1942–3* (Robert Hale, London, 1987).

Gibson, Walter, *The Boat* (George Mann, Maidstone, 1973).

Gilbert, G. M., *Nuremberg Diary* (Eyre and Spottiswoode, London, 1948).

Gleichauf, Justin F., *Unsung Heroes: The Naval Armed Guard in World War II* (Naval Institute Press, Annapolis, 1990).

Gretton, Vice-Admiral Sir Peter, *Crisis Convoy: The Story of Convoy HX231* (Peter Davies, London, 1974).

Hadley, Michael L., *Count Not the Dead: The Popular Image of the German Submarine* (McGill-Queens University Press, Montreal, 1995).

Hague, Arnold, *The Towns* (World Ship Society, Kendal, 1988).

Hague, Arnold, *Convoy Rescue Ships, 1940–1945* (World Ship Society, Gravesend, 1998).

Hancock, H. E., *Wireless at Sea* (London, 1950).

Hancock, H. E., *Semper Fidelis: The Saga of the 'Navvies', 1924–1948* (General Steam Navigation Co., London, 1949).

Hancock, W. K., *Problems of Social Policy* (HMSO, London, 1950).

Hancock, W. K. and Gowing, M. M., *British War Economy* (HMSO, London, 1949).

Hashimoto, Mochitsura, *Sunk: The Story of the Japanese Submarine Fleet* (Panther (p), London, 1955).

Hawkins, Doris M., *Atlantic Torpedo* (Cedric Chivers reprint, Bath, 1969).

Hendrie, Andrew, *Short Sunderland in World War II* (Airlife, Shrewsbury, 1994).

Hessler, G., *German Naval History: The U-Boat War in the Atlantic, 1939–1945* (HMSO, London, 1992).

Hickham, Homer H., *Torpedo Junction: U-Boat War off America's East Coast, 1942* (US Naval Institute Press, Annapolis, 1989).

Hinsley, F. H., *British Intelligence in the Second World War: Its Influence on Strategy and Operations*, 5 vols, (HMSO, London, 1979–88).

Hirschfeld, Wolfgang, *Hirschfeld: The Story of a U-Boat NCO, 1940–1946* (Orion (p), London, 1997).

[Hitler, Adolf], *Fuehrer Conferences on Naval Affairs 1939–1945* (Greenhill Books, London, 1990).

Hope, Stanton, *Ocean Odyssey: A Record of the Fighting Merchant Navy* (Eyre and Spottiswoode, London, 1944).

Hope, W. E. Stanton, *Tanker Fleet: The War Story of the Shell Tankers and the Men Who Manned Them* (Anglo-Saxon Petroleum Company, London, 1948).

Hopkins, J. A. H., *Diary of World Events* (National Advertising Company, Baltimore, 1942).

[Houlder Brothers], *Sea Hazard, 1939–1945* (Houlder, London, 1947).

Howarth, Stephen, and Law, Derek (eds), *The Battle of the Atlantic, 1939–1945. Proceedings of the 50th Anniversary International Naval Conference* (Greenhill Books, London, 1994).

Hudson, Kenneth and Nicholls, Ann, *The Book of Shipwrecks* (Macmillan, London, 1979).

Hughes, Robert, *Flagship to Murmansk: A Gunnery Officer in HMS Scylla, 1942–43* (Kimber (p), London, 1961).

Hurd, Archibald (ed.), *Britain's Merchant Navy* (Odhams Press, London, n.d. but circa 1942–45).

Hurd, Sir Archibald, *The Battle of the Seas: The Fighting Merchantmen* (Hodder and Stoughton, London, 1941).

International Military Tribunal, *Trial of the Major War Criminals*, vols 1, 5, 13, 22, 25, 40 (Tribunal Secretariat, Nuremberg, 1948).

Infield, Glenn, *Disaster at Bari* (New English Library (p), London, 1976).

Irving, David, *The Destruction of Convoy PQ17* (Corgi (p), London, 1970).

James, Robert Rhodes (ed.), *'Chips': The Diaries of Sir Henry Channon* (Weidenfeld (p), London, 1993).

Jones, Guy Pierce, *Two Survived* (Hamish Hamilton, London, 1941).

Kaplan, Philip, and Currie, Jack, *Convoy: Merchant Sailors at War, 1939–45* (Aurum Press, London, 1998).

Kemp, Paul, *Convoy: Drama in Arctic Waters* (Arms and Armour Press, London, 1993).

Kennedy, J., *When Singapore Fell: Evacuations and Escapes, 1941–1942* (Macmillan, Basingstoke, 1989)

Kennedy, Ludovic, *Pursuit: The Sinking of the Bismarck* (Collins/Fontana (p), London, 1975).

Kerr, J. Lennox (ed.), *Touching the Adventures of Merchantmen in the Second World War* (Harrap, London, 1953).

Kerslake, S. A., *Coxswain in the Northern Convoys* (William Kimber, London, 1984).

King, G. A. B., *A Love of Ships* (Kenneth Mason, Emsworth, 1991).

Knox, Collie, *Atlantic Battle* (Methuen, London, 1941).

Krancke, Theodor, and Brennecke, H. J., *Pocket Battleship* (Tandem (p), London, 1973).

Lamb, James B., *The Corvette Navy: True Stories from Canada's Atlantic War* (Futura (p), London, 1979).

Lane, Tony, *The Merchant Seaman's War* (Manchester University Press, Manchester, 1990).

Lee E. C. B. and Lee, Kenneth, *Safety and Survival at Sea* (Greenhill Books, London, new edn 1989).

Lenton, H. T., *British Escort Ships* (Macdonald and Jane's, London, 1974).

Lloyd, E. A., *Hypothermia and Cold Stress* (Croom Helm, London, 1986).

Lund, Paul, and Ludlam, Harry, *PQ17: Convoy to Hell: The Survivors' Story* (New English Library (p), London, 1969).

Lund, Paul, and Ludlam, Harry, *Night of the U-Boats* (New English Library (p), London, 1974).

McCance, R. A., Ungley, C. C., Crosfill, C. C. W., and Widdowson, E. M., *The Hazards to Men in Ships Lost at Sea, 1940–44*, Medical Research Council Special Report No. 291 (HMSO, London, 1956).

Macdonnell, J. E., *Object Destruction* (Horwitz (p), Sydney, 1970).

Macintyre, Donald, *The Battle of the Atlantic* (Pan (p), London, 1969).

Macintyre, Donald, *Sea Warfare, 1939–1945* (Salamander Books, London, 1975).

McKee, Alexander, *The Coal-Scuttle Brigade* (New English Library (p), London, 1973).

Male, H. G., *Being in All Respects Ready for Sea* (Janus, London, 1992).

Mason, David, *U-Boat: The Secret Menace* (Pan/Ballantine, London, 1972).

Mason, John T., Jr, (ed.), *The Atlantic War Remembered: An Oral History Collection* (Naval Institute Press, Annapolis, 1990).

Medical Research Council, *A Guide to the Preservation of Life at Sea after Shipwreck* (HMSO, London, 1943).

Mellanby, K., *Human Guinea Pigs* (Merlin Press, London, 1973).

Metzler, Jost, *The Laughing Cow: A U-Boat Captain's Story*, (William Kimber (p), London, 1960).

Middlebrook, Martin, *Convoy: The Battle for Convoys SC122 and HX229* (Allen Lane, London, 1976).

Miller, Nathan, *War at Sea: A Naval History of World War II*, Scribner, New York, 1995.

Mohr, Ulrich, and Sellwood, A. V., *Atlantis: The Story of a German Surface Raider* (Werner Laurie, London, 1955).

Morison, Samuel Eliot, *History of United States Naval Operations in World War II*, i, *The Battle of the Atlantic, 1939–1943* (Little, Brown and Co., Boston, 1970).

Morison, Samuel Eliot, *History of United States Naval Operations in World War II*, x, *The Atlantic Battle Won, 1943–1945* (Little, Brown and Co., Boston; 1970).

Muggenthaler, Karl August, *German Raiders of World War II* (Pan (p), London, 1980).

Müllenheim-Rechberg, Baron Burkhard von, *Battleship Bismarck: A Survivor's Story* (The Bodley Head, London, 1981).

Murphy, Mark, *83 Days: The Survival of Seaman Izzi* (E. P. Dutton, New York, 1943).

Murray, William, *Atlantic Rendezvous* (Futura (p), London, 1975).

Norris, Alan, *High Fronts and Low Backs* (Professional Authors' and Publishers' Association, London, 1994).

Ott, Wolfgang, *Sharks and Little Fish* (Arrow (p), London, 1960).

Padfield, Peter, *War Beneath the Sea: Submarine Conflict, 1939–1945* (John Murray, London, 1995).

Padfield, Peter, *Dönitz: The Last Führer* (Victor Gollancz (p), London, 1993).

Peillard, Leonce, *U-Boats to the Rescue: The Laconia Incident* (Coronet (p), London, 1976).

Pitt, Barrie et al., *The Battle of the Atlantic* (Time-Life Books, USA, 1977).

Poolman, Kenneth, *Periscope Depth: Submarines at War* (William Kimber, London, 1981).

Poolman, Kenneth, *Focke-Wulf Condor: The Scourge of the Atlantic* (Book Club Associates, London, 1979).

Pope, Dudley, *73 North: The Battle of the Barents Sea* (Pan (p), London, 1976).

Powell, Michael, *The Last Voyage of the Graf Spee* (New English Library (p), London, 1973).

Rayner, D. A., *Escort* (Futura (p), London, 1974).

Robertson, Terence, *The Golden Horseshoe* (Pan (p), London, 1957).

Robin, Bernard, *Survival at Sea: A Practical Manual for Yachtsmen* (Stanley Paul, London, English edn 1981).

Rogge, Admiral Bernhard, *Under Ten Flags: The Fantastic Story of Germany's Deadliest Raider, The Atlantis* (Four Square (p), London, 1960).

Rohwer, Jürgen, *Axis Submarine Successes, 1939–1945* (Patrick Stephens, Cambridge, 1983).

Rohwer, Jürgen, *The Critical Convoy Battles of March 1943* (Ian Allan, London, 1977).

Roskill, S. W., *The War at Sea*, 3 vols (HMSO, London, 1954–61).

Roskill, S. W., *A Merchant Fleet in War: Alfred Holt and Company, 1939–1945* (Collins, London, 1962).

Roskill, S. W., *Naval Policy between the Wars* (Collins, London, 1968).

Roskill, S. W., *The Navy at War, 1939–1945* (Wordsworth (p), Ware, 1998).

Ruegg, Bob, and Hague, Arnold, *Convoys to Russia, 1941–1945*, (World Ship Society, Kendal, 1992).

Runyan, T. J., and Copes, J. M. (eds), *To Die: The Battle of the Atlantic* (Westview Press, San Francisco, 1994).

Russell of Liverpool, Lord, *The Knights of the Bushido* (Chivers Press, Bath, 1985 edn).

Salter, Lord, *Memoirs of a Public Servant* (Faber and Faber, London, 1969).

Sandbach, Betty, and Edge, Geraldine, *Prison Life on a Pacific Raider* (Hodder and Stoughton, London, 1941).

Saunders, H. St. George, *Valiant Voyaging: A Short History of the British India Steam Navigation Company in the Second World War, 1939–1945* (Faber and Faber, London, 1948).

Savas, Theodore P. (ed.), *Silent Hunters: German U-Boat Commanders of World War II* (Savas Publishing, Campbell, California, 1997).

Scarlett, R. J. (compiler), *Under Hazardous Circumstances: A Register of Awards of Lloyds War Medal for Bravery at Sea, 1939–1945* (Arms and Armour Press, Dallington, 1992).

Schmoeckel, Helmut, *Menschlichkeit im Seekrieg?* (Mittler und Sohn, Herford, 1987).

Schofield, B. B., *The Russian Convoys* (Pan (p), London, 1971).

Schofield, B. B., and Martyn, L. F., *The Rescue Ships* (William Blackwood, Edinburgh, 1968).

Seamer, Robert, *The Floating Inferno: The Story of the Loss of the Empress of Britain* (Patrick Stephens, Wellingborough, 1990).

Shakespeare, Geoffrey, *Let Candles be Brought in* (Macdonald, London, 1949).

Shankland, Peter, and Hunter, Anthony, *Malta Convoy* (Fontana (p), London, 1963).

Sharpe, Peter, *U-Boat Factfile: Detailed Service Histories of the Submarines Operated by the Kriegsmarine, 1935–1945*, (Midland Publishing (p), Earl Shilton, 1998).

Sibley, David, *The Behar Massacre* (A. Lane, Stockport, 1998).

Smith, Anthony, *Survived!* (Quintin Smith (p), London, 1998).

Smith, Peter, *Pedestal: The Malta Convoy of August 1942* (William Kimber, London, 1970).

Smith, Peter, *Convoy PQ18: Arctic Victory* (New English Library (p), London, 1977).

Stern, Robert C., *Type VII U-Boats* (Arms and Armour Press, London, 1991).

Talbot-Booth, E. C., *What Ship is That?* (Sampson Low, London, n.d.).

Talbot-Booth, E. C., *Ships and the Sea* (Sampson Low, London, 7th edn 1942).

Tarrant, V. E., *The Last Year of the Kriegsmarine, May 1944 to May 1945* (Arms and Armour Press, London, 1994).

Taylor, Fred (trans. and ed.), *The Goebbels Diaries, 1939–1941* (Sphere Books (p), London, 1982).

Terraine, John, *Business in Great Waters: The U-Boat Wars, 1916–1945* (Leo Cooper, London, 1989).

Terrell, Edward, *Admiralty Brief: The Story of Inventions that Contributed to Victory in the Battle of the Atlantic* (Harrap, London, 1958).

Thomas, Gabe, *Milag: Captives of the Kriegsmarine: Merchant Navy Prisoners of War* (Milag p. o. w. Association, Pontadarwe, 1995).

Topp, Erich, *The Odyssey of a U-Boat Commander: Recollections of Erich Topp* (Praeger, Westport Connecticut, English edn 1992).

Trevor Roper, H. R., (ed.), *Hitler's Table Talk*, (Weidenfeld, London, 1953).

Turner, L. C. F., Gordon-Cumming, H. R., and Betzler, J. E., *War in the Southern Oceans* (O.U.P., London, 1961).

Tusa, Ann, and Tusa, John, *The Nuremberg Trial* (Papermac, London, 1954).

United Kingdom, H.M. Government, *British Merchant Vessels Lost or Damaged by Enemy Action During the Second World War* (HMSO, London, 1947, reprinted in *British Vessels Lost at Sea, 1939–1945*, Patrick Stephens, Cambridge, 1980).

United Kingdom, H.M. Government, *Strength and Casualties of the Armed Forces and Auxiliary Services of the United Kingdom, 1939–1945*, White Paper Cmd 6832 (HMSO, London, 1946).

United Kingdom, Ministry of Information for MWT, *Merchantmen at War: The Official Story of the Merchant Navy, 1939–1944* (HMSO, London, 1944).

United Kingdom, Ministry of Information for Air Ministry, *Coastal Command: The Air Ministry Account of the Part Played by Coastal Command in the Battle of the Seas, 1939–1942* (HMSO, London, 1942).

United States Congress (Senate), 67th Congress, 2nd session, document 126, *Conference on the Limitation of Armament* (Washington, 1922).

van der Vat, Dan, *The Atlantic Campaign: The Great Struggle at Sea, 1939–1945* (Hodder and Stoughton, London, 1988).

van der Vat, Dan, *The Pacific Campaign: The US-Japanese Naval War* (Hodder and Stoughton, London, 1992).

Vause, Jordan, *U-Boat Ace: The Story of Wolfgang Luth* (Airlife, Shrewsbury, 1992).

Vernon, B. D., *Ellen Wilkinson, 1891–1947* (Croom Helm, London, 1982).

Vince, Charles, *Storm on the Waters: The Story of the Life-Boat Service in the War of 1939–1945* (Hodder and Stoughton, London, 2nd edn 1948).

von der Porten, Edward, *The German Navy in World War Two* (Pan (p), London, 1972).

Watts, Anthony J., *Axis Submarines* (Macdonald and Jane's, London, 1977).

Watts, Anthony J., *Battleships* (Macdonald and Jane's, London, 1978).

Watts, Anthony J., *Axis Cruisers* (Jane's Publishing Company, London, 1979).

Wemyss, Commander D. E. G., *Relentless Pursuit* (New English Library (p), London, 1974).

West, F., *Lifeboat Number Seven* (William Kimber, London, 1960).

Weyher, Kurt, and Ehrlich, Hans-Jürgen, *The Black Raider* (Elek Books, London, 1955).

Williams, David, *Wartime Disasters at Sea: Every Passenger Ship Loss in World Wars I and II* (Patrick Stephens, Sparkford, 1997).

Williams, Mark, *Captain Gilbert Roberts RN and the Anti-U-Boat School* (Cassell, London, 1979).

Winton, John, *Ultra at Sea* (Leo Cooper, London, 1988).

Winton, John (ed.), *The War at Sea, 1939–45* (Pimlico (p), London, 1994).

Woodward, David, *The Secret Raiders* (New English Library (p), London, 1975).

Partworks

Images of War, issue 39.

Purnell's History of the Second World War, numbers 2, 11, 49.

World War II, numbers 5, 14, 30, 34.

Articles

Ahuja, Anjana, 'Living to Tell the Tale', *The Times*, 30 September 1996, p. 14.

Baker, Richard, 'Sequel to a Sea Battle', *Sea Breezes*, 67 (1993), pp. 878–81.

Borrer, R., 'Loss of the *Stentor*', *Sea Breezes*, 64 (1990), pp. 410–15.

Davies, Sid, 'In Memory of Idris Thomas, Lost at Sea', *Sea Breezes*, 66 (1992), pp. 935–38.

Drew, J. H., 'An Alternative Method of Breasting-Out Ships' Lifeboats in Lieu of Booms', *Merchant Navy Journal*, April 1942, p. 69.

Elderton, Sir William, 'Merchant Seamen during the War', *Journal of the Institute of Actuaries*, 83 (1946), pp. 250–84.

Ewart, J. N., 'Escape from the *Empress of Asia*', *Sea Breezes*, 64 (1990), pp. 328–31.

Fifield, Len, 'To Archangel', *Sea Breezes*, 71 (1997), pp. 952–56.

Fisher, Robert C., 'Group Wotan and the Battle for Convoy SC 104', *Mariner's Mirror*, 84 (1998), pp. 64–75.

Franklin, G. D., 'A Breakdown in Communication: Britain's Over Estimation of ASDIC's Capabilities in the 1930s', *Mariner's Mirror*, 84 (1998), pp. 204–14.

Harwood, Patrick, 'The Long Road Home', *Sea Breezes*, 65 (1991), pp. 308–15.

Heaton, P. M., 'The Lamport and Holt Fleet – Part IV: The *Lassell* Incident', *Sea Breezes*, 51 (1977), pp. 589–97.

Heaton, P. M., 'The Lamport and Holt Fleet – Part V', *Sea Breezes*, 51 (1977), pp. 665–75.

Lewis, Keith P., 'The *Athenia*, First of the Many', *Sea Breezes*, 63 (1989), pp. 602–607.

Lovell, Robert, 'Survivors Sailed in a Sea of Cigarettes', *Sea Breezes*, 69 (1995), pp. 225–27.

McMillan, G. H. G, 'Care of World War II Convoy Casualties in the Kola Area of North Russia', *Journal of the Royal Naval Medical Service*, 81 (1995), pp. 221–30; and 82 (1996), pp. 61–79.

McNee, J. W., 'Convoy Rescue Ships', *Journal of the Royal Naval Medical Service*, 31 (1945), pp. 1–7.

Messimer, Dwight R., 'Heinz-Wilhelm Eck: *Siegerjustiz* and the *Peleus* Affair', in Theodore P. Savas (ed.), *Silent Hunters: German U-boat Commanders of World War II* (Savas, Campbell, California, 1997), pp. 138–83.

Milner, M., 'The Battle of the Atlantic', *Journal of Strategic Studies*, 13 (1990), pp. 45–66.

Molnar, G. W., 'Survival of Hypothermia by Men Immersed in the Ocean,' *Journal of the American Medical Association*, 131 (1946) pp. 1046–50.

Mulligan, T. P., 'German U-Boat Crews in World War II: Sociology of an Elite', *Journal of Military History*, 56 (1992), pp. 261–81.

Murray, W. E. P., '*Upwey Grange: Torpedoed*', *Ships Monthly*, March 1978, pp. 14–16.

Sheehan, Fred, 'The Last Voyage of the *St Usk*', *Sea Breezes*, 72 (1998), pp. 145–50.

Syrett, D., 'The Battle of the Atlantic: 1943, the Year of Decision', *American Neptune*, 45 (1985), pp. 46–64.

Syrett, D., 'Prelude to Victory: The Battle for Convoy HX231, 4–7 April 1943', *Historical Research*, 70 (1997), pp. 98–109.

Thowsen, Atle, 'The Norwegian Merchant Navy in Allied War Transport', in Stephen Howarth and Derek Law (eds), *The Battle of the Atlantic, 1939–1945* (Greenhill Books, London, 1994).

Till, Geoffrey, 'The Battle of the Atlantic as History', in Stephen Howarth and Derek Law (eds), *The Battle of the Atlantic, 1939–1945* (Greenhill Books, London, 1994).

Vause, Jordan, 'Victor Otto Oehrn: The Ace with No Name', in Theodore P. Savas (ed.), *Silent Hunters: German U-Boat Commanders of World War II* (Savas, Campbell, California, 1997), pp. 109–35.

Wharton, J. D., 'Loss of the *Empire Mersey*', *Sea Breezes*, 55 (1981), pp. 562–69.

Williams, Peter R., 'Loss of the *Gloucester Castle*', parts 1, 2 and 3, *Sea Breezes*, 67 (1993), pp. 348–52, 431–35, 515–19.

Wood, John, 'The Last Stand of the *Chilean Reefer*', *Sea Breezes*, 63 (1989), pp. 688–89.

Internet

http://www.uboat.net/

Index

Ships named are all British unless otherwise indicated.
Plates are shown in bold.